The Air-Raid Warden Was a Spy

The Air-Raid Warden Was a Spy

And Other Tales from Home-Front America in World War II

William B. Breuer

CASTLE BOOKS

This edition published in 2005 by
CASTLE BOOKS ®
A division of Book Sales, Inc.
114 Northfield Avenue
Edison, NJ 08837

This edition published by arrangement with and permission of
John Wiley & Sons, Inc.
111 River Street
Hoboken, New Jersey 07030

Library of Congress Cataloging-in-Publication Data:

Breuer, William B.
The Air-Raid Warden Was a Spy / William B. Breuer.
p. cm.
Includes bibliographical references and index.

ISBN-13: 978-0-7858-1994-3
ISBN-10: 0-7858-1994-0

Printed in the United States of America

Dedicated to four-star
GENERAL BARRY R. McCAFFREY (Ret.),
a valiant warrior who received
two Distinguished Service Crosses
and three Purple Hearts during
four combat tours.

We have a distinct spy menace.
The peril is the deep penetration
of the United States by subversives.

— J. Edgar Hoover,
FBI Director
(1941)

Contents

Part Four—A Nation in Total War

Introduction

DURING WORLD WAR II, few civilians realized that home-front America was under seige, that the German and Japanese warlords had planted a large number of spies, saboteurs, and propagandists who were bent on wreaking as much havoc as possible.

Many of these subversives were "sleepers," who had been recruited by the Germans or the Japanese years earlier and ordered to blend in with their communities until it was time to spring into action.

To hold down panic on the home front, the U.S. government slickly covered up the fact that these predators were blowing up factories and key installations, causing enormous damage and loss of life, and that they had set ablaze millions of acres of forests. These fires were attributed to careless smokers.

At the same time the saboteurs were striking blows at home-front America, German spies were radioing reports on departing convoys to submarines lurking off the eastern seaboard, resulting in the sinkings of hundreds of merchant vessels. Nazi submarine skippers had become so bold that one even took his undersea craft into New York harbor.

Meanwhile, life on the home front went on as nearly normal as possible. Professional sports continued. Hollywood created movies. There were countless acts of heroism, patriotism, and sacrifice. Thousands grieved over the loss or serious wounding of loved ones on the far-flung battlefields of the world. As with the young men doing the fighting, the human will prevailed on home-front America.

Part One

Shock Waves
Hit America

"On the Ground, by God!"

AMERICA'S MAGNIFICENT CAPITOL, its huge white dome topped by a twenty-foot-high statue of Freedom, was keeping watch over sprawling Washington, D.C., on this bleak, frigid Sunday of December 7, 1941. Although Japan had been saber rattling in the Pacific in recent weeks, most of America's top military and government leaders were casually going about leisure-time pursuits.

That afternoon, Masuo Kato, a reporter for Domei, the Japanese news agency, was riding in a taxi to attend funeral services for Colonel Kenkichi Shijo, the assistant military attaché in the Japanese embassy, who had died of pneumonia.

Suddenly, at 2:26 P.M., the music on the taxi radio halted and an excited announcer stated: "This is a bulletin from the White House. Japanese airplanes are bombing Pearl Harbor!" And, from that moment the nation became galvanized as one.

The angry driver shouted to his passenger: "Goddamn those slanty-eyed Jap bastards! We'll lick the hell out of those sons of bitches now!"

Near Topeka, Kansas, word was received by a group of the State Field Dog Trials. One man voiced the sentiment of all: "I guess our hunting will be confined to those goddamn Jap bastards from now on!"

In New Orleans, some four hundred grim citizens stood in front of the Japanese consulate and watched officials there burning papers in the courtyard. A stiff breeze caused papers to float up at times while they were still burning. The Japanese chased them about the yard. Like fans at a football game, the Americans roundly hissed and booed each chase.

A fire engine rushed to the Japanese consulate in San Francisco when the diplomats had been so rapidly burning documents that they set the building afire.

Members of a labor union in Chattanooga, Tennessee, unanimously voted its own declaration of war against the Japanese Empire, and those in the Rotary Club in Kodiak, Alaska, pledged to let their beards grow until Japan was whipped.

Arthur A. Names, a man who had flown in France in World War I, sent a message to the White House, in Washington, offering to become what later would be known to the Japanese as a kamikaze. "I will personally fly a plane

A few days before Pearl Harbor, a newspaper published Washington's supersecret plan for defending against any attack. The information had been stolen by a mole in the War Department. (Chicago Tribune)

load of explosives against any enemy battleships wherever and whenever the [president] may deem it necessary and expedient."

There were exceptions to the instant belligerence. Ernest Vogt and his family were eating a late chicken dinner at their home in New York City when they heard a radio report. Vogt was skeptical: "I think it's another Orson Welles hoax."

Back on October 30, 1938, twenty-three-year-old Orson Welles presented a radio play, *Invasion from Mars.* To make the fantasy seem credible the script simulated newscasts announcing that forces from Mars had landed in New Jersey, were heading across the Hudson River to New York City, and were devastating the region with death rays. It was brilliant radio—and America panicked. It was several days before the last visages of terror had vanished.

As the Pearl Harbor bulletins began to saturate the air almost continually, panic struck. That night at a military post a nervous sentry challenged three times, received no answer, and shot an army mule.

At Fort Sam Houston in Texas, an obscure brigadier general named Dwight D. Eisenhower got an urgent telephone call from Washington. Wife Mamie heard him say, "Okay, I'll get there right away." As he rushed off to catch a plane for Washington, he said he hoped to be back soon. "Soon" would be four years.

In Pittsburgh, Senator Gerald Nye had arrived to address some three thousand members of America First, an isolationist organization whose most prominent figure was Charles A. Lindbergh, the first man to have flown the

Atlantic alone. America First had some 100,000 members and claimed that "the warmonger Roosevelt" was taking the nation down a rocky road to war.

Now, just before Senator Nye took to the podium a reporter told him about the attack on Pearl Harbor. Nye snapped: "It sounds terribly fishy to me."

A few days earlier, Eleanor Roosevelt, the president's wife, had invited Edward R. Murrow, who had gained world fame while broadcasting back to the United States on short-wave radio the German bomber attacks on London in 1940, and his wife to dinner at the White House on December 7. Now Murrow's wife telephoned Mrs. Roosevelt: Was the couple still expected for dinner?

"We all have to eat," the First Lady replied. "So come anyway." Later that night the president and the radio newscaster were in the White House study. Clearly, Roosevelt was angry. Pounding a table, he described to Murrow how American planes were destroyed "on the ground, by God, on the ground!"[1]

Dispute in the President's Office

LATE ON THE NIGHT OF DECEMBER 7, President Roosevelt went to the Oval Office. At about 10:30 P.M., a procession of grim-faced leaders of the Senate and House filed into the room and took seats. Behind his highly polished desk, Roosevelt gave the lawmakers a briefing on the Pearl Harbor debacle. He pulled no punches.

The group listened in dead silence, clearly astonished that such a disaster would be "allowed" to occur. "The principal defense of this country and the whole West Coast of America has been seriously damaged today," the president declared. Lawmakers were flabbergasted. What Roosevelt was saying was that a Japanese invasion of California might be forthcoming.

It was an informal gathering. Roosevelt was puffing on his trademark cigarette and long holder. Nearly everyone was casually dressed, having been urgently summoned only an hour or two earlier. Now the president dropped another blockbuster.

"There is a rumor, I don't know if it's true, that two of the planes [in the bombing] were seen with [Nazi] swastikas on them," he said. "I don't discount German participation in the air strike."

Senator Thomas T. Connally, chairman of the Foreign Relations Committee, had become steadily more angry during the briefing. It appeared to him that Roosevelt and his armed forces secretaries had cooked up excuses for the catastrophe. Suddenly, Connally called out: "Hell's fire, didn't we do anything?"

Roosevelt flushed at this outburst, then replied evenly: "That's about it." Connally then turned his guns on Secretary of the Navy Frank Knox, demanding to know, "Well, what in the hell did we do?"

Knox started to sputter a response when the irate Connally interrupted him. "Didn't you say just two weeks ago that we could lick the Japs in two weeks? Didn't you say that our Navy was so well prepared and located that the Japs couldn't hope to hurt us at all?"

Knox appeared shaken and fumbled for a reply. But Connally wasn't finished. "Why did you have all the ships at Pearl Harbor crowded in the way you did?" he exclaimed. "I am amazed by the attack by Japan, but I am still more astounded at what happened to our Navy. They were all asleep. Where were our patrols?" Knox made no reply.[2]

Calls for Retreat to Rockies

THE FLOOD OF GLOOMY REPORTS from Hawaii triggered near hysteria among many of the nation's best-known leaders. One even telephoned the White House and, almost shouting, declared that the West Coast was not defensible, that Japanese forces would land there soon, and recommended that a battle line be organized in the Rocky Mountains to halt a cross-country Japanese drive to capture Washington.[3]

Submarines Off West Coast

AT THE TIME THE BOMBERS HIT PEARL HARBOR, the Japanese had nine submarines submerged a short distance off the West Coast of the United States. They were lying in wait from San Diego in the south to Seattle in the north.

The submarine skippers had strict orders not to fire torpedoes or surface until the precise moment the first bombs exploded on Pearl Harbor. Only a few minutes before the deadline, the captain on one underwater craft spotted the freighter *Cynthia Olsen* in his periscope. The ship was loaded with lumber and bound for Hawaii.

Glancing steadily at his watch, the skipper raised one arm to signal his gunner. Suddenly, he brought the arm down and a torpedo flew out of its hatch. Minutes later the *Cynthia Olsen* disappeared below the waves—probably the first U.S. ship to be sunk in the open sea.

A few days later the liner *Mauna Loa*, carrying thousands of Christmas turkeys, sailed for Honolulu. Suddenly, the ship was ordered to return to port. In the haste of making a run for safety with a Japanese submarine on her tail, the *Mauna Loa* ran aground northwest of the Columbia River. Most of the turkeys washed ashore, providing hundreds of residents of that Oregon region with their Christmas dinners.

At about the same time, the tanker *Emido* was sailing southward, along the coast from Seattle to San Pedro, California. Off Cape Mendocino, Califor-

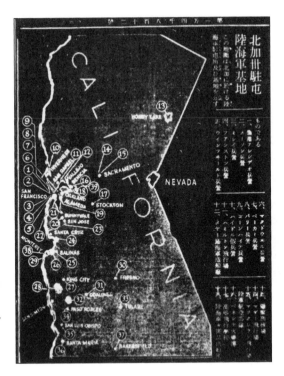

Japanese invasion map of California found on a spy arrested by the FBI. The numbers identify barracks, army posts, naval bases, shipyards, and airfields. (Author's collection)

nia, a Japanese submarine, probably having exhausted its torpedoes, surfaced and pumped six shells into the unarmed ship. Hastily, the crew abandoned her, but the *Emido* didn't sink. Instead, it meandered along the shore aimlessly until it came to rest on a rock pile north of the shelling site. None of these actions on the front doorstep of home-front America became known to the citizens. The Navy kept the Japanese attacks secret.[4]

Roosevelt Rallies the Nation

WASHINGTON, D.C., WAS GRIPPED BY A BITTER COLD on the morning of December 8, 1941. Outside the Capitol, squirrels scampered along the leafless tree branches. Inside the building a few minutes after noon, a procession of government leaders walked solemnly down the long corridor in the Capitol and through the broad rotunda. Behind Senate Majority Leader Alben Barkley and Minority Leader Charles McNary, the delegation entered the cavernous chamber of the House of Representatives.

Next came the justices of the Supreme Court in their flowing black robes, and behind them as they took seats down front were hundreds of grim members of the House and Senate. In the front row were silver-haired General George C. Marshall, Army chief of staff; Admiral Harold "Betty" Stark, chief of

President Franklin Roosevelt signing the joint resolution of Congress declaring war on Japan. (Library of Congress)

Naval Operations; and members of the cabinet. At 12:31 P.M. Speaker of the House Sam Rayburn of Texas rapped his gavel and called out: "The president of the United States!"

There was thunderous applause as Franklin Roosevelt painfully entered the room on the arm of his thirty-four-year-old son, Marine Captain James Roosevelt. Crippled by polio at the age of thirty-nine, the president wore a fifteen-pound brace on each leg.

Struggling up to the podium, the chief executive opened a black loose-leaf notebook. A hush fell over the assembly. He began to read: "Yesterday, December 7, 1941—a date which will live in infamy—the United States of America was suddenly and deliberately attacked by naval and air forces of the Empire of Japan."

A pin could have been heard had it dropped in the room. Roosevelt then went on to describe the sneak attack on Pearl Harbor and Army Air Corps fields in Hawaii. "As commander-in-chief of the Army and Navy, I have directed that all measures be taken for our defense. Always will our whole nation remember the character of the onslaught against us," he said.

Suddenly, as though some supernatural force had pressed a button, those in the chamber leaped to their feet and began cheering and applauding madly.

As the speech continued, Roosevelt was interrupted numerous times by heavy applause. Finally, he said, "With confidence in the armed forces, with the abounding determination of our people, we will gain the inevitable triumph. So help us God!"

In closing, the president stated: "I ask that Congress declare that since the unprovoked and dastardly attack by Japan on Sunday, December 7, 1941, a state of war has existed between the United States and the Japanese Empire."

Roosevelt slowly closed the notebook. The chamber exploded with handclapping, shouting, whistles, and rebel yells.

Only one vote kept the verdict from being unanimous. Sixty-one-year-old Republican Representative Jeannette Rankin of Montana, the first woman elected to Congress, voted "present."

Across the land most Americans applauded, too. Roosevelt had articulated what was in their hearts. In most instances, people reacted with one enormous angry voice. Partisan politics and beliefs were tossed aside, at least for the present.

Senator Burton K. Wheeler, who had long been one of the staunchest isolationists, summed up the collective view of his colleagues: "Now all there is to do is whip the hell out of the Japs!"[5]

Eavesdropper in the German Embassy

AMONG THE PEOPLE who had been glued to radio sets during Roosevelt's call for war against Japan was Hans Thomsen, at the German embassy on Massachusetts Avenue. Inside the dreary old brick building, Thomsen, whose title was chargé d'affaires, had built up in recent years the most conspiratorial den of spies found in any Third Reich embassy in the world. Undercover operatives were planted across the land.

Earlier the clever Thomsen had cabled Berlin that "a close friend" of the U.S. attorney general was providing him information. Through this mole, Thomsen had been sending Berlin a steady stream of reports on what had been transpiring in Roosevelt's cabinet meetings and elsewhere in Washington's corridors of power.

Now, in a cable to Berlin, Thomsen detected a ray of light in Roosevelt's address: "The fact is that [Roosevelt] did not mention Germany with one word shows that he will try to avoid war with us."

That night, the Nazi spymaster fired off another upbeat cable: "War with Japan means transferring all U.S. energy to its own rearmament, a corresponding shrinking of guns and war accoutrements to England, and a shifting of all activity to the Pacific."

No doubt tipped off by a high-ranking mole in the Roosevelt administration, Thomsen's observation had been entirely accurate. It was indeed the administration's plan to focus on licking Japan with all available resources.

When Roosevelt had been conferring with confidants on what to include in his address to the joint session of Congress, there had been pressure on the president to include Germany and Italy in his call for a declaration of war. But the cagey Roosevelt vetoed the recommendation. He decided to wait and see if the often impetuous führer, Adolf Hitler, might declare war on the United States. Such an action by Hitler would solidify opposing American factions behind the war, Roosevelt envisioned, for it would establish Nazi Germany as the "aggressor" against the United States instead of the other way around.

Four days later, on December 11, Hitler performed precisely as Roosevelt had predicted. Before a cheering Reichstag (parliament), he thundered that Roosevelt had provoked the war in order to cover up the failure of his (economic policies).

When the führer, a spellbinding orator, began to announce that he was going to war against the United States, the frenzied deputies leaped to their feet and drowned his words in bedlam.

Later that day, Benito Mussolini, the bombastic Italian dictator and Hitler's close crony, also declared war on the United States.[6]

A Television Pioneer

WHILE PRESIDENT ROOSEVELT had been galvanizing a divided America into one with his historic six-and-a-half-minute address to Congress, the largest radio audience in history—estimated at 90 million people—had ears glued to Philco and Atwater Kent sets. At the same time, a newfangled electronic apparatus known as television had carried the speech—but not the president's image.

Television cameras and equipment were so bulky that they were immobile. So to give the Roosevelt telecast "picture," an American flag was placed before the studio camera and an unseen whirling electric fan caused Old Glory to flutter majestically while the president was speaking.

At the time, there were only six television stations operating in five U.S. cities: New York (two), Chicago, Philadelphia, Los Angeles, and Schenectady. Only some two thousand television sets were scattered about the nation. Most were playthings for the rich. Programming was primitive and sporadic.

A few months prior to Pearl Harbor, the CBS television station in New York City had sprung a novelty on whatever viewers may have been watching— a fifteen-minute newscast. Richard Hubbell was the "news narrator" (the exalted title of "anchor" was a decade way). Hubbell, a true television pioneer, was on the screen each day, but hardly anyone outside the studio recognized him, except perhaps for his family.

War news was the principal fare. Hubbell stood in front of a wall map, and with the aid of a pointer explained what was happening on the battlefronts of the world.

It made no difference if the narrator was pointing at the correct locale—TV sets were so crude and screens so small that viewers could barely make out Hubbell, much less the map.

After Roosevelt's speech, American industry was ordered to cut back sharply on any production not vital to the war effort. Construction of new television sets ceased, and operating outlets cut down televising from four to five nights a week to one. The six U.S. television stations had virtually gone out of business "for the duration," the popular phrase of the era.[7]

Instant Psychologists

IN THE WAKE OF THE JAPANESE STRIKE, a confused, humiliated, and furious home-front America was trying to discern the reason for the Pearl Harbor disaster. Radio and press "experts" who had no true facts, gazed into crystal balls and blessed America with their analyses.

In Iowa, Paul Mallon wrote in the *Sioux City Journal*: "The Hawaiian attack was obviously a demonstration designed more for psychological effect than for military damage." A classic example of pure guesswork.

Other media geniuses stated that the bombing had been done by madmen. "And how can one make sense of the motives of madmen?" it was reasoned.

Many reporters thought it would have been impossible for Japan to pull off such a gargantuan caper on its own. The *Chicago Times* declared: "Had it not been for Adolf Hitler, Japan would never have ventured on such a suicide course."

That stark declaration would have come as news to the führer. He had been as surprised as U.S. leaders about the bombing. *New York PM* agreed with the Hitler-ordered-the-attack theory. "The German government is masterminding the Japanese policy," *PM* proclaimed.

The clones in the U.S. media jumped aboard the Hitler-did-it bandwagon. Because of the surprise and daring of the air attack, declared the *Tulsa Daily World*, "Japan had been carefully coached in such proceedings by the Germans."

Columnist Upton Close declared that the Pearl Harbor bombing might have been as big a surprise to Emperor Hirohito and his government as it had been to President Roosevelt and official Washington.

Billed as a Far East expert, Close elaborated: "It is very possible that there is a double-double-cross in this business. It is possible . . . that this is a coup engineered by the Germans and with the aid of German ships in the Pacific."

Other columnists also became instant psychologists. At least three analysts pointed out that the Japanese were suffering from the "Runt's Complex." Boake Carter declared the Japanese had "suicidal tendencies."[8]

Strange Doings across the Land

ACROSS THE WIDTH AND BREADTH of America, millions of people were swamped by rumors and often reacted in strange ways. In Washington's Tidal Basin an incensed man chopped down four Japanese cherry trees. Bellboys on the roof of the Statler Hotel in Boston used gallons of black paint to hide the huge arrow pointing to the airport.

In upscale Scarsdale, New York, mothers spent long, tedious hours sitting in parked cars outside of schools, ready to spirit their children home if bombers were to appear. In Norfolk, Virginia, site of the major U.S. naval base, the chief of police had his men round up and jail all fourteen people of Japanese ancestry living in that city.

In Denison, Texas, the mayor and city council convened in emergency session and were debating buying a machine gun for the police department. An excited man rushed into the chamber and called out that New York City was being bombed. So the mayor proposed that, instead of one machine gun, the city buy two.

Various local governments organized armed civilian bands to thwart potential saboteurs, and the vigilantes stood watch over likely targets: bridges, railroad trestles, water reservoirs, docks, tunnels, dams, and public buildings. Most of these modern-day Minute Men were armed with a motley collection of weapons: antiquated pistols, shotguns, hunting rifles, even knives. Few had had military training.

A woman driving across the San Francisco Bay Bridge failed to hear a challenge by a band of armed civilians, one of whom shot at and seriously wounded her.

On Lake Michigan, sentries shot and killed a duck hunter and wounded his companion.

The public safety director of Newark, New Jersey, ordered police to board trains and arrest "all suspicious Orientals" and "other possible subversives," leaving it up to the individual policeman to determine who "looked suspicious" and who did not.

North Carolina's governor ordered state police cars to be painted black (presumably to make them inconspicuous at night) and instructed his officers to make arrests without warrants, otherwise they could not act "even if they saw an offender preparing to blow a bridge."

Oregon's governor proclaimed a state of emergency, although he explained he didn't know what kind of emergency he was heralding.

In Galveston, Texas, a civilian guard thought a blinking light in a house was flashing signals to unseen enemy ships offshore, so he fired a rifle round into the building.

Farmers armed with shotguns posted themselves at each end of the Missouri town of Rolla and carefully inspected each passing vehicle, halting those that "looked suspicious."

In the northeastern United States, a week-long spy scare erupted after the Army released aerial photographs showing fields that appeared to have been plowed in such a way that arrows pointed in the direction of several aircraft factories. Law enforcement officers took into custody two farmers and grilled them for several hours.

After three days, the badly frightened "suspects" were released when it was found that the photographs were a hoax perpetrated by an Army public-relations officer who was gifted with more zeal than brains. He explained that his goal had been to shock Americans into realizing that Nazi spies could be everywhere.

At the same time on the Pacific shore sixty miles north of Los Angeles one night, a man, his voice dripping with anxiety, telephoned the local police department. A spy was sending signals with a flashlight to Japanese submarines.

Two policemen rushed to the scene and detected the subversive—an elderly woman who was prowling around in the dark outside her house in search of her cat.[9]

A Stop-and-Go Railroad Trip

ALMIRA BONDELID, A SOUTH DAKOTA SCHOOLTEACHER, was married to a marine taking boot training at Parris Island, South Carolina. On the day after Pearl Harbor, her husband telephoned and asked her to come there immediately. A few hours later the young bride was on a train rolling southward.

The trip was frustrating. Each time the train approached a bridge, the engineer halted the train while the crew got out to see if a bomb had been placed on the span.

After crawling around under the bridge for a period of time, the crew would get back on the train, and it would continue to the next bridge.

This stop-and-go technique was followed all the way to Chicago, where Almira changed trains. The remainder of the trip to South Carolina was routine.[10]

"San Francisco Is Being Bombed!"

ONLY TWENTY-FOUR HOURS after the Japanese attack, Fiorello La Guardia, the rotund, feisty mayor of New York City, and Eleanor Roosevelt, the First Lady, boarded a plane outside Washington to fly to the West Coast. La Guardia was the director of the Office of Civilian Defense (OCD), an agency created only the previous spring, and Eleanor was his assistant, whose task it was to mobilize woman power and keep up the physical fitness of those on the home front.

They were a curious duo, many journalists held. La Guardia spoke rapidly with a rash of arm waving. Eleanor was regal, even reserved. They did not always agree on priorities, but they learned to compromise to keep the OCD program rolling.

La Guardia was fearful of perceived danger to New York City and Washington. At a press conference before departing for the West Coast, he told reporters that "we who live on the Atlantic Coast are in as much danger of being bombed as our countrymen who were bombed yesterday in Honolulu."

Doom and gloom seemed to be hovering over the airplane carrying the two officials. It took off into the blackness and was soon gripped by bad weather. Perhaps halfway on the trip, the pilot came back into the cabin and excitedly told the OCD officials: "I just picked up an Associated Press report on the radio. San Francisco is being bombed!" They told him to continue the flight course as planned. Actually, the nearest Japanese war plane was a few thousand miles away.

Early the next morning, the mayor and the president's wife met with the California State Council of Defense, and La Guardia gave a fire-eating speech. California Governor Cuthbert Olson interrupted the speaker and said his aide in New York City was on the telephone with word that the Big Apple, as it was called, was under an alert and expecting a bombing attack.

Did La Guardia wish to speak to his aide? No, he replied, just tell him to follow the instructions already given. With that he continued his speech.

The closest German bomber was in France, more than three thousand miles from New York City.

When La Guardia returned to the East Coast, he was proud of the way New Yorkers had handled the air-raid alert. "City Nonchalant as Sirens Wail," a *New York Times* headline exclaimed.

There was good reason for the easy going response. Few citizens had even heard the weak-toned and widely scattered sirens.[11]

Watching for Enemy Paratroopers

IN WASHINGTON, the Office of Civilian Defense tried to bring order out of chaos, but it was fighting an uphill battle. Most communities, large and small, set up their own operations.

In Florida, the North Dade County Volunteers published a booklet called *When the Sirens Scream*. It was chiefly concerned with an attack by German paratroopers. "If there is any danger of having parachute drops from the skies, everyone must lock and mobilize his car as he leaves it," citizens were warned. "We do not wish to provide transportation for the enemy."

In Wake County, North Carolina, the Defense Council consisted of members of the United Daughters of the Confederacy, Daughters of the American Colonists, Colonial Dames, and Daughters of the American Revolution. Ages ranged between the late forties and the early nineties. Presumably this group would defend the region against German paratroopers.

Vancouver, Washington, had among its messengers a blind man with a seeing-eye dog. In case of an attack, this man and his canine companion could make their way better than sighted people through blackouts and bomb rubble.

In California, the State Council of Defense accepted deaf people in various localities. It was reasoned that the enormous cacophony of exploding bombs and antiaircraft-gun shells would make normal conversation difficult or impossible. So the deaf member's ability to read lips would be most helpful.

One dark night the air-raid siren screamed in Smithville, Georgia. The town promptly blacked out, and volunteer firemen rushed to their appointed civil-defense posts. So dedicated were they to this task that a large building burned to the ground when the firefighters refused to leave their assigned posts.

Enemy paratroopers were a deep concern of many California residents. State Attorney General Earl Warren was inundated by letters in which citizens wanted to know if it was legal to shoot the intruders from the sky. Warren's legal opinion: fire away.

Across the land in these early weeks of America at war there were countless false alerts. One of these, at San Pedro, California, triggered near panic in that city. Just as a flight of U.S. fighter planes winged overhead on a black night, a thunderclap and lightning bolt rocked the region. Hundreds of people rushed for basements and other shelter and braced for an expected rain of bombs.[12]

A Covert Raid into Mexico

AT THE HEADQUARTERS of the Western Defense Command at the Presidio, outside San Francisco, Lieutenant General John L. DeWitt was burdened by an awesome task: security for an enormous stretch of real estate that stretched from Alaska southward to the Mexican border.

DeWitt was sixty years of age, and leadership of the Western Defense Command was to be his final assignment before retirement. Mild mannered in appearance, the general was hard-nosed, a no-nonsense, outspoken type. Two days after Pearl Harbor, DeWitt publicly blasted San Francisco civic leaders for "criminal, shameful apathy" for ignoring blackout regulations.

DeWitt ordered a curfew along the West Coast and commended anti-aircraft outfits for firing at "unidentified planes."

On the day after Pearl Harbor air reconnaissance pilots reported to the Presidio that a Japanese fleet of thirty-four ships had been spotted between Los Angeles and San Francisco. (The enemy force turned out to be fifteen fishing boats.) Three days later the phantom enemy fleet was detected again, one hundred and seventy miles west of San Francisco.

No doubt based on the flood of rumors reaching the Presidio, Army officers developed a theory that the Japanese had secretly massed a large force on Baja California, a peninsula in Mexico south of San Diego, to launch a blow against the United States. Baja would be an excellent locale in which to hide an army, having desertlike regions heavy with scrub brush and desolate mountains.

The theory became more pronounced with reports that all of the Mexican fishing boats along Baja had mysteriously vanished. Presumably these vessels had been confiscated by the Japanese force. Then more rumors indicated that the (nonexistent) enemy airplanes that had been flying over San Diego, Los Angeles, San Pedro, and other West Coast cities had been and were using Baja California as a base.

Submarines, it was reported, were bringing in bombs and fuel to the hostile bomber force under cover of darkness. How did bombers get nine thousand miles from Japan to Baja California? They were sneaked in from aircraft carriers.

General DeWitt secretly negotiated with Mexican officials (presumably those in the consulate in San Francisco) and was granted permission to send a scouting party across the border to look for the assembled Japanese army and bomber force. Operating in the utmost secrecy, an Army captain with a platoon of heavily armed soldiers slipped across the border in six jeeps at night and roamed about the Mexican territory. They found no sign of Japanese activity.

At the same time, the Federal Bureau of Investigation in Washington apparently had sent one or more disguised agents across the border into Baja California to check the reports. The covert search was fruitless. One rancher of Japanese ancestry was encountered, described in the FBI report as "a toothless old man."

The rumor about the secret hostile base in Mexico refused to die. A few weeks after the scouting of Baja California, the FBI office in Los Angeles received an unsigned letter in which the writer claimed that a coordinated bombing attack would be launched from the phantom Mexican base against San Francisco, San Pedro, and San Diego, probably on New Year's Day. The Pearl Harbor bombing had been early on Sunday morning when many members of the U.S. fleet were caught sleeping off hangovers. Now, the letter writer declared, the looming raids would hit on New Year's Day morning for the same reason.

This anonymous report had a new twist. The assaults on the three U.S. cities would be by German planes that had been in hiding for several weeks awaiting the signal to attack. Beleaguered General DeWitt held another clandestine meeting with Mexican officials and received permission from the U.S. Army Corps to fly a limited number of reconnaissance missions over Baja California to search for the phantom Luftwaffe bomber force.

No matter how preposterous were the alarms and excursions inundating the Presidio, DeWitt had to investigate them. Privately, he told aides: "I don't intend to be another General Short!"

DeWitt was referring to Lieutenant General Walter C. Short, who had been in command of the Army's Hawaiian Department when the Japanese struck. A scapegoat for the disaster was needed in Washington, so Short was being measured for horns.

DeWitt had to deal not only with real or perceived hostile threats to the West Coast, but much of his time was spent hassling with state and local officials. He coerced California Governor Cuthbert Olson to close down all houses of prostitution, an act, wags declared, that caused the "ladies" to peddle their wares on street corners. It had not been made clear how whorehouses had been jeopardizing the security against Japanese attacks.[13]

Fear for Roosevelt's Life

SINCE WORD HAD FIRST REACHED Secretary of the Treasury Henry Morgenthau Jr. about the Japanese treachery, he had been obsessed with President Roosevelt's security. A component of the Treasury, the Secret Service was directly responsible for protecting the chief executive on an around-the-clock basis.

American intelligence officers told the Secret Service that Abwehr, the German espionage agency, had for years planted agents in and around Washington. They had been instructed, said the report, to lay low, to blend in with their neighborhoods until given a signal from Berlin. Then, it was said, these moles would put on the German uniforms they had brought with them, dig out the weapons they had hidden, and, under cover of night, assault the White House and murder President Roosevelt.

Police in Washington were told to be on the lookout for suspicious characters lurking about in civilian clothes and promptly arrest them with no regard for their legal rights. How one "looks suspicious" was left to the judgment of the policemen.

An armored Packard sedan was acquired for Roosevelt, and Morgenthau established a tight procedure for admission into the White House. No doubt he recalled to his horror and embarrassment the time two teenage boys had slipped into the White House on New Year's Day 1939 and prowled around the building without being challenged. They had walked in on the president and his wife and asked the astonished couple for autographs.

Fearing a bombing raid, Morgenthau insisted that Roosevelt take shelter in the thick vault of the Treasury Building, which is located near the White House. (A tunnel would soon connect the two structures.) The president quipped that he would take refuge there only if he could play poker with the guards and use Morgenthau's twenty-dollar gold pieces for chips.

Morgenthau wanted to obtain four tanks from the Army to guard the approaches to the White House. Roosevelt said no. The treasury secretary then planned to bring in a battalion of heavily armed soldiers. Again, Roosevelt rejected the idea, agreeing to have only one soldier posted every one hundred feet along the iron fence that circles the grounds.

Without Roosevelt's prior approval, Morgenthau arranged to have a company of soldiers manning World War I machine guns deployed around the White House grounds. On the roof of the building were two ancient antiaircraft guns, along with shells that had been in wooden crates for twenty years.

Among the president's aides there was a heated debate over the subject of blacking out windows in the White House to thwart enemy bombers. The president was opposed to it, but those in favor won out. So like any housewife in Tupelo, Mississippi, or Springfield, Illinois, Henrietta Nesbitt, the housekeeper, was dispatched to scour Washington stores for blackout material.

Although she represented the nation's most powerful figure, Nesbitt was able to pry loose only three bolts of cloth, a fraction of the amount that would be needed. So the problem was solved by using black sateen shades and painting windows black.[14]

FBI Joins in Sinking Submarine

TWO WEEKS AFTER AMERICA was bombed into a global conflict, operators at the Radio Corporation of America Communications (RCAC) radio station at Point Reyes, about fifty miles northwest of San Francisco, heard two strange radio outlets exchanging messages. Using directional antenna, they figured that the strong station was probably one in Japan and the weaker station a submarine a short distance off the California coast.

The RCAC operators contacted the Federal Bureau of Investigation, which sent an agent to the station. "Wish you'd monitor that wave length when you have time," the G-man said. "If you hear anything, give us a call."

About noon five days later, one of the operators telephoned the FBI man. "That station is sending again," he said. "Sounds like a mobile marine unit at 6908 kilocycles, and it could be close to shore."

Several FBI agents rapidly put in telephone calls to the Pan American Airways Station at Treasure Island, in San Francisco Bay, and the Federal Communications Commission (FCC) monitoring stations at Portland, Oregon, and Santa Anna, near Los Angeles. These facilities were asked to tune in and take a directional reading on the mystery station. The telephone lines were held open.

In less than five minutes, the operator in the Pan American post said over the telephone lines: "According to my charting, that offshore station is sending from about eight miles off Point Mendocino, which is about two hundred miles northwest of here."

The FBI agent immediately telephoned the information to the Pacific Naval Coastal Frontier headquarters, which promptly relayed the data to the PBY (amphibious airplane) on patrol.

Ten minutes later the navy post called back to report receipt of a message from the PBY: "Attacking enemy submarine."

Two bombs were dropped, one landing behind the submarine and the other ahead of it. Then Army bombers arrived and dropped several depth charges on the now submerged submarine. Minutes later a large oil slick rose to the surface and spread over the water.

Men in the Army bombers felt they had destroyed the underwater vessel. But its fate would never be known for a certainty. As for the G-men who had worked on the case, they liked to think that they had played a key role in the destruction of a Japanese submarine.[15]

Rounding Up Subversive Suspects

MONTHS BEFORE WAR ERUPTED in the Pacific, J. Edgar Hoover, the peppery director of the Federal Bureau of Investigation, had been getting his agency prepared for emergency operations. Now he put the FBI on a twenty-four-hour schedule. Annual leaves were cancelled. The entire force was faced with its greatest challenge—rapidly rounding up a few thousand subversive suspects from a list put together in recent months.

Prior to late 1939, when Hoover was designated by President Roosevelt to take sole control of the battle against spies and saboteurs, the United States had been a subversive's paradise. Spies and saboteurs could and did roam the nation at will.

During the 1930s, Adolf Hitler's espionage apparatus had invaded America with the most massive penetration of a major nation that history had known. Nazi agents stole nearly every military, industrial, and government secret. Hoover and his men had nailed scores of spies, but there were a large number still burrowed into the fabric of American society.

With the invasion of America's West Coast a distinct threat in the early weeks of the war, Hoover was especially concerned that the Tokyo warlords had received a massive amount of military and industrial secrets obtained by

Lieutenant Commander Hideki Tachibana, who had projected himself as a language officer in the Japanese consulate in Los Angeles.

Back in May 1941, the FBI reported to Secretary of State Cordell Hull, who had been born in a log cabin in the Tennessee mountains, that G-men had uncovered widespread espionage activities by Tachibana. His diplomatic post had allowed him to travel up and down the West Coast unchallenged.

Hull gave the green light to arrest Tachibana, and he was taken into custody. A few days later the new Japanese ambassador to the United States, Kichisaburo Nomura, pleaded with Hull to release Tachibana in the interest of promoting good relations between the two governments.

For whatever the reason, Hull, who no doubt had the approval of President Roosevelt, agreed to free the Japanese spy, who was promptly deported. No doubt he took with him a huge cache of American secrets.

Now, after the G-men around the nation had been put on the alert, they waited impatiently for the order. From San Francisco, Special Agent in Charge N. J. L. Pieper telephoned Louis Nichols, an assistant FBI director in Washington, and said: "The boys are getting jumpy. Shouldn't we get going?"

"Not yet," Nichols replied. "We've got to wait for the proper papers to be signed after President Roosevelt issues an emergency proclamation."

In the meantime, Director Hoover, rated in public opinion polls as the second most popular American (just behind Roosevelt), had turned his office suite in the Justice Department Building into a militarylike command post. When the green light came from the White House, Hoover leaped into action. Hour after hour, he barked orders on the telephone as his agents fanned out across the nation and Hawaii, Alaska, and Puerto Rico.

Assisted by local police, sheriffs' departments, and military intelligence officers, the G-men moved with speed and coordination. Within the first seventy-two hours after Pearl Harbor, 3,846 subversive suspects were taken into custody. Each had a hearing before a civilian board and was represented by a court-appointed lawyer.[16]

A Feud over Wiretapping

ALTHOUGH CONFRONTED BY the most serious threat in America's history, squabbles over jurisdiction broke out after President Roosevelt designated the FBI to "take charge of communications censorship." J. Edgar Hoover promptly put a halt to all communications to Japan.

Federal Communications Chairman James J. Fly and his aides were outraged over what they considered to be an intrusion onto their bailiwick. Fly fired off a message to the communications companies, calling on them to ignore the FBI order. However, Fly's order was ignored.

Hard on the heels of that brouhaha, the FCC and the FBI got into another fuss over the FBI's right to make security checks (that is, wiretaps) on messages being sent to Tokyo, Rome, Berlin, Moscow, and other world capitals. Hoover maintained that it was the responsibility of his agency to make these checks, because Roosevelt had designated the FBI to be in charge of security on home-front America.

Curiously, with the United States at war, Chairman Fly and his FCC bureaucrats held that wiretapping or interception of messages was illegal, an interpretation of the law not shared by Attorney General Francis Biddle, who was Hoover's boss, and legal experts in the Justice Department. Biddle's view was that authorized wiretaps and intercepts were legal as long as the information obtained was not divulged to unauthorized persons.

Friction intensified when Fly and the FCC refused to turn over to the FBI the fingerprint cards of some 200,000 radio operators and communications employees. Fly pointed out that the prints had been taken only to check the citizenship of the workers and that turning over the prints might be regarded by the people fingerprinted as a serious breach of faith on the part of the FCC. Besides, Fly stated, the workers' union leaders objected to the transfer.

Attorney General Biddle fired off a sharp letter to Fly. "The evidence is strong that messages have been surreptitiously transmitted to our enemies by radio [from the United States]," Biddle stated. "Military attacks upon the territory of this country may have furthered and facilitated thereby. . . . I should hate to have something serious happen which might have been easily avoided."

Fly continued to balk. The cards should not be kept in FBI files because "it would be unfortunate if the employees were subjected to disclosure of past misdemeanors and other crimes that had nothing to do with national security matters."

Biddle was unmoved. "If there is anyone in a position to do real harm in the present states of affairs, certainly the radio operator is included," he responded to Fly. "Unless the cards are filed with the FBI, a person could be discharged for subversion by one federal agency and hired by another with no one the wiser."

Months later the FBI received the fingerprint cards from the FCC. No doubt President Roosevelt himself had intervened in the dispute.[17]

Mission: Halt Ambassador's Hara-Kiri

IN WASHINGTON, Assistant Secretary of State Breckenridge Long was charged with containing the diplomats who were in the Japanese embassy when war broke out in the Pacific. If furious Americans were to break into the building and kill Ambassador Kichisaburo Nomura, U.S. diplomats waiting repatriation

Japanese Ambassador Kichisaburo Nomura was reported to be planning hara-kiri while in U.S. custody. (National Archives)

in Tokyo might also be murdered. Consequently, heavily armed law enforcement officers guarded the Japanese embassy around the clock.

Ambassador Nomura and his staff had been trapped in the building for the first week after Pearl Harbor. The warlords in Tokyo had kept Nomura in the dark about the sneak attack, so such provisions as food soon ran out. A staff member telephoned for groceries and paid the deliveryman with a check. Soon the American was back with the check. Banks would not accept it. So forty people in the embassy pooled U.S. currency to pay the bill.

There were sleeping accommodations for only ten people, but four times that number were holed up in the embassy. So most of them had to sprawl on the floor at night without blankets or mattresses.

After the eight days of confinement, the Japanese delegation was moved to West Virginia and Virginia, where they were ensconced in luxury resort hotels to await an exchange for Americans in Japan.

A few days later Breckenridge Long received an alarming report: Nomura was preparing to commit hara-kiri, the historic ritual in which disgraced Japanese kill themselves.

Accelerating Long's problem in dealing with his potentially explosive situation was the fact that the media got hold of the report and began speculating in print and on the air. Could the suicide be performed on foreign soil, or did it have to be done in Japanese controlled territory?

In this thorny situation, Long called on Charles Bruggmann, the Swiss minister in Washington, to intervene. He was a fifty-two-year-old career diplomat who was married to the sister of Henry A. Wallace, the vice president of the United States. The Swiss had met Mary Wallace in Washington and the couple was married the next year in Paris.

Unbeknownst to Breckenridge Long (or anyone else in Washington) Bruggmann had dispatched a series of telegrams to Bern, Switzerland, after the Japanese bombing of Pearl Harbor. These messages described in detail what had transpired in President Roosevelt's office on the afternoon of December 7.

Bruggmann told Bern that the U.S. fleet was a twisted, smoking mass. This fact was to be kept from Japan. However, copies of the communications were stolen and sent on to Berlin by a German agent (code named Habakuk) who had been planted a year earlier in the Swiss Foreign Ministry in Bern.

Habakuk advised his superiors in Berlin that the information about the destruction of the U.S. fleet had to be authentic, because, he pointed out, Vice President Wallace had to be the source.

Within hours, Berlin flashed the high-grade intelligence to Tokyo. For the first time, the Japanese warlords knew that their sneak strike had been a rousing success.

Now, in Washington, Bruggmann was driven to the resort hotel where he pleaded with Ambassador Nomura not to kill himself because that action would cause grave consequences for many people. The Swiss might as well have saved his breath. Nomura soon made it clear that he had no intention of committing hara-kiri.[18]

A Field Marshal Is Shocked

CHRISTMAS 1941 WAS NEARING WHEN Field Marshal John Dill arrived in Washington to take up his new duties as British Prime Minister Winston S. Churchill's liaison officer to the U.S. War Department. Accustomed to many months of wartime austerity in Great Britain, Dill was flabbergasted by the prosperous lifestyle of Americans and by the belief in official Washington that the Japanese and Germans could be quickly polished off without undue disruption of normal conditions on the home front.

"This country is the most highly organized for peace that you can imagine," Dill wrote to Field Marshal Alan Brooke, chief of the Imperial General Staff in London. "At present this country has not—repeat not—the slightest conception of what war means, and their armed forces are more unready for war than it is possible to imagine."

Closing his gloomy analysis, Dill declared: "The whole organization belongs to the days of George Washington."[19]

Lieutenant Reinhardt Hardegen took his U-boat into New York harbor early in 1942. Eventually his crew sank twenty-three Allied ships, most of them along the eastern seaboard of the United States. (National Archives)

Nazi U-Boat in New York Harbor

BLOND, AUDACIOUS KRIEGSMARINE (German Navy) Lieutenant Reinhardt Hardegen was steering his U-boat in the blackness toward New York harbor. It was January 13, 1942, the first day of Operation Paukenschlag (Drumbeat), a plan conceived and launched by Grossadmiral Karl Doenitz, chief of the submarine service. His goal was to blockade America's Atlantic ports and cut her crucial shipping lanes to the British Isles.

Doenitz had selected Reinhardt Hardegen and eleven other bold U-boat skippers to stalk America's eastern seaboard, directing Paukenschlag from the submarine base in Lorient, France. As reports flowed in from harbor spies in New York, Boston, Norfolk, and other eastern ports, the U-boat chief, like a chess master adroitly moving pawns, shifted his underwater wolves into position to intercept departing ships.

Now, at midnight, Lieutenant Hardegen's *U-123* surfaced off the port of New York. He and his crewman were astonished by the dazzling sight before them. Even though the United States had been at war for more than a month, Manhattan was aglow with thousands of lights that twinkled through the night like fireflies.

"It's unbelievable!" Hardegen exclaimed to Second Officer Horst von Schroeter. To dramatize how close the *U-123* was to America's largest city, Hardegen quipped in a radio signal to Lorient: "I can see couples dancing on the roof garden atop the Astor Hotel in Times Square."

With daylight approaching, the *U-123* nestled silently on the ocean bottom of Wimble Shoal, a few miles south of New York City. Throughout the day, Hardegen's radio man reported sounds of ships overhead. "*Gott!*" the skipper exploded. "Can you imagine what we could do with twelve U-boats in here [New York harbor]?"[20]

A Journalist Prowls the *Normandie*

EDMOND SCOTT, A REPORTER for a New York City newspaper, *PM*, was assigned to a curious investigation. He was to masquerade as a longshoreman and look into repeated reports that the waterfront was wide open to sabotage. It was mid-January 1942.

Dressed in work clothes, Scott got a job with a crew hired to lug furniture aboard the French ocean liner *Normandie* at Pier 88 on the Hudson River. Taken over by the U.S. Navy and rechristened the *Lafayette*, the huge vessel was being converted into a badly needed transport, and some fifteen hundred civilian workers were swarming about on her.

Scott was appalled by the almost total lack of security for this highly valuable ship. A private firm had been hired to guard the vessel, and anyone who had fifty dollars for a union initiation fee could become a stevedore and board the *Normandie*.

Alone and unchallenged, the disguised Scott prowled all over the ship, and he was struck by how simple it would be to set fire to the vessel. A pocketful of incendiary pencils, he visualized, could be used with devastating impact.

Eight hours after "longshoreman" Scott had boarded the *Normandie*, he had learned her destination, when she would leave New York, how many guns she would mount, and the thickness of armor being put over portholes—secret information obtained from loose-tongued workers and foremen.

Back at his newspaper, Scott handed his blockbuster story to editors. They were flabbergasted, calling the account a "blueprint for sabotage," one that could advise enemy saboteurs how to destroy the world's third largest ship (only a few feet shorter than the *Queen Mary* and the *Queen Elizabeth*). So publication was held up.

However, the alarmed editors did report Scott's amazing adventure to Captain Charles H. Zearfoss, the U.S. Maritime Commission's antisabotage chief. He angrily denied the findings (the editors would say) and ordered: "Get your reporter off there before he gets shot!"[21]

The Salesman's Luck Runs Out

THIRTY-SIX-YEAR-OLD Waldemar Othmer led the life of the average young American. A blond, blue-eyed personable man, he supported his wife and son by selling Electrolux vacuum cleaners in and around Norfolk, Virginia, site of the Navy's largest base and headquarters of the Atlantic Fleet.

Neighbors were fond of Othmer, who always had a kind word to say and took his family to church each Sunday. He had volunteered his services to the Red Cross and each day raised an American flag in front of his modest house. Neighbors noticed that Othmer often was gone for several days at a time, but they presumed he was selling vacuum cleaners. What they didn't know was that he was a slick Nazi spy.

In 1937, Othmer, a naturalized American of German birth, had returned to the fatherland on a visit. Impressed by Adolf Hitler's cause, he volunteered to spy in America. His German controller instructed him to "lay low" in the United States (a sleeper agent) until he was called to active duty. That summons came in 1940 when President Roosevelt began rearming the nation to counter the Nazi threat.

Othmer had been ordered to serve his espionage apprenticeship at the Brooklyn Navy Yard, where he passed his test with flying colors. Later he obtained a job as a civilian electrician at a Marine Corps training base in North Carolina, and then he was told to establish a residence in Norfolk.

From his vantage point in the Virginia port—he often paid visits to the naval base without undue challenge—Othmer was able to pass on to his German controllers in Hamburg the status of American and British warships and merchant vessels being repaired there and when they sailed.

In 1943, Othmer's days of betraying his adopted country came to a sudden halt. Arrested by FBI agents, he was tried in court, found guilty of espionage, and sentenced to twenty years in prison.[22]

Part Two

America under Seige

Joe Louis Contributes Huge Purse

SIX WEEKS AFTER PEARL HARBOR, Joseph Louis Barrow did what no other boxer had done before or since: he risked a million-dollar-plus heavyweight championship to make a major financial contribution to his country. Known professionally as Joe Louis, the Brown Bomber, as he was called, was going to put his title on the line against a promising fighter, Buddy Baer. At two hundred and thirty pounds, the challenger would outweigh the champion by twenty-five pounds. In his bout against Baer, Louis would donate his $100,000-plus purse (equivalent to $1.2 million in 2002) to Navy Relief for needy families of sailors.

Born to cotton-picking parents in tiny Lexington, Alabama, Louis had won the world title in June 1937 when he knocked out James Braddock in the eighth round in Chicago. Sports writers claimed Louis had the fastest hands ever for a heavyweight.

On the afternoon of the fight, the Navy held a luncheon, and Louis was asked to speak to the twenty-five-hundred guests. Poker-faced (as he always was during his fights) and soft-spoken, he said that he was going to join the Army. "We will win the war," he added, "because we are on God's side."

That night the champion demolished Buddy Baer in the first round. The next morning Louis was sworn into the Army as a private.[1]

A Grieving Father Joins Navy

ON JANUARY 4, 1942, fifty-one-year-old Walter Bromley called at a Seattle recruiting station and tried to enlist in the Navy. He was rejected. Six years too old.

Bromley persisted, and a few hours later the Navy recruiter was suddenly struck with blurry vision and he wrote on the application that Bromley was forty-five. Minutes later he was sworn into the service, possibly the oldest seaman in the Navy.

Bromley had explained that his two sons had been killed at Pearl Harbor.[2]

Self-Appointed Do-Gooders

WITH THE BULK OF America's young men in uniform or about to enter the armed forces, do-gooders in the civilian sector took it upon themselves to stand guard over the morals of the GIs. The Minnesota Anti-Saloon League passed a resolution—unanimously of course—that called for the War Department to establish so-called "dry zones" around Army camps.

Church groups fired off letters to members of Congress about the evils of Demon Rum and demanded that prostitutes not be permitted any closer to military installations than five miles.

Other segments of American society, however, were not eager to "eliminate" prostitution around military bases—if such a goal actually could be achieved. Many leaders in the armed forces felt that young men required sexual activity, that the urge was uncontrollable. Large numbers of local government officials looked on prostitution as an industry that brought heavy revenue to the city halls.

In early 1943, headlines in the sensationalist press screamed that venereal disease had reached epidemic proportions around military bases and demanded that Washington take action to wipe out this plague.

No doubt responding to pressure from Congress, whose members were being bombarded with letters from worried mothers, Surgeon General Thomas Parren published a report that scalded armed forces leaders for not doing enough to halt the spread of venereal disease, which he called the "number one saboteur of our defense."

Parren's document gave detailed and lurid descriptions of "our country's newly organized panzer prostitutes."

Newspapers, even so-called staid ones like the *New York Times*, eagerly published long excerpts from the racy Parren report.

President Roosevelt, always the consummate politician, instructed the Army and Navy to take action to curb the nation's "number one saboteur." Secretary of the Navy Frank Knox responded by holding a private session with the House Committee on Naval Affairs, on February 23, 1943.

Knox, a former publisher of the *Chicago Daily News*, brought with him an article from the current issue of *American Mercury*, a small-circulation magazine, entitled: "Norfolk—Our Worst War Town." The piece detailed how easy it was to obtain illicit liquor and sex in and around Norfolk, site of the nation's largest naval base. In that Virginia city of some 200,000 population, the Navy had its largest supply depot and the headquarters of the Atlantic Fleet.

Immediately after the session with Knox, Naval Affairs Committee Chairman Carl Vinson appointed a seven-person panel, headed by Ed Izac, to rush to Norfolk and hold hearings. The only woman in the group was Margaret Chase Smith, whom the media promptly dubbed the Vice Admiral. Forty-five years of age, she had become a Republican member of the House in 1940.

Smith sat at the end of a long table at the hearing in Norfolk, decidedly uncomfortable about being surrounded by only men and the topic—sex and whores. In that era, such gross subjects were not discussed in front of refined ladies.

Smith was deeply disturbed by the lurid disclosures. Norfolk officials testified that professional prostitutes were no longer the main source of venereal disease proliferation. Taking the place of the whores as the primary source of contagion were young girls, some only twelve to fourteen years of age.

Labeled "good-time Charlottes," "patriotic amateurs," or "khaki-wackies," these girls, the Norfolk chief of police testified, were "unable to resist a man in uniform."

Margaret Smith was horrified to learn of the steps being taken by law enforcement officers to "control" venereal disease around the naval base. Civilian curfews resulted in the arrest of women "with no visible means of support," leaving it to the police officer to determine if the women were "promiscuous."

Between sessions, without telling her colleagues, the congresswoman slipped away to inspect the Norfolk jail. After her visit, she held a press conference and stated that she had seen ninety-one women and female teenagers at the Norfolk jail held in a crowded space meant for twenty-five. Filthy mattresses and blankets were on the dirty floor. There was one toilet.

Smith angrily told reporters that the females sometimes had to wait weeks or even months before being sentenced or released. Most of the younger girls had been picked up when they were alone on the street trying to find a brother or boyfriend, she said. A few married women told Smith that their Navy husbands had been sent overseas. Bored, lonely, worried, they went out unescorted and were arrested for being "promiscuous."

Despite bold newspaper headlines across the nation resulting from the Norfolk hearings, the congressional subcommittee accomplished nothing. Although expressing concern for the increasing number of teenage "patriotic amateurs," Navy and Norfolk authorities privately held to the belief that arresting and detaining "promiscuous women" was the only practical means for controlling venereal disease. Certainly the 80,000 Navy men in Norfolk on weekends couldn't be put in jail.[3]

A Hollywood Victory Committee

WHILE AMERICA WAS MOBILIZING to confront the extreme dangers to her freedoms, requests for Hollywood stars to appear at bond rallies and other patriotic functions across the land began pouring in. Consequently, a Hollywood Victory Committee of leading lights in the movie industry was formed to coordinate these activities.

Appointed chairman of the Screen Actors Division of the organization was thirty-nine-year-old Clark Gable, one of Tinsel Town's brightest stars, who had skyrocketed to global fame in his role as Rhett Butler in the classic *Gone With the Wind.* He was known as the King of Hollywood.

Hundreds of enthusiastic members turned up at the Hollywood-Roosevelt Hotel for the first meeting of the Victory Committee. All the big names were there: actors, actresses, producers, directors, and studio heads. Gable made a stirring speech, calling on each luminary to pledge his or her support to the war effort.

Earlier, a few hours after the Japanese sneak attack, Gable had fired off a letter to his friend at 1600 Pennsylvania Avenue in Washington, D.C., offering his services and those of his movie star wife, beautiful Carole Lombard, in "any capacity."

In due time, President Roosevelt replied, expressing his gratitude for the offer, but reminding Clark and Carole that entertainment was a vital factor in wartime morale. They could serve the nation best by continuing what they were doing in Hollywood, Roosevelt stated.

With the arrival of the year 1942, Clark Gable was scheduled to begin shooting *Somewhere I'll Find You,* with Lana Turner. Before reporting on the set, however, he flew to Washington and buttonholed another friend, the chief of the Army Air Corps, General Henry H. "Hap" Arnold.

Gable pleaded with Arnold to "get me off the sidelines," and put his stardom to use in some productive endeavor. The general echoed what Roosevelt had written earlier.

Gable flew back home deeply disappointed. Carole thought he should promptly receive a commission. "She won't settle for anything else than a colonel," Clark quipped to friends.[4]

Actress Dies for Her Country

EARLY IN JANUARY 1942, a request arrived at the Victory Committee in Hollywood asking that Carole Lombard, an Indiana native, be the featured attraction at the nation's first War Bond rally. Sponsored by Governor Henry F. Schricker, the event would be held in Indianapolis on January 15.

Anxious to serve her country, Carole eagerly accepted the invitation. The thirty-one-year-old blond and glamorous actress had been born Jane Peters in Fort Wayne, Indiana, and she had fought her way to superstar status from playing bit parts in Western movies at a salary of seventy-five dollars per week.

Carole's journey was as carefully synchronized as a key military operation. She traveled on a special train, with brief stops at Salt Lake City, Chicago, and points in between. At each place she made platform talks and gave media interviews, plugging the need for Americans to buy War Bonds.

Carole Lombard and husband Clark Gable a short time before she died in an airplane crash while serving her country. (MGM)

During the rail safari of several days duration, Carole and Clark talked on the telephone numerous times at her various stops. He had always called her "Ma" and she referred to him as "Pa."

On the appointed day, tens of thousands of people stood in the bitter cold in front of the state house in Indianapolis. A galaxy of political celebrities was on hand. Governor Schricker introduced Carole as the "little Hoosier girl who's made it big in Hollywood."

As the actress strolled to the podium, a thunderous cheer went up. In her short speech, she concluded by calling out, "Heads up, America! Let's give a cheer that will be heard all the way to Tokyo and Berlin!"

Moving aside to a table in the crowded rotunda of the state house, Carole exclaimed in her pleasant voice, "Okay, let's go." The throng moved forward to buy War Bonds. Each purchaser received a certificate bearing the actress's picture and a message from her: "Thank you for joining with me in the vital crusade to make America strong."

Young, old, men, women, many holding infants, patiently awaited their turn. Carole had a friendly word for each one.

"Glad to see you. Thank you, I'm fine, and so is Clark. How many? Thanks. How nice of you."

Carole never stopped to eat. Just past noon she asked an official: "How are we doing?" "Past the million-dollar mark!" "Great! Let's go for two!"

That night a crush of more than ten thousand people gathered in Cadle Tabernacle to hear Carole introduced as "Indiana's number one saleslady" who had sold more than two million dollars in bonds that day.

"Are you tired?" one official asked the nearly exhausted actress.

"Oh, no," she replied. "It's all been great fun!"

At midnight, the hoopla and festivities concluded. Carole had been scheduled to return to Hollywood on the train, but she told a companion she wanted to get back to Pa, so she would fly home. She reached the Indianapolis airport at four o'clock in the morning, and her plane took off for Albuquerque, New Mexico. There fifteen Army pilots got aboard to fly to a base on the West Coast, and the plane lifted off for Las Vegas, Nevada. Then it was on to Los Angeles.

That night, Gable got a telephone call at home. He was shocked. Carole's plane was down, its location unknown. Clark and four friends chartered an aircraft and they arrived at the sheriff's office in Las Vegas. Soon a radio report came in from a pilot of a commercial airline: "Plane crash on a mountain."

Clark's face whitened. He knew immediately what that meant.

A rescue party with a pack train of mules and horses started up the barren, snow-covered mountain. After a tortuous seven-mile climb, the group reached the crash site and radioed back a terse message: No survivors.

A friend approached the distraught Gable. "Ma's gone," Clark said simply.

Grief-stricken, Gable returned to the couple's ranch. Telephone calls and telegrams poured in. President Roosevelt wired:

> Carole brought great joy to all who knew her and to millions who knew her as an artist. She gave unselfishly of her time and talent to serve our country in peace and in war.

Newspapers throughout the nation carried glowing editorial tributes to Carole. The *New York Times* stated: "Like the Army pilots who fell in the burning plane with her, she too died in the service of her country."

Later a Liberty ship that hauled weapons and supplies to fighting men around the globe was named the *Carole Lombard*. Noted Hollywood actress Irene Dunne christened the vessel.[5]

Dismantling a Nazi Spy Network

HOME-FRONT AMERICA, still reeling from the catastrophe at Pearl Harbor, was astonished once again to read and hear that nine men and women, some of them U.S. citizens, would stand trial on espionage charges in a federal court in New York City. Proceedings began on February 3, 1942.

The media labeled the defendants the Ludwig Gang, after the network's leader, Kurt Frederick Ludwig. An insignificant looking man of small physical stature with a nervous manner, he had been born in Fremont, Ohio, but had

Leader of a widespread Nazi spy ring in New York City area was Kurt Ludwig. His principal associate was nineteen-year-old Lucy Boehmler. (FBI)

been taken to Germany as a child. His wife and three children were still living in Munich.

A successful businessman in Germany, Ludwig knew many figures high on the Nazi totem pole, including Gestapo chief Heinrich Himmler. In 1939, shortly after Adolf Hitler had triggered war in Europe by sending his panzers plunging into neighboring Poland, Ludwig told Himmler that even though he was still an American citizen, he was eager to contribute to Germany's war effort. Himmler replied that Ludwig could best serve the Third Reich by spying in the United States.

So after learning secret codes, invisible inks, radio communication, and other espionage techniques at what was called The Academy in Hamburg, Germany, Ludwig, in the guise of a leather goods salesman, arrived in New York City in March 1940. His orders from the Gestapo were to organize his own spy network and report to Germany details on America's armed forces, aircraft production, and the routing of convoys between the United States and England.

Ludwig took to spying as a duck takes to water. He rapidly created a smoothly functioning ring consisting of eight high-grade agents in the New York–New Jersey area, along with a swarm of scouts, couriers, informants, and straphangers. Shrewd, industrious, and innovative, Ludwig, who went by the alias Joe Kessler, was soon flooding intelligence agencies in Germany with much top-secret information.

Ludwig had a powerful automobile—courtesy of Adolf Hitler's billfold—and he loved to race along the highways at the breathtaking speed (for the era) of eighty miles per hour. Hidden in his car was a portable shortwave radio set over which he sent coded signals to clandestine Nazi stations in Brazil or to U-boats off the eastern seaboard of the United States for relay to Germany.

Like any "corporation," Ludwig's organization had a high overhead and required regular infusions of funds. Ludwig seldom knew the source of the money, some of which came from wealthy American citizens. He would receive a message to be at a certain place at a specific time and meet a stranger, whose appearance would be described. On one occasion Ludwig was told to go to Child's Restaurant on 34th Street in Manhattan and watch for a man carrying a *New York Times* in his left hand.

Ludwig took up position near the door and soon spotted the Nazi bagman, who slid into a booth and began reading the *New York Times*. The master spy joined him, the two men exchanged passwords, and the stranger gave Ludwig an envelope containing five hundred dollars (a sizeable sum at the time).

Ludwig casually finished drinking a coffee, then sauntered leisurely out into the crowded sidewalk. Neither man would see the other again.

Piecing together countless tiny clues, agents of the Federal Bureau of Investigation got on the tail of "Joe Kessler," and through tedious probing, secured enough evidence to arrest the Nazi spy and eight key members of his spy ring. Blaring newspaper headlines and radio news reports about their trial intensified spy-mania across America.

Mathias F. Correa, an able young U.S. attorney, and his associates presented a huge collection of devastating evidence—all of it collected by the FBI. There were three hundred exhibits and in excess of two thousand pages of interrogations.

After five weeks of listening to the incriminating evidence, the jury returned a guilty verdict against all of Ludwig's gang. Only Ludwig failed to take the stand in his defense. No doubt he knew that his wife and children in Munich would be handed over to the Gestapo should he talk.

Although the trial was held when the United States was at war, the espionage had taken place before Pearl Harbor, so the defendants were sentenced under peacetime laws. Ludwig was given the maximum penalty—twenty years in prison. Receiving the same penalty was fifty-five-year-old Paul Borchardt, a major in the German army, who had come to the United States in February 1940 under the auspices of a New York City Catholic organization whose function was to spirit refugees out of Hitler's Europe.

Also receiving a twenty-year term was René Froelich, a thirty-four-year-old native of Germany who was drafted into the U.S. Army in early 1941. Stationed at Fort Jay on Governor's Island in New York harbor, he was a clerk in the post hospital. Patients from area camps were admitted to the Fort Jay medical facility, where each day a list of new admissions and discharges was drawn up and placed on the desk of the commanding officer. Copies of the lists were stolen by Froelich and handed over to Ludwig.

The spy-ring leader was elated. The lists revealed, for example, that a discharged patient was Sergeant John Smith of the 76th Field Artillery. This knowledge permitted Ludwig to inform Hamburg that the 76th Field Artillery was stationed at Fort Dix, New Jersey.

In consideration of her cooperation with the FBI, Lucy Boehmler, a nineteen-year-old full-bosomed beauty, was handed the lightest sentence—five years. Born in Germany and brought to New York City at age five, she had been one of Ludwig's first recruits.

Ludwig had spotted this seemingly all-American schoolgirl at a social function. Bit by bit, he lured her into espionage work. She had been fascinated by his spy tales and finally joined him in search of "excitement."

The spymaster noted that Lucy possessed a hidden talent that was invaluable in espionage activity—a phenomenal memory. She soon became one of his slickest agents, shielded in part from suspicion by her schoolgirl charm and appearance.

Another agent, Helen Mayer, a Brooklyn housewife, had invited Grumman Aircraft Corporation employees to her home. After plying the unwary dupes with liquor she subtly picked their brains for military secrets. She received a term of fifteen years.

Also sentenced to fifteen years was Hans Pagel, a short, fair-haired youth who was one of Ludwig's most fanatical agents. Pagel looked harmless enough. But his special job had been to cover the New York waterfront and report on ship sailings, information that was relayed to German U-boats lurking off the eastern seaboard.

Karl Victor Mueller, another of Ludwig's key foot soldiers, was born in a small Austrian village and became a naturalized American. He was thirty-five years of age, but deep furrows in his brow and a prematurely old countenance caused him to look elderly. He even walked like an old man, his skinny body leaning forward and his head bobbing with each step.

Mueller carried a camera on spy jaunts, and even though he spoke with a thick Teutonic accent, guards and attendants at war production plants and airfields often went out of their way to help the "harmless old man" get the photographs he sought.

Mueller's true allegiance was to Nazi-occupied Austria, to which he hoped to return as a national hero. Instead he would spend the next fifteen years in a U.S. prison.

Twenty-one-year-old Frederick Edward Schlosser had initially been a reluctant spy. Tall and blond, he had been a pal of Hans Pagel and was engaged to Pagel's sister.

At first Schlosser had resisted Pagel's incessant pleas to become a spy, but he finally consented. Ludwig put the youth to work trekking up and down New York City piers culling shipping information. Soon the newcomer was caught up in the excitement, as he termed it, and he even stole a piece of a new antiaircraft gun from a factory where he worked. He was given twelve years internment.

Carl Herman Schroetter refused to testify against his confederates and was sentenced to ten years. He had an ideal "cover"—skipper of a charter boat, *Echo of the Past*, based in Miami. Swiss-born Schroetter, who had two sisters living in Germany, cruised the Atlantic coast of Florida while shepherding paid tourists and mailed to Ludwig in New York City a stream of coded messages on ship movements.

A few days after Schroetter entered the federal penitentiary in Atlanta, he hanged himself with a sheet in his cell. Presumably he had anguished over the probable fate of his two sisters at the hands of the Gestapo in Germany.[6]

A Debacle in Manhattan

PIER 88 ON THE NEW YORK CITY WATERFRONT was a beehive of activity in early 1942. Tied up there was the French luxury liner *Normandie*, which had been in the port in September 1939 when France and England declared war on Nazi Germany and was taken over by the U.S. Navy after France fell in mid-1940. It was being converted to a troop transport.

There was enormous urgency to the renovation task. It was to be finished by February 28, after which the ship would sail to Boston. There ten thousand soldiers would climb aboard, along with weapons and equipment, before sailing into the Atlantic Ocean under sealed orders.

Because of the rush, only cursory checks had been made on the backgrounds of the civilian workers. Likewise, no background investigations were conducted for the hundreds of men who brought building materials and furnishings on board.

On the afternoon of February 9, less than three weeks before the *Normandie* was to sail for Europe, fire broke out on the gray-painted ship. Flames began whipping rapidly through corridors, and in an hour the liner was an inferno. New York City firemen later would state that the heat was the most intense that they had experienced.

As the flames spread, some three thousand civilian workers, crewmen, and others began scrambling over the sides of the ship or dashing down gangplanks. Hardly had the last man escaped, at 2:32 P.M., than the doomed liner, listing heavily from tons of water poured into her by New York City fireboats, rolled onto her side and lay still in the Hudson's gray ice.

At the time when every ship was vital to the war effort, the United States had lost its largest transport. Frank Trentascosta was killed when he received a fractured skill in a fall down a ladder. Some two hundred and fifty others suffered burns, cuts, bruises, or lung irritations.

Converted French ocean liner Normandie *ablaze under mysterious circumstances in New York harbor. (U.S. Navy)*

Hardly had the *Normandie* capsized than several groups launched investigations to pinpoint the blame. A congressional Naval Affairs subcommittee concluded that "the cause of the fire [is] directly attributable to carelessness by [civilian workers]."

Millions of Americans refused to agree. They felt that they knew the real culprits—German saboteurs.

The people's suspicions would have been reinforced had they known the government investigations had either failed to report on the role played by the Oceanic Service Corporation or else had chosen to keep silent about it. Oceanic had handled the hiring of many of the guards and workers on the *Normandie*.

Oceanic had been founded by William Dreschel, who had formerly been a superintendent of the North German Lloyd Steamship Line. A few years earlier he had admitted to a House committee that he had supplied $125,000 bail (equivalent to $1.5 million in 2002) for Nazi agents who had been arrested in the United States. In 1938, during the trial of eleven men and women who had been charged with conducting anti-Nazi demonstrations on the deck of the German ocean liner *Bremen* when it was at a New York City pier, Dreschel was asked by the defense counsel: "Do you owe allegiance to Adolf Hitler?" The answer was a loud: "Yes!"

After Hitler declared war on the United States, the ownership and the identity of the officials of the Oceanic Service Corporation had not been investigated by U.S. officials. So the firm had been placing its people on the *Normandie* at the pier without question.

Ten days after the *Normandie* capsized and lay on its side like a huge beached whale, Congressman Samuel Dickstein took to the House floor and stridently charged that William Dreschel had put Nazi guards on the liner.

Calling Dreschel "the nation's number one spy," the congressman thundered: "He organized the Oceanic Service Corporation and through that agency was supplying guards to ships, piers, and warehouses in New York City. He placed more than thirty Nazi agents on the *Normandie!*"[7]

The Battle of Los Angeles

AT A PRESS CONFERENCE in the Oval Office of the White House on February 17, 1942, President Roosevelt dropped a blockbuster in an offhand manner. He declared that it was possible that an American city could be shelled and bombed without warning. Did he have any particular cities in mind? Yes, New York and Detroit. Curiously, by omission Roosevelt seemed to indicate that Washington was not a target for any enemy force.

Six days after Roosevelt's pronouncement, as if to dramatize his viewpoint, a Japanese submarine surfaced at night off Goleta, California, eight miles north of Santa Barbara, and pumped twelve to fifteen shells from a deck gun into a large oil complex. A derrick was blown apart, but little other damage was done.

However, it was a psychological victory for the people of Japan. A Tokyo newspaper headline screamed: "Our Submarines Destroy Large U.S. City."

American intelligence officers concluded that the Japanese submarine had been tuned in to California commercial radio broadcasts because the shelling erupted at the precise time that President Roosevelt was giving one of his folksy fireside chats.

A night after the oil field shelling, three million people in the Los Angeles region were rousted from sleep when sirens began blaring throughout the sprawling complex. Minutes later, scores of powerful searchlights began stabbing long fingers of white into the black sky. Army antiaircraft guns barked and fired more than fifteen hundred rounds at the phantom enemy bomber forces.

Citizens were terrified. Many fled to basements. Others crawled under beds. Adding to the raucous din, police cars dashed about with sirens screeching. An hour after lookouts had spotted the nonexistent bombers, an eerie silence descended upon Los Angeles.[8]

"We Poison Rats and Japs"

ANGER AND NEAR-HYSTERIA continued to saturate the U.S. home front weeks after the Japanese treachery. These deep emotions intensified after what turned

A *"dangerous subversive"* looks in bewilderment at an armed guard. No incident of betrayal by Japanese Americans ever occurred. (U.S. Army)

out to be false rumors seeped out that Japanese civilians in the Hawaiian Islands had pinpointed targets for the air armada.

Americans reacted with a gut impulse for revenge, and erupted in a rage against General Hideki Tojo, the warlord, and the Japanese nation as a whole. In their fury, American civilians turned on some of their own neighbors and fellow citizens—the 125,000 men, women, and children of Japanese birth or descent who lived in the continental United States. Nearly all of them resided on the West Coast, mainly in California. Some 70,000 had been born on U.S. soil, a fact that made them bona fide citizens.

In the shock and terror that followed the debacle at Pearl Harbor, General John DeWitt, in charge of West Coast defenses (which were virtually non-existent), snapped: "A Jap's a Jap! It makes no difference if he is an American or not!"

DeWitt had plenty of company. Milkmen refused to deliver their products to Japanese Americans (known as Nisei); grocers refused to sell them food; insurance companies cancelled their policies. The state of California revoked their licenses to practice law or medicine.

At first, the Japanese Americans were encouraged to leave California voluntarily and go inland to other states. Some eight thousand Japanese Americans followed the suggestion, thereby triggering angry voices from politicians and the media.

"If the Japs are dangerous in California, they are likewise dangerous in Nevada," declared the Nevada Bar Association. Said Governor Chase Clark of Idaho, "I don't want them taking seats in our universities."

"Japs are not wanted or welcome in Kansas," said Governor Payne Ratner, who ordered the state patrol to bar them from using the highways.

The thousands of wandering Japanese Americans were harassed at every turn. Many restaurants refused to serve them and ordered them out. Some eating places hung signs in their windows that read: "We poison rats and Japs." Gas station employees wouldn't fill their tanks with fuel. Small town cops threw some of the refugees in jail for "loitering" or as "suspicious subjects" before releasing them the next day.

In the weeks ahead, angry voices were raised across the United States, a resounding chorus demanding that every man, woman, and child of Japanese descent be evacuated from the West Coast. Perhaps the most powerful voice was that of Walter Lippmann, whose syndicated columns on politics and foreign affairs were carried in hundreds of newspapers.

Harvard-educated Lippmann may well have been the nation's most influential journalist. It was said that Washington politicians read his columns as though Moses had brought them down from the mountain. Among Lippmann's most ardent fans was President Franklin Roosevelt.

In those confused early days of the war, Lippmann wrote a strident column:

> It is a fact that the Japanese navy has been reconnoitering the Pacific Coast. . . . It is a fact that communication takes place between the enemy at sea and enemy agents on land.
>
> I submit that Washington [meaning President Roosevelt] is not defining the problem on the Pacific Coast correctly and that it is failing to deal with the practical issues.
>
> The Pacific Coast is officially a combat zone; some part of it may at any moment be a battlefield. Nobody's constitutional rights include the right to reside and do business on the battlefield.

Lippmann had substituted rumor and theory for facts. Never had there been any known incident of anyone on the Pacific Coast signaling Japanese submarines offshore.

Other influential voices joined the evacuation cacophony, including California Attorney General Earl Warren and Secretary of the Treasury Henry Morgenthau.

J. Edgar Hoover, the Federal Bureau of Investigation chief, strongly opposed the mass upheaval, describing any such action as being "a capitulation to public hysteria." Hoover told Morgenthau that arrests should not be made "unless there are sufficient fact [probable cause] upon which to justify the arrests"; that the rights of American citizens should be protected.

Hoover was a voice crying in the wilderness. No doubt responding to demands from influential public sources and segments of the media, President Roosevelt, on February 19, 1942, signed Executive Order No. 9066. It authorized Secretary of War Henry Stimson to "establish military areas" on the West Coast and "exclude from them any and all [suspicious] persons."

The ink had hardly dried on Roosevelt's order than a mass evacuation of Japanese civilians and Nisei began. They were given forty-eight hours in which to dispose of their businesses, homes, and automobiles before reporting, with whatever belongings they could carry as hand luggage, to fifteen Army-run Assembly Centers, as they were officially designated.

On arrival, the detainees were given medical examinations and identification cards and herded into hastily thrown-up barracks. They were penned in by barbed-wire fences and constantly watched by patrolling Army military police. At night, searchlights swept the bare ground outside the wire.

Altogether, with brutal swiftness, 110,000 people—nearly the entire Japanese and Nisei community in the West—had been driven out of their homes and into virtual captivity.

Incredibly, almost without exception, the young men endured the internment and its humiliation with their faith in the United States unimpaired. Many of the Japanese Americans insisted that they be allowed to prove their loyalty to the United States by serving in frontline combat. One of them behind barbed wire, Henry Ebihar, wrote Secretary of War Stimson: "I only ask that I be given a chance to preserve the principles that I have been brought up on and which I will not sacrifice at any cost. Please give me a chance to serve in your armed forces."

In response to the clamor from the young men in the internment camps, Congress authorized the formation of an all-Nisei combat unit, and on January 28, 1943, the Army announced it would accept volunteers. Some twelve hundred signed up and eventually joined the newly formed 442nd Regimental Combat Team.

Meanwhile in Honolulu, another Nisei, seventeen-year-old Daniel K. Inouye, graduated from McKinley High School, where he was an honor student, only four months after the Pearl Harbor catastrophe. Perhaps because of his youth, he was not regarded by older Caucasians as a suspected subversive or threat to the United States, although he received his share of snubs and insults.

The oldest of four children, Inouye was born in Honolulu. His father, Hyotaro, had immigrated to Hawaii as a child from a village in Japan, worked as a file clerk to support the family in what Daniel would later describe as "respectable poverty."

Shortly after receiving his high school diploma, Daniel enrolled in the premedical program at the University of Hawaii. But he dropped out of college to enlist as a private in the 442nd Regimental Combat Team, whose motto was "Go for Broke!"

Twenty-one-year-old Lieutenant Daniel Inouye, who would receive the Congressional Medal of Honor fifty years later for an action in which he was seriously wounded. (Courtesy Senator Daniel Inouye)

Mild-mannered, soft-spoken Dan Inouye proved to be a tiger in combat, a natural leader of men, and he was awarded a battlefield commission as a second lieutenant.

In late April 1945, Lieutenant Inouye was leading his platoon in an assault to capture a heavily fortified German position that included several machine guns and a company of grenadiers (infantrymen) in the Po Valley of Italy. A blistering firefight erupted. Swarms of bullets hissed and sang overhead.

Inouye began slithering toward three spitting machine guns. Moments later, a rifle grenade exploded next to him, and jagged chunks of red-hot metal tore into his right arm. Dazed, bleeding profusely, his arm hanging in shreds, the lieutenant continued edging toward the German force. Then bullets ripped into his stomach and legs.

Through superhuman effort, Inouye managed to pull a pin from a grenade, rise up and toss the lethal missile. It exploded in the midst of one machine-gun crew. Twice more he lobbed grenades, wiping out the other two automatic weapons. Then he collapsed, unaware that his feats had permitted his platoon to charge forward and seize that objective.

After a few weeks in Army hospitals in Italy, where doctors had saved his life, Lieutenant Inouye was flown to the United States and became a patient at the Percy Jones Medical Center in Battle Creek, Michigan. The facility focused on rehabilitation of seriously wounded soldiers. Two other patients there were Robert Dole of Kansas, and Phillip Hart of Michigan. None of these three maimed servicemen had any way of knowing that years later all would be serving together in Washington as U.S. senators.

Inouye spent two years in Army hospitals, recovering from his wounds and from amputation of his right arm at the shoulder. During these long, lonely hours, he had plenty of time to ponder his future—if indeed a twenty-one-year-old Nisei veteran with one arm had a future.

Unhappy, morose, nearly despondent, and usually dependent upon others, Inouye tried not to think of tomorrow. Yet his thoughts came back to his role in the civilian world.

He pledged not to let his physical disability thwart him from achieving useful goals in the years ahead. So he decided to change career directions and go into law and politics, instead of becoming a physician.[9]

Goal: Coalition of Africa and Japan

ON FEBRUARY 28, 1942, violent racial strife erupted in Detroit, a vital center for war production. At the Sojourner Truth housing project prospective Negro tenants were assaulted by white men armed with clubs, knives, and rifles. There were scores of injuries and more than one hundred arrests.

Two of the white men taken into custody were members of a hate group that had been distributing pro-Nazi propaganda in the project. However, the rabble-rousers igniting violence in the Detroit region were five black men. They included Robert Jordan, a West India native, whose goal was to form a coalition of Africa and Japan to dominate the world.

In Berlin, Adolf Hitler's propaganda genius, Paul Josef Goebbels, used racial discord in the United States in the Nazi's worldwide disinformation apparatus. The Sojourner Truth riot in Detroit triggered an enormous outburst of propaganda. *Die Wehrmacht*, the Nazi newspaper aimed at the German armed forces, published a full page of pictures on the Detroit violence.[10]

Mysterious Malady on Ships

DURING A THREE-WEEK PERIOD beginning on March 1, 1942, a mysterious malady struck several cargo ships after they sailed out of Boston, New York, and Philadelphia bound for hard-pressed Soviet forces. Each vessel was making the dangerous trek separately.

The freighters were loaded with tanks, munitions, airplane parts, artillery pieces, and other war supplies. A few days out in the Atlantic, as though on cue, each ship foundered and was unable to continue to its destination.

Guns, tanks, and trucks broke loose, careened over the deck, smashed other war goods, and plunged into the heavy swells of an angry ocean. Crippled by the shifting loads, each vessel was forced to slow, and then turn around and head back to its home port. A few ships never made it.

One of the vessels, the SS *Collmar*, a sitting duck, was torpedoed and sunk with the loss of ten crewmen, as it limped along toward Philadelphia.

The National Maritime Union smelled Nazi skullduggery in American ports and launched an investigation. It was found that, in several instances, cotter pins had not been in place on the shackles holding the deck cargoes.

On March 26, Joseph Curran, president of the Maritime Union, testified before a House committee in Washington that the shifting cargoes had hardly ever been a problem in peacetime. "We, as seamen, have been sailing ships that carried heavy deck loads, sometimes as high as you could get them, and we never lost any of that cargo," Curran declared. "We never had a problem with deck loads."[11]

The FBI and the OSS Feud

DURING THE EARLY MONTHS OF 1942, William J. "Wild Bill" Donovan, a wealthy Wall Street lawyer and Congressional Medal of Honor recipient in World War I, dashed about Washington and New York City like a demon possessed in a search of recruits. A few weeks before Pearl Harbor, Donovan had been appointed by President Franklin Roosevelt to a new post: Coordinator of Information (COI).

It was a deliberately vague title. Roosevelt, a consummate politician, had privately instructed Donovan to launch political warfare against America's enemies, using the president's unvouchered funds. Actually, Donovan was to be the nation's first official spymaster.

Establishing the COI had been a landmark in U.S. history and was designed to fill a crucial need for a worldwide intelligence apparatus. In an often hostile and volatile world, the United States had been stumbling around without eyes and ears.

After Pearl Harbor, the energetic Donovan, who had connections worldwide, conducted a nonstop personal recruiting campaign for his fledgling cloak-and-dagger outfit. At posh cocktail parties, in Wall Street law firm suites, in the cloistered halls of Ivy League universities, in multibillion-dollar banks and investment firms, and along countless byways and highways, the indefatigable spymaster gave his sales pitch.

Flocking to Donovan's siren call was a strange mixed bag: multimillionaire bluebloods and union organizers, athletes and ministers, bartenders and missionaries, a former Russian general, a big-game hunter, a former advisor to a Chinese warlord, and professors. There were corporate executives, lawyers, editors, scientists, labor leaders, ornithologists, code experts, and anthropologists, wild-animal trainers, safe-crackers, circus acrobats, paroled convicts, and a bullfighter. Scores of rough-and-ready individuals were, as Donovan described them, "hell raisers who are calculatingly reckless, of disciplined daring, eager for aggressive action, and enjoy slitting throats."

Understandably, two strong-willed men competing on the same turf—Bill Donovan and J. Edgar Hoover of the FBI—soon clashed. Their ongoing duel intensified in mid-January 1942, six weeks after Pearl Harbor. No doubt Donovan privately approved a caper in which his agents "penetrated" (that is, broke into at night) the Spanish embassy in Washington. The dark intruders busily photographed the top-secret codebooks and assorted official documents of Generalissimo Francisco Franco's pro-Nazi government.

When Hoover heard about the intrusion on his domain he was furious but did not register a formal complaint with President Roosevelt.

Three months later, Donovan's boys paid another nocturnal call at the Spanish embassy to practice their photographic skills. They were tailed to the site by FBI agents in two unmarked cars.

Waiting while the intruders broke into the building, the FBI men pulled their vehicles in front of the embassy and parked. A few minutes later, the G-men turned on their sirens, whose strident sounds pierced the black stillness.

For blocks around, citizens dashed into the streets to determine the reason for the shrill noise. Was Washington about to be bombed by German planes?

Then the FBI cars sped away, just before the "burglars" scurried hell-bent out of the embassy.

Learning of the squabble between two of his elite agencies, President Roosevelt issued strict orders that implied the "legal burglary" of embassies in Washington was to be the sole domain of the FBI.

Donovan reportedly accepted the executive decision with a shrug, and continued to expand his agency, whose name would be changed to the Office of Strategic Services (OSS).

The new designation stirred up the fussing-and-feuding pot. The U.S. Army's chief of intelligence refused to even speak to a *reserve* officer and communicated with Donovan through an intermediary when absolutely necessary. Hoover and the head of the U.S. Navy intelligence were embroiled in a squabble of their own, but each managed to find time to take potshots at Wild Bill and his fledgling OSS.[12]

Hijinks on a Hospital Roof

SHORTLY AFTER PEARL HARBOR, Navy Lieutenant Commander John "Pappy" Ford set up a small temporary office in Washington. A famed Hollywood movie director, Ford had been acclaimed with Academy Awards for such blockbusters as *The Grapes of Wrath, Stagecoach, Young Mr. Lincoln,* and *How Green Was My Valley.*

Famed Hollywood director John "Pappy" Ford (left) and a top assistant, Robert Parrish. Ford headed an OSS combat intelligence unit. (Courtesy of Robert Parrish)

Back in mid-1940, with America starting to partially mobilize in the wake of the threat of Adolf Hitler's powerful military juggernaut, Pappy Ford, then forty-five years old and holding the reserve rank of Navy lieutenant commander, formed Field Photographic, an ad hoc unit without official Navy status. He signed up some of the biggest names in Hollywood: cameramen, soundmen, special effects, film editors, and script writers.

Ford organized his talented cinema civilians into a martial-type unit, taught them the basics of military discipline, then tried tenaciously to get Washington naval brass to absorb Field Photographic into the official reserves. For more than a year, Ford pleaded his case, but he was given the cold shoulder.

Ford was about to give up on his crusade as a lost cause when, just before Pearl Harbor, lightning struck from an unexpected source. Field Photographic was swept up intact by Bill Donovan, who felt that the moving-picture unit would be a valuable tool for cloak-and-dagger operations.

A few weeks later in Washington, Commander Ford called in two of his young petty officers, Robert Parrish and Bill Faralla, who had labored in the vineyards of the Hollywood movie industry. Ford instructed them to test a new type of combat camera that had been developed by Ray Cunningham, a technician at RKO Studios. The revolutionary moving-picture camera was mounted on a .30-.30 rifle stock; all the photographer had to do was point the camera and squeeze the trigger.

Rising from his desk, Pappy Ford spit in the direction of a wooden box he kept in the corner for that function, lit his pipe, and said to Parrish and Faralla, "Give me a complete photographic report on the State Department Building next to the White House. Cover it from all angles, outside, inside, what have you. Don't take any crap from anyone. If they give you a hard time, show them your OSS card."

Parrish and Faralla, wearing their navy uniforms, entered a hospital across from the White House, climbed up stairs to the roof, and were accosted by a nurse. "Who are you men and what are you doing here?" she demanded to know, suspiciously eyeing the gunlike camera and other paraphernalia the strangers were carrying.

"We're here on official business, Ma'am," Parrish responded as Faralla flashed his OSS card. "We're from the OSS."

"Oh, yes," the nurse replied. "The OSS. Well, continue with your work." Faralla and Parrish were convinced that the dedicated nurse had no clue as to what OSS even stood for, much less what its function was. They set up a tripod, attached the odd-looking camera to it, and aimed what appeared to a marine on the roof of the State Department Building to be a machine gun. The sentry waved furiously, but the pair kept shooting moving pictures, including footage of a World War I machine gun "guarding" the White House.

Glancing back toward the State Department roof, Parrish froze as he saw a squad of marine reinforcements point their old bolt-action rifles at the unknown intruders on the hospital roof. With their first "combat photography" under their belts, Parrish and Faralla surrendered.

Parrish and Faralla were ensconced in a "detention chamber" in the sub-basement of the State Department Building. There they remained incommunicado, from 4:30 P.M. on Sunday until Tuesday at 11:00 A.M. They were handled much as espionage suspects would be. Guards confiscated their OSS cards ("We never heard of no OSS," one explained), the expensive combat camera (which was closely inspected for German and Japanese markings), and personal belongings.

Parrish kept telling the marine captain that the two men had been on a mission for Lieutenant Commander John Ford, the famous Hollywood director. The marine was unmoved. He said the suspects would remain until the camera-gun (as he called it) had been checked out by ballistic technicians. The film had been sent to other authorities to be developed and scrutinized.

Presumably John Ford had not been notified that two suspicious men claimed to be working for him because it was more than forty hours before Tom Early, a top aide to OSS boss Bill Donovan, arrived at the "jail."

Faralla and Parrish were relieved to know that the visitor was the brother of Stephen Early, President Roosevelt's press secretary. Hopes were quickly dashed. Tom Early advised the detainees that the marine captain was insisting that they be court-martialed by the Navy.

Finally, Commander Ford got into the act. He told the marine that his two men were only doing their jobs. "I think we should lock their film in a vault and dismiss any charges," Ford declared. "Do you agree, Captain?"

After pausing briefly, the marine replied, "I agree, Commander."

Bob Parrish and Bill Faralla were free men again.

Pappy Ford and Bill Donovan had hit it off from the beginning; each was a rugged individualist with a touch of the maverick in him. They would have been failures as diplomats for each said precisely what was on his mind. In mid-1942, Donovan called a meeting at OSS headquarters in Washington for precisely 8:00 A.M. Hard-driving, hard-drinking Ford had been carousing the city until daylight, and when he walked silently into the conference room, his eyes concealed behind dark glasses, the others had already taken their seats.

"Commander Ford," Donovan barked. "If you can see well enough, we'll get started!"

"General," Pappy replied evenly, "I can see one thing—you've got that ribbon for your Congressional Medal of Honor on the wrong place on your uniform!"

Donovan joined in the chorus of laughter.[13]

Suspicions Run Rampant

IN FEBRUARY 1942, rumors continued to deluge home-front America. People in southern Florida spread the word that a German submarine captured off-shore had a galley (kitchen) with milk bottles from a Miami dairy. Never mind that no German submarine had been captured. The tale was too good not to pass along. For many weeks home-delivery drivers from this dairy were the subjects of much suspicion—even scorn.

A good story can always stand elaboration, so in a variation of the Miami dairy yarn word raced through Virginia that bread from a Richmond bakery had been found on the "captured" U-boat.

No matter how absurd, these rumors were tracked down and deflated by the overburdened Federal Bureau of Investigation. But the probes did little, if anything, to shut off the rumor mills.[14]

"German Officers" Stalk Harbor

SUBVERSION WAS ON THE MINDS of newspaper editors, and much ink was devoted to warn the public to be on the lookout for "suspicious persons." Hoping to dramatize the lax security at war plants (and to sell more newspapers), two Philadelphia reporters donned the uniforms of officers of the Kriegsmarine (German Navy), complete with swastika armbands. It was early February 1942.

For the most of one day, the reporters stalked up and down the Philadelphia docks, stopping on occasion to point at a U.S. Navy ship and speaking with thick German accents. Not once were they challenged. The only time they received "official" attention was when a Philadelphia policemen told them that their automobile (a prewar German make) was parked illegally. When he saw that they were "navy boys," the policeman did not give them a parking ticket.[15]

Commercial Radio's First War

THROUGHOUT HOME-FRONT AMERICA, millions of citizens kept ears glued to one of the 836 broadcast outlets that reached into homes day after day, night after night. Commercial radio had taken its first wobbly steps only nineteen years before Pearl Harbor, so this was the medium's first war.

In the early weeks of the global conflict, radio advertisers displayed an enormous appetite for bad taste when they tied their pitches to the war. Said one ad: "Use Gillette blades which will last longer, and thereby conserve steel for national defense." The message was clear. Any man who didn't buy Gillette products was unpatriotic, perhaps even unwittingly helping Adolf Hitler and Emperor Hirohito.

Another radio commercial tried to get listener's ears by having an authoritative-sounding announcer suddenly shout: "Here is an important late news bulletin! Use Smith Brothers cough drops."

One New York City station and its advertiser collaborated on an incredible stunt. After a newscaster launched a spiel about American casualties overseas, the advertiser (a funeral parlor and cemetery) had an announcer state: "You never know when to expect bad news so be prepared. Buy a family lot now."

Aware of a backlash from an angry public, radio moguls began correcting the avalanche of bad taste spewing from advertisers. Commercials trying to capitalize on the war were refused in most instances. Announcements using gunfire, airplane engines, the revving of tank motors, and the blast of a destroyer's horn to sell Pall Mall cigarettes or other goods were banned by the networks.

Radio commentators on home-front America enjoyed a freedom of speech that could not be found in any other nation. If so inclined, a commentator perched comfortably on his throne could, and did, lambast President Roosevelt, his administration chiefs, the armed forces high command, the conduct of the war, and the British, French, and Soviet allies.

These commentators made no pretense of objective or unbiased reporting. Most hammered at their favorite targets, often using as weapons gossip and unfounded rumor. This approach was puzzling to millions of Americans who tuned into programs listed in their newspapers as "news" and instead were assaulted by prejudiced commentaries.[16]

Two years after America went to war, German U-boats were still stalking the eastern seaboard. This oil tanker was torpedoed in sight of bathers on a Florida beach near Miami. (U.S. Navy)

U-Boats "Ruining" Tourist Season

ALTHOUGH MEDIA on home-front America were free to blast President Roosevelt and other leaders, newspapers and radio were forbidden to give even a hint about the bloody carnage being inflicted by German U-boats in sight of citizens along the east coast.

Aware that the U.S. coastal defenses were virtually nonexistent, the submarines became steadily more brazen. Almost within view of the mighty naval base at Norfolk, Virginia, on March 13, 1942, an Allied freighter was sunk and the U-boat remained on the surface for four hours, shining a yellow light in its conning tower.

Soon the bold U-boat captains became so smug that they began sinking ships in broad daylight. Thousands of bathers at Coney Island, New York; Virginia Beach, Virginia; Atlantic City, New Jersey; and Miami, Florida, watched in horror as oil tankers were torpedoed, causing the vessels to explode in balls of fire and thick black smoke. Surviving crewmen, most heavily burned, mutilated, and cover with oil, struggled ashore.

U-boat skippers began referring to their zones of operations as the American Front. The U.S. Navy concluded that German submarines were being guided by lights and electric signs in cities along the Atlantic coast. Howls of protest erupted from Atlantic City southward to the tip of Florida when Washington ruled that the illuminations would have to be extinguished.

"Such an extreme action would ruin the tourist season," one large-hotel owner in Miami complained. It would be two more months before the last light blinked out.[17]

Helping a German POW Escape

A TALL, RUGGEDLY HANDSOME, blond man in civilian clothes walked up to the front door of a Detroit home occupied by Margaretta Johanna Bertlemann, a thirty-six-year-old housewife. Glancing quickly around, the man knocked on the door. It was March 12, 1942.

When Bertlemann, who lived alone, answered the summons, the man asked for a drink of water. Once inside, he identified himself as Lieutenant Hans Peter Krug, a bomber pilot in the Luftwaffe, who had not been at all happy with accommodations at his prisoner-of-war camp in Ontario, Canada. Comrades in the enclosure had found Bertlemann's name and address written on a slip of paper and concealed in a pair of socks that had been sent in a gift package from the Third Reich.

A few weeks earlier, Krug had been chafing over the dreary humdrum of life behind barbed wire. His mind flashed back more than a year to the time another Luftwaffe pilot, Oberleutnant Franz von Werra, had gained world fame by escaping from Canada, sneaking into the United States, and eventually making his way back to Germany. Krug had been determined to follow in von Werra's footsteps.

With the aid of fellow POWs, a dummy had been rigged from newspapers and straw and carried to the predawn roll call. The dummy was crude, but it had masked Krug's absence long enough for him to get a good running start after slipping out of the camp. He made his way to Windsor, Ontario, and crossed the Detroit River into the United States.

Now in her home, Margaretta Bertlemann accepted his identification after the escapee displayed the epaulets he had cut from his Luftwaffe uniform. She provided breakfast for the famished German, and told him she knew a man who could assist him in his flight. He was Max Stephen, a naturalized U.S. citizen who owned a Detroit restaurant that was a gathering place for members of the German-American Bund, the Nazi organization of U.S. citizens.

Stephen was contacted, and he plunged enthusiastically into the task. He gave Krug shelter and money, coached him on how he should act to avoid suspicion, and bought him a bus ticket to Chicago. Then the restaurant operator, who had a framed picture of Adolf Hitler hanging on the wall in his home, outlined a detailed escape plan. Krug, who spoke only sketchy English, was to proceed by stages toward the Rio Grande River in Texas, then slip over into Mexico and board a ship back to the Third Reich.

The escape plan unfolded as prescribed, and Krug reached San Antonio, Texas, in routine fashion. There he registered in a dingy hotel as Jean Ette, and went to his room. In the morning, he would catch a bus that would take him to the Mexican border.

That night Krug was deep in slumber when he awakened with a start. Three men had crashed through the locked door and pounced on the German. They flashed their badges and called out: "FBI!"

Krug gave up with a struggle. The hotel clerk had recognized the escapee from an FBI wanted notice.

In the days ahead, J. Edgar Hoover's sleuths linked Max Stephen to the escape, and the Detroit man was taken into custody. He was convicted of treason—the first American to be found guilty and sentenced to death.

Later President Roosevelt commuted Max Stephen's sentence to life imprisonment. Presumably the rich restaurant owner had squealed on other Nazi agents in the Detroit region to save his life.[18]

Strange Scenario in San Francisco

ON MARCH 31, 1942, three men in civilian clothes were conferring intensely in a secluded booth in a San Francisco restaurant. No one in the room paid attention to the men, so the other diners and waitresses were unaware that the occupants of the booth were plotting a military operation that would soon electrify the entire free world: bombing Tokyo.

Planning the mission was Vice Admiral William F. "Bull" Halsey, who had the good fortune of being at sea with a task force of aircraft carriers when the Japanese bombers hit Pearl Harbor; Commander Miles R. Browning, Halsey's chief of staff; and Air Corps Lieutenant Colonel James H. "Jimmy" Doolittle, who had gained peacetime fame as a stunt flyer.

The cloak-and-dagger touch (civilian clothes, rendezvousing in a public restaurant) resulted from the quite real possibility that Japanese spies might be lurking in San Francisco. Halsey and Doolittle were well known and might have been spotted by hostile eyes had they been in uniform and going into a Navy building. Should the Tokyo warlords learn that Halsey, who commanded a force of aircraft carriers, and Doolittle, leader of a group of two-engine B-25 bombers, were secretly conferring, the Japanese might have deduced the nature of the forthcoming operation and taken steps to smash it.

Halsey and Doolittle shook hands and left the restaurant separately. Their next meeting would be out in the Pacific Ocean.[19]

Silencing a Priest Rabble-Rouser

IN APRIL 1942, Attorney General Francis Biddle asked the postmaster general to cancel the second-class mailing privileges of *Social Justice*, claiming that it echoed the enemy's propaganda line. That permit was the type that gave special low rates to media, without which most newspapers and magazines could not exist.

Father Charles E. Coughlin, a Detroit priest, was publisher of *Social Justice*, a monthly publication with a circulation in excess of 200,000. Coughlin charged that Jews and Communists had tricked the American people into supporting the war.

Coughlin, apparently, was delighted with the government action. Now he could gain enormous publicity for his views by testifying before a grand jury.

Biddle, for his part, had no intention of converting Coughlin into a martyr. So he quietly asked a prominent lay Catholic, Leo T. Crowley, to explain the situation to Archbishop Edward Mooney of Detroit. Within seventy-two hours, Mooney ordered Coughlin to be silent (or be defrocked). *Social Justice* went out of business.[20]

Nazi Agents in Key Industry Posts

FOUR MONTHS AFTER Adolf Hitler and Benito Mussolini declared war on the United States, members of the German-American Bund were holding key executive posts in American public utilities and manufacturing plants. In New Jersey in April 1942, Herman von Busch, state treasurer of the Bund, was in charge of the gas works of the Public Service Corporation, which was providing gas to a large section of New Jersey's defense industries.

Composed mainly of U.S. citizens sympathetic to the Nazi cause, the German-American Bund received its directions and heavy secret financing from Berlin.

Busch had plenty of help at the gas works in Harrison. Chief operator at the facility was Wilhelm Koehne, also a staunch Bund member. General foreman at the gas works was Fritz Kunze, who had been fired from the same plant during World War I because of his pro-German sympathies. After that conflict he was rehired and eventually promoted to the top executive post.

John Wilkins, in charge of a blower room at the Harrison works, had a son in Adolf Hitler's army. The chief purification operator, George Haag, openly kept a photo of the führer at his workstation.

Amazingly, neither New Jersey state officials nor the federal government had taken steps to remove this potentially dangerous powder keg. Only after a New York City newspaper published a blockbuster story that detailed how these Bundists had been provoking disputes and absenteeism among the Harrison workers and that much equipment had been mysteriously damaged did the New Jersey governor order the Bundists to be fired.

This incredible situation was not unique to the Harrison gas works. In New York, armed guards were patrolling the outside of the Liquidometer plant, which produced crucial parts for airplanes. Inside, a clique of strident Bundists was doing all it could to slow production. Machinist Julius Weber, who had served in the German navy in World War I, strolled around the plant giving the Nazi salute.

John Blaeser, a department supervisor at Liquidometer, told his workers not to be too concerned about production, that there was no hurry. At the same time he was distributing pro-Hitler propaganda sheets to the employees.

It was not until government inspectors discovered a rash of defective airplane components after they had received an official U.S. Navy stamp of approval that the Federal Bureau of Investigation was called in. After interviewing scores of employees who had been angered over the conduct of their Bund superiors, the Nazi agents were booted out.

At four plants of the Brewster Aeronautical Company, a large number of supervisors and employees strutted about at work giving the Heil Hitler salute. One of these Bundists was found to have bought over $7,500 (equivalent to $90,000 in 2002) worth of *Rueckwanderer* marks, which were special funds sold at a discount in Nazi Germany. These were deposited in his name in a Third Reich bank.

By late April 1942, the four Brewster plants had failed to deliver a single vitally needed airplane. Again the FBI was called in, and days later, five supervisors and twenty-seven employees were discharged.[21]

Blasts Rock Defense Facilities

DURING THE EARLY MONTHS OF 1942, the Federal Bureau of Investigation and other law enforcement agencies were confronted by a deluge of catastrophes that was destroying vital war materials and badly damaging facilities involved with defense. In January alone, a fire gutted an Army administration building at Voorheesville, New York. Another blaze, also of undetermined origin, seriously damaged a building under construction that would make Garand rifles for the Army, at Springfield, Massachusetts.

In February, the mysterious carnage continued. An explosion wrecked a Navy TNT facility in southeast Washington, killing three people and injuring four others. In Dearborn, Michigan, a Ford Motor Company plant being converted to manufacture airplanes was hit by a blaze that broke out in the middle of the night. J. Cohen, a New York City firm supplying lumber to Army camps, had huge amounts of its product destroyed by a raging fire that erupted at about midnight.

In March, the fourth month of America's involvement in the war, the series of unexplained calamities accelerated:

- Just as a shift was changing at an ordnance plant in Iowa, a blast killed seven persons and injured twenty others.
- Two died and thirteen were hurt when an oil barge exploded in the Gulf of Mexico off the Texas shore.
- Four were killed and more than one hundred others were injured when a munitions truck exploded outside New York City.
- A third ship fire in four days broke out on the Philadelphia waterfront.
- The telephone system in southern California was widely disrupted after several key cables were cut.
- A blaze badly damaged a San Diego firm manufacturing silk for Army parachutes.
- Flames swept a warehouse used by the Army in San Francisco.
- Two were killed and five injured when a blast rocked the Welland Chemical plant in Buffalo, New York.
- Army officers launched a probe into the origin of a fire at an Air Corps base in South Carolina.
- In Easton, Pennsylvania, thirty-one persons lost their lives when an explosion erupted at a quarry under contract to the Army.
- The Remington Arms Company plant in Sheboygan, Wisconsin, was shaken by a blast that knocked down several walls.
- Fire leveled the Cortland Boat factory that had a defense contract in Connecticut.

Officials in the War Department in Washington were astonished by the wave of mass destruction that was striking home-front America from coast to coast. Said Secretary of War Henry Stimson to confidants: "Teutonic efficiency."[22]

Eastern America Set Ablaze

IT WAS NEAR MIDNIGHT on April 20, 1942, when U.S. Forest Service District Ranger J. B. Fortin was patrolling the mountains near his base in Brevard, North Carolina. Suddenly, he looked up to see "perhaps twenty fires" break out on Sunburst Mountain. The veteran forester had never seen anything to compare with the sight that greeted his eyes. Radioing his headquarters, he exclaimed: "All twenty started at almost the same time. It had to be saboteurs!"

This strange happening was no isolated event in western North Carolina. A series of forest blazes continued for a week and wiped out thousands of acres of valuable timber that was earmarked for Army-camp construction.

During that same week raging fires swept through the forests of New Jersey, destroying more than five thousand acres of woodland. One hundred and sixty-eight different fires were reported burning. Much of the woods were cedar and pine, which was in heavy demand for war activities. A force of twenty-five hundred soldiers, fire wardens, and volunteers finally brought the conflagrations under control.

District Fire Warden John Wiley noted that, in addition to the destruction of huge amounts of badly needed timber, the fires had been set by saboteurs at a time the wind was blowing toward a large Army post in New Jersey.

A few days after the New Jersey blazes were finally brought under control, ten or twelve forest fires broke out in Rhode Island along a fifty-mile wide swath. Governor J. Howard McGrath was deeply alarmed, and he proclaimed martial law in four towns and collected a fire-fighting force of some three thousand soldiers, sailors, and forest service wardens.

After the blazes were extinguished, James R. Simmons, district supervisor of the Forest Service, noted that the suspicious fires had been burning in a region where nearly 2 million feet of timber to be used for defense production were stored in several lumber yards.

"It seems strange to me that these fires would suddenly spring up where the United States government has such a huge amount of lumber stored," Simmons told a Providence newspaper.[23]

The Mysterious Shangri-la

SUDDENLY, PROGRAMMING ON MILLIONS of American radios was interrupted. After several moments of silence, a voice said that President Franklin Roosevelt would have an important message to deliver at 10:00 A.M. (eastern standard time). It was April 20, 1942.

Listeners braced for another bitter dose of disastrous news from the Pacific, as had been the case since Uncle Sam had gone to war more than four months earlier. Many feared that California had been invaded. Instead, the president was barely able to keep the glee out of his voice.

A force of bombers led by Lieutenant Colonel James J. "Jimmy" Doolittle had lifted off from Shangri-la and bombed Tokyo, the president stated.

Americans were electrified. Spirits soared. Japan's greatest city, the capital of its empire, had been attacked from the air.

Actually, Doolittle's sixteen, twin-engine B-25 bombers, after practicing the revolutionary technique on land many times, had taken off from the aircraft carrier *Hornet,* part of Admiral William "Bull" Halsey's task force, which had sneaked to within a few hundred miles of Tokyo.

In the wake of the raid, the people in Tokyo were near panic. They had been assured many times that no American planes would ever get near the homeland. A spokesman for the government now spoke over the radio to assure the nervous citizenry that this "mistake" would never happen again.

Doolittle's men dropped bombs on Tokyo, Yokohama, Kobe, Nagoya, and Yokosuka, causing minimal property damage, but the psychological impact on the Japanese home front was devastating. Curiously, the raid had taken place on the 167th anniversary of Paul Revere's fabled ride.

In Tokyo, the Imperial General Staff was bewildered by Roosevelt's mention of Shangri-la, unaware that it was a mythical Himalayan retreat in James Hilton's novel, *Lost Horizon.* Scouring maps, the generals concluded that Roosevelt had used the code name for Midway Island, the nearest U.S. post, twenty-one-hundred miles east of Tokyo.[24]

Comic Strip Puzzles Tokyo Warlords

IN THE WAKE OF the surprise bombing of Tokyo, Japanese warlords were trying to unravel the mystery—and significance—of a full page of comic strips that had appeared in hundreds of American newspapers on the same day that Jimmy Doolittle's raiders struck.

That comic strip—by an amazing coincidence—featured the hero American pilot, Barney Baxter, sneaking his airplane through Japanese defenses and bombing Tokyo.

Apparently the Japanese leaders believed that the comic-strip artist was somehow connected to the cloak-and-dagger operations and that he had a direct pipeline into the office of General George C. Marshall, the Army chief of staff, in Washington. Many puzzled Americans had reached the same conclusion.[25]

Disaster Impacts Two U.S. Towns

IN THE SPRING OF 1942, America suffered its worst military disaster in history. Racked by disease, starving, exhausted, and out of ammunition, some 75,000 U.S. and Filipino soldiers on Bataan and Corregidor in the Philippines were forced to surrender.

Despite their pitiful physical condition, the POWs were forced to trudge on foot for fifty-five miles in what came to be known as the Death March. During the trek to a prison camp, 2,300 Americans and about 9,000 Filipinos perished from being bayoneted, shot, or tortured.

Only later would the citizens of two small towns tucked away in obscure corners of America feel that they had been struck by some biblical plague. Salinas, California, with a population of 11,596, had contributed 152 men to the tragedy of Bataan and Corregidor, and Harrodsburg, Kentucky, population 4,673, had lost 76 of its sons.[26]

"A Date with Destiny"

A WEEK AFTER the American tragedy in the Philippines, Secretary of War Henry Stimson telephoned thirty-seven-year-old Oveta Culp Hobby, an executive with the *Houston Post* in Texas. Congress had been shocked into realizing that the United States was fighting for its existence and would have to fully mobilize. Consequently, on May 13, 1942, it authorized the creation of a Women's Auxiliary Army Corps (WAAC), and now Stimson asked Hobby to take charge of the new organization.

Hobby promptly accepted and became America's first woman colonel. Her role was to train members of WAAC for certain army jobs to free able-bodied men for combat duty.

Colonel Hobby plunged into the demanding and frustrating task of building the WAAC from scratch. Often she met hostility rather than cooperation from the War Department. Male reporters at her first press conference bombarded her with irrelevant questions. "Can officer WAACs date men who are privates?" "Will WAACs underwear be khaki?" "What if an unmarried WAAC gets pregnant?"

For months to come, newspapers and magazines carried stories about America's new "petticoat army, Wackies, and powder magazines." Despite the boos and catcalls, Hobby persevered, and within weeks she had recruiting, staffing, facilities, uniforms, and training programs operational.

Hobby set the tone when she addressed the WAAC Officer Candidate students at Fort Des Moines, Iowa, in July 1942. "You have taken off silk and put on khaki," the colonel said. "And all for essentially the same reasons—you have a debt and a date. A debt to democracy, a date with destiny."[27]

A Tumultuous Homecoming

EARLY ON THE MORNING of May 8, 1942, Alice Bulkeley drove to La Guardia Airport with her father-in-law, Frederick Bulkeley. Alice was the wife of Navy Lieutenant John Bulkeley, who two months earlier had rescued General Douglas MacArthur from Japanese-surrounded Corregidor island in the Philippines.

After American and Filipino forces had been forced to surrender, Lieutenant Bulkeley escaped to Australia. Now he was coming home.

Alice hoped to have a private reunion with her husband, who had earned every decoration for valor—some of them twice—that the United States had to offer. Soon her hopes were dashed: awaiting the arrival of the PT-boat squadron skipper was a throng of many thousands, including a herd of reporters and photographers, along with camera teams from Paramount and Movietone News.

At 10:22 A.M. a United Airlines plane rolled to a stop, and out hopped Bulkeley and two other PT-boat officers, Lieutenants Robert Kelly and Anthony Akers. An enormous roar from the crowd echoed across La Guardia and into adjacent locales.

Alice noticed her husband, who had been a boxer on the West Point team, looked thin—he had lost thirty pounds since Pearl Harbor. He explained: "You don't get fat on a steady diet of salmon and tomcat."

Bulkeley was dragooned (as he later would term it) before the newsreel cameras and bombarded with questions. His resolute spirit was still intact. "The Japs are tough, courageous fighters," he declared. "But one of our boys can lick hell out of five them!"

A squad of hard-pressed but smiling New York City policemen escorted the Bulkeleys through the milling throng to their private automobile. On the drive home, the Navy officer said he was looking forward to a "few days of peace and quiet."

Tranquility would have to wait. When the Bulkeleys arrived at Alice's apartment, hundreds of people had gathered in the street, and their rousing cheers rocked the neighborhood as John stepped from the automobile.

In the days and weeks ahead, the Navy hero, who was preparing to return to the Pacific with a new squadron of PT boats, was trailed everywhere by reporters and photographers. Two days after reaching home, he was honored with a parade in the New York City borough of Queens, riding with Alice in a car followed by three thousand marchers and scores of floats.

On May 13, New York City gave one of its rousing welcomes to the Wild Man of the Philippines. Some 500,000 cheering men and women, ten rows deep, lined both sides of Seventh Avenue. John and Alice rode in a convertible. Ticker tape and confetti streamed down from the windows in towering buildings.

A huge sign stretched across Seventh Avenue: "All New York Welcomes John D. Bulkeley."

Four days later, on May 17, 1.3 million men, women, and children (by police estimate) stood shoulder to shoulder in New York's Central Park mall and overflowed onto Fifth Avenue and Central Park West. They were there to honor John Bulkeley on "I Am an American Day." Public officials said it was the largest crowd ever assembled in one place in the nation's history.

Along with Bulkeley, the speakers' platform was loaded with celebrities: heavyweight boxing champion Joe Louis; composer Irving Berlin; Supreme Court Justice Hugo Black; operatic stars Lily Pons, James Melton, and Marion

Lieutenant Commander John D. Bulkeley receives the Congressional Medal of Honor from President Franklin D. Roosevelt in the Oval Office of the White House. (Courtesy of Alice Bulkeley)

Anderson; orchestra leaders Fred Waring and Andre Kostelanetz; and a host of Hollywood stars.

As each celebrity was introduced, the crowd applauded vigorously. But a thunderous roar went up for John Bulkeley. For nearly five minutes, rousing cheers echoed around mid-Manhattan.

Paul Muni, one of the great names of stage and screen history, recited an anonymous poem dedicated to the dead of Bataan, which said in part: "They are what this war is about / Do not ask them why they died / They wouldn't know how to tell you, were they alive / They were just plain fighting men — who died for you."

Elsewhere in New York City, Dave Elman, a popular WABC-radio personality, had been conducting a Victory Auction at 9:00 A.M. each weekday. Elman solicited personal items from celebrities to be sold on the air, and the winning bidder paid by buying War Bonds in the amount bid.

At the request of Elman, John Bulkeley contributed his PT-boat tie clasp and the collar rank insignia of a lieutenant that he had worn at the time he had rescued General MacArthur. These items had a combined monetary value of perhaps two dollars. Bidding was furious. Finally, the two small items were purchased by Arthur J. White, a New York City restaurant owner, for the War Bond equivalent of $16,000 ($185,000 in the year 2002).[28]

Lord Haw-Haw and His Spies

COLONEL EDSON D. RAFF was seated in his small, spartan office at Fort Bragg, North Carolina, perusing orders he had just received from Washington. His crack 509th Parachute Infantry Battalion was going overseas. It was mid-May 1942.

Before departing for the New York City port of embarkation, Raff informed his five hundred paratroopers that the entire trip to their yet unknown destination would be conducted under the utmost secrecy. Therefore, they would have to shed their "badges of honor"—parachute wings, jump boots, paratrooper patches on caps, and the word "parachute" sewn to sleeves at the shoulders.

The reason for this covert action was to conceal from German agents the fact that the first American paratrooper outfit to go overseas was bound for the British Isles.

Under the veil of night, Colonel Raff and his paratroopers boarded a train, whose crew had been sworn to secrecy about the trip, and headed for Fort Dix, New Jersey.

On June 4, wearing the unadorned uniforms of regular soldiers (straight legs, the parachutists called them), the battalion climbed onto another train at Fort Dix. After a short ride across the New Jersey flatlands and into bustling New York City, the train halted at a pier along the Hudson River. Then the troopers climbed aboard a huge, gray-painted ship, the peacetime British luxury liner *Queen Elizabeth.*

Converted to a troop transport after war had erupted in Europe, the ship carried 14,000 soldiers. Due to its speed, the *Queen* would cross the Atlantic unescorted—hopefully avoiding German U-boats.

A few days after sailing from New York harbor, the *Queen* arrived at Greenock, Scotland, the port of Glasgow, in the Firth of Clyde. Still garbed as regular GIs, the paratroopers debarked onto the dock and boarded yet another train. A friendly Scot official asked the battalion surgeon, Captain Carlos C. Alden Jr. of Buffalo, New York, "What kind of an outfit are you?" Replied Alden: "We're USO entertainers."

Soon the train was racing southward and finally reached the battalion's new home: Nissen huts on the grounds of the estate of U.S.-born Lady Ward, at Chilton Foliat in Berkshire, England.

Still in plain uniforms, the troopers tuned in Radio Berlin, over which the British renegade, William Joyce, broadcast Nazi propaganda using the name Lord Haw-Haw.

"Welcome to England," Lord Haw-Haw said pleasantly. "You men of the 509th Parachute Infantry have come to die in [British Prime Minister Winston] Churchill's war. I want to particularly welcome your leader, Colonel Raff." Then the propagandist gave a facetious greeting to other officers in the battalion by name.

Among the paratroopers there was no doubt how Lord Haw-Haw had obtained such detailed information about their outfit: Nazi spies in the United States were alive and well.

A day later, Colonel Raff told his men that they could put back on their badges of honor.[29]

Part Three

A Sleeping Giant Awakens

Invasion Target: California

DURING THE SPRING OF 1942, generals and admirals in Washington were astonished by the power, speed, and skill of the Japanese blitzkrieg (lightning war), which dwarfed Adolf Hitler's remarkable conquests in Europe and the Mediterranean. A grim conclusion was reached by the Army and Navy: with full mobilization of American manpower and resources, and at a frightful cost in lives, reconquering the Pacific would take at least ten years.

Japan's 36 million citizens were in a state of euphoria. *Hakko-ichiu* (bring the eight corners of the world under one roof) had become the national slogan. Emperor Hirohito, whom most Japanese revered as a god, now reigned over one-seventh of the globe. His empire radiated from Tokyo for five thousand miles in several directions.

Japan's war of "liberations" (as Tokyo called it) had only begun. The warlords were planning an invasion of California. First, however, they would have to capture Midway Island, as a base for the next leap to Hawaii, eleven hundred miles to the southwest. Then it would be on to Los Angeles and San Francisco.

However, Admiral Isoroku Yamamoto, the Harvard-educated commander of the Combined Imperial Fleet and architect of the sneak attack on Pearl Harbor, was unaware that the United States had cracked Japan's "unbreakable" navy code. So when Yamamoto sent a formidable naval force to seize Midway, two American armadas, which included three aircraft carriers, intercepted the Japanese fleet near Midway on June 4.

The smashing American triumph had not been cheap. The U.S. carrier *Yorktown* and a destroyer were sunk and about one hundred and fifty airplanes were lost. But for the first time since Pearl Harbor, six months earlier, the warlords' dreams of capturing Los Angeles and San Francisco had been turned into a nightmare.[1]

Washington: Chaotic Capital

DURING THE EARLY MONTHS OF 1942, Washington, D.C., skyrocketed into a boomtown and a center of monumental chaos. Hordes of people flooded into the city on every bus and every train—every hour. Washington's population rapidly soared from some 700,000 to double that figure.

Throngs of employers arrived in search of juicy defense contracts. Business executives by the thousands descended on the city to take up wartime appointments in the government. Many were known as dollar-a-year men. Wags held that most of them were worth every penny of it.

Starry-eyed teenaged girls and young women flocked to the capital, mainly from small towns across America, looking for the only commodity not in short supply—jobs. They had come in response to pleas of the U.S. Civil Service Commission to help in the war effort—and to collect fatter paychecks. There were thousands of positions paying $1,440 a year, perhaps three times what these girls and women had been earning.

Also arriving by the hundreds to take advantage of what promised to be a financial bonanza was another coterie of women of all ages—prostitutes.

Washington residents were confronted daily with a wide variety of shortages. However, there was never a scarcity of paper generated by the new people who came in to help run the war. Each night of the week, a thirteen-car train chugged out of the Washington railroad yard with a cargo of wastepaper.

"Where were these mountains of paper going?" an enterprising newspaper reporter asked a railroad official. "Can't comment on that," he replied. "Security. There's a war on." No doubt the German and Japanese warlords would have been aided greatly in their strategic planning should they learn where wastepaper was being dumped.

Soon office space for the mushrooming government was almost unobtainable, even though large contingents of carpenters began throwing up ramshackle temporary structures. Military officers, many wise in the capital scheme of things, jumped in and seized much of the available office space. Growled the head of one large new civilian agency: "If the Army can capture territory as well as it grabs office space, the war will soon be over!"

In an effort to alleviate the acute shortage of office space, the government took over several large apartment buildings and converted them into makeshift offices. Even the bathrooms were used as work space. This was achieved by laying a sheet of plywood over the bathtub. On it was placed a typewriter. A cushion was put on the toilet seat to provide a chair for the typist.

Sleazy nightclubs sprang up in and around Washington. The booze was expensive—and awful. Few customers complained. Entertainers at these joints were billed as being "direct from Broadway"—meaning Broadway Street in Paducah, Kentucky, or West Overshoe, Montana.

A degree of fantasy soon began to color wartime Washington, mainly in Hollywood patterns. In Tinsel Town, a favorite pastime was to dine at the chic Brown Derby or Chasen's and rubberneck as Hedy Lamarr, or Mickey Rooney, or Bob Hope strolled in regally. In Washington, the dining rooms at the Mayflower, Statler, Willard, and other major hotels were jammed with people who craned their necks when Secretary of War Henry Stimson, General George Marshall, or Treasury Secretary Henry Morgenthau arrived.

Legends began to circulate about the housing shortage. No one recognized this critical need more than President Roosevelt, who fancied himself as an architect. Despite shouldering burdens heavier than ever had to be carried by a president, he found time to sit at his desk in the White House Oval Office and use a pencil to design on paper his version of temporary housing.

Roosevelt's designs were called "absurd" by one White House official who pleaded anonymity. No one ever said anything to the president about his creations, and he may have conjectured to himself on occasion why nothing he designed was ever built.

Innovative classified advertisements appeared in Washington newspapers: "Urgently needed, two room apartment. Will leave my wife as security." "Returned wounded infantry office desperately needs house for self, wife, and one infant. References on everything, including infant."

A favorite tale making the rounds in the capital concerned the man who had fallen into the Potomac River. His cries for help brought a passerby. Instead of hauling the man from the water, the stranger demanded to know: "What is your name and where do you live?"

"John Smith, 26 South L Street. Help!"

The passerby leaped in his car and drove to 26 South L Street. He told the landlady: "I want to rent John Smith's room. He just drowned."

"You're too late," the woman replied. "It was just rented by the man who pushed him in."

Under wartime pressures, the federal government grew so speedily that nobody—including President Roosevelt—could fathom everything that was transpiring. Executive orders flew like confetti out of the White House—and the president did not comprehend many of them.

Crippled by archaic procedures, Congress was often unable to function with the speed required by wartime decisions, so it often signed checks for billions of dollars, then left it to Roosevelt to decide how the funds should be spent.

A rash of wartime "alphabet agencies" (OWI, WPB, COE, FEPC, CWIRC, WLD, FCA, among many) sprang up. They confused both the home front and the Washington government. Roosevelt had a distaste for firing people who didn't measure up—often they were old cronies—or had failed in some manner. Instead of chopping off their heads, the president let these bureaucrats remain, then he created new alphabet agencies to get the job done.[2]

A Young Reporter Is Awed

As the war progressed, President Roosevelt held two regular press conferences each week. One was in the morning to give afternoon newspapers first crack at his remarks or disclosures, and the other was in the afternoon for the convenience of the morning sheets.

Carlton Smith, the NBC Washington manager, like those with other media in the capital, decided that the network would have to cover these presidential press conferences. Smith, in his wisdom, decided that NBC's correspondent would have to possess these qualifications: tall, white, neatly dressed, Protestant. Consequently, he selected a newcomer to Washington, David Brinkley, in his early twenties, whose background was in United Press bureaus in middle-sized cities in the South.

Strangely, the awed Brinkley reflected, Smith had never asked him if he was highly conversant with the complicated national and global affairs with which Roosevelt had to deal daily. Had the boss done so, Brinkley's answer would have to be "no."

Brinkley began a crash course of self-education. Scanning through hundreds of Washington newspapers from the past year, he gained a working knowledge of the subtleties and nuances of the White House and its foremost resident.

When the young man from Wilmington, North Carolina, walked into the Oval Office for his first press conference in mid-1942, he felt as though his knees had turned to jelly. For the first time, he saw President Roosevelt—close-up. In those days, the White House press corps was small, and the correspondents gathered in a semicircle around the presidential desk.

Brinkley was also intimidated by being in the company of famous media figures whom he had known only by reputation, such as James B. "Scotty" Reston of the *New York Times*, among others. A few of the reporters continued the peacetime affectation of the famous statesmen they were covering, wearing homburg hats, striped pants, and pince-nez glasses.

For fear that he would show his ignorance, Brinkley covered Roosevelt's conferences for more than two months in total silence. But he learned. And a decade and a half later, David Brinkley would become a household name on television across home-front America—and to an extent, around the world.[3]

"Doll Woman" an Enemy Agent

IN PORTLAND, OREGON, on the afternoon of May 10, 1942, a mailman delivered a letter to the home of Mrs. Sarah Garland (not her real name). Stamped on the envelope were the words: "Addressee unknown." It had been returned from Buenos Aires, Argentina, and Mrs. Garland's name was given on the return address.

She had never seen the letter before and didn't know anyone in Buenos Aires. Puzzled, she took the letter to the Federal Bureau of Investigation.

It was a gentle letter and seemed innocent. It started in part:

I just secured a lovely Siamese Temple Dancer; it had been damaged, that is tore in the middle. But it is now repaired and I like it very much. I could not get a mate for this Siamese Dancer, so I am redressing just a small plain doll into a second Siam doll.

In the FBI laboratory in Washington, cryptographers studied the letter and concluded that "Siamese Temple Dancer" meant "warship." The seemingly insignificant talk about dolls translated into a sinister meaning:

I just secured information of a fine aircraft carrier, it had been damaged, that is torpedoed in the middle. But it is now repaired and I like it very much. They could not get a mate for this so a plain ordinary warship is being converted into a second aircraft carrier.

The FBI took note of the fact that this letter, dated May 20, had been written a few days after the aircraft carrier *Saratoga* left Puget Sound in the state of Washington for San Diego.

The name signed to the doll letters was Marilyn Byers (not her real name), who now received a visit from a G-man. She knew nothing about the letter and certainly hadn't written it. Then did she have any idea who might have used her name?

Byers thought a few seconds, then her eyes blazed. "I'll bet it's that damned Velvalee Dickinson in New York City," she snapped. "I bought some dolls from her and because I couldn't pay her right away she's been after me with some nasty letters."

Hostile letters written to Marilyn Byers by Dickinson were compared to the letter sent to Buenos Aires. They had been produced on the same typewriter.

In New York City, FBI men began probing into Dickinson's background and daily routine. Then they confronted her. The one hundred dollar bills she had been taking from a safe-deposit box in a bank had been left to her as part of her late husband's estate, she explained. When the agents began to shoot holes in this story, she changed it. Her late husband had been paid $25,000 (equivalent to some $275,000 in 2002) by the Japanese naval attaché, Ichiro Yokoyama, on November 16, 1941. That date was eleven days before the Pearl Harbor attack. Why did the Japanese officer pay such a whopping amount of money? Because he wanted information on the U.S. Navy, Dickinson replied.

She insisted vehemently that her husband had been the spy, that she had had nothing to do with obtaining and providing the information. However, FBI evidence indicated that she, not her husband, had been the spy for the Japanese.

Velvalee Dickinson was indicted on espionage charges, but the federal prosecutors agreed to accept her plea of guilty to violating censorship because, it was held, the evidence was circumstantial. However, Judge Shackelford Miller verbally scalded her: "It is hard to believe that [you] do not realize that our nation is engaged in a life and death struggle. You were certainly engaged in espionage. You were fortunate that the government did not have you tried on espionage charges which could have resulted in death or life imprisonment for you."[4]

Panic Erupts at Concert

SIX MONTHS INTO THE WAR, much of the nation was still gripped by the jitters, a hangover from the flood of wild rumors that flowed seemingly without end. At an outdoor concert in St. Louis, Vladimir Golschmann was conducting the *1812 Overture* before thousands of people. In the rousing finale of the piece, two shotguns were fired into the air offstage.

Near panic erupted as hundreds of spectators scrambled for the exits, thereby attracting the St. Louis police department's riot squad.[5]

Standard Oil Aids the Nazis

IN EARLY 1942, HOME-FRONT AMERICA was stunned by testimony given at a hearing before the Senate Committee to Investigate the National Defense Program, chaired by Missouri's Harry Truman. Better known as the Truman Committee, the panel's crucial task was to root out waste, extravagance, and inefficiency.

Thurman Arnold, assistant U.S. attorney general in charge of antitrust prosecutions, testified before the Truman Committee that the development of vitally needed synthetic rubber and oil production in the United States had been delayed because of German agreements with Standard Oil of New Jersey.

Arnold disclosed that Standard Oil had helped Nazi Germany in 1939 to design facilities for manufacturing synthetic aviation gasoline. At the same time, the American company was induced by Adolf Hitler's officials to withhold essential information necessary for the building of synthetic oil and rubber plants in the United States.

A battery of high-powered lawyers vigorously defended Standard Oil, but documents from the firm's files subpoenaed by the Truman Committee indicated otherwise.

In a report, the Truman Committee declared: "The conclusion remains that whether or not Standard Oil so wished, it put itself in the position of furnishing information to the German company, through which it was available to the German government, while withholding the same information from the United States."

Back in 1930, the investigators discovered, Standard Oil of New Jersey and the huge German conglomerate I.G. Farbenindustrie organized a chemical company in the United States. Called Jasco, Inc., its function was to develop and exploit new processes for making chemical products out of natural and refined gases.

Although the joint enterprise was ostensibly a partnership, it was actually under tight German control. Jasco built a large plant near Baton Rouge, Louisiana, and lengthy experiments resulted in a new process of making acetylene, a component of acetyl acid used in making plastics, rayon, film, paints, and pharmaceuticals.

Under German orders, the experimentation at Baton Rouge was halted in 1935 at a time Adolf Hitler announced to the world that he was rearming Germany. All future experiments were carried out in the Third Reich, as Hitler called his empire after he had become dictator two years earlier.

On September 6, 1939, five days after Hitler sent his legions plunging into neighboring Poland to ignite what would be called World War II, the Germans ordered Standard Oil to dismantle the plant at Baton Rouge.

In 1942, three years after the Louisiana facility was demolished, Assistant Attorney General Thurman Arnold told the Senate Patents Committee in Washington that the Nazi government "was undoubtedly anxious to facilitate the destruction of any plant in the United States that might be useful if America were to go to war against Germany."[6]

A Guidebook for Nazi Spies

LONG AFTER AMERICA went to war, Nazi espionage operations in the United States continued to function masked as legitimate business concerns. One of these was Chemnyco, Inc., located in New York City. The company was affiliated with I.G. Farbenindustrie of Germany and served as a center for the collection of detailed information about American war production.

In late May 1942, agents of the Federal Bureau of Investigation raided Chemnyco headquarters and hauled off a vast collection of espionage materials, including a copy of the Index of American Industry.

It was an exhaustive document of many pages. A summary was given of the nature of each American business listed. In many instances, it named and classified each worker politically and by race and religion, what he or she had done in the past, and how he or she might be used by Nazi saboteurs or spies in the future.

In many respects, the FBI discovered, more detailed information on a business firm could be found in the Index of American Industry than was available anywhere else in the United States.[7]

They Came to Blow Up America

JUST PAST EIGHT O'CLOCK on the dark night of June 12, 1942, the U-boat *Innsbruck* surfaced off Long Island, one hundred and five miles east of New

York City. Propelled by its nearly silent electric motors, the submarine edged closer to the beach. On board and preparing to be paddled ashore were four men wearing the uniforms of German marines.

Five nights later, a thousand miles to the south, a similar scenario was unfolding. U-boat *201* made landfall on a dark stretch of shore off Ponte Vedra Beach, twenty-five miles south of Jacksonville, Florida. Silently taken onto the sandy beach were four men in German marine garb.

These eight intruders were members of Operation Pastorius, one of the boldest and largest single sabotage missions ever undertaken. All of the saboteurs were German-born but had lived in the United States for extended periods before returning to the Third Reich. They were to receive hefty monthly salaries and promised high-paying jobs in Germany—or the United States—after Adolf Hitler had won the war.

The Pastorius saboteurs were:

- Ernest Peter Burger, who had worked as a machinist in Detroit and Milwaukee and been a member of the Michigan National Guard
- George John Dasch, alias George Davis, alias George Day, who at age thirty-nine was the oldest of the group, had been a waiter in New York, and had served in the U.S. Army Air Corps
- Herbert Hans Haupt, who had worked for an optical firm in Chicago and at twenty-two was the youngest of the saboteurs
- Heinrich Heinck, alias Henry Kanor, who had been employed as a waiter in New York City
- Edward Kerling, alias Edward Kelly, who had been with a New Jersey oil corporation and had been a butler
- Hermann Neubauer, alias Herman Nicholas, who had been a cook in Chicago and Hartford hotels
- Richard Quirin, alias Robert Quintas, who had worked in the United States as a mechanic
- Werner Thiel, alias John Thomas, who had been employed in Detroit automobile plants

Masterminding the elaborate sabotage scheme had been pudgy, bull-necked Lieutenant Walter Kappe, who had beat the propaganda drums for Nazi-front groups in New York City and Chicago in the 1930s. Returning to Germany in 1937, he had been given a commission in the Abwehr, the Third Reich's cloak-and-dagger agency.

Kappe had recruited the eight saboteurs and put them through a rigorous routine of secret writing, incendiaries, explosives, fuses, timing devices, grenade-pitching, and rifle shooting. Each man had to memorize scores of targets in the United States. They rehearsed phony life stories over and over, backgrounds that were documented with bogus birth certificates.

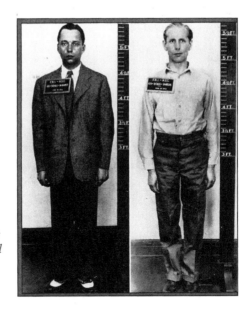

Operation Pastorius ringleaders were Ernest Burger (left), a former member of the Michigan National Guard, and George Dasch, who had served in the U.S. Army Air Corps. (FBI)

On May 23, 1942, the saboteurs were divided into two teams and given their boom-and-bang assignments in the United States.

Team No. 1 would be led by the "old man," George Dasch, and include Burger, Heinck, and Quirin. It was to destroy hydroelectric plants at Niagara Falls, New York; blow up Aluminum Company of America factories in East St. Louis, Illinois; Alcoa, Tennessee; and Massena, New York; blast locks in the Ohio River between Louisville, Kentucky, and Pittsburgh, Pennsylvania; and wreck a Cryolite plant in Philadelphia.

Team No. 2 would be under the command of Edward Kerling, and his companions would be Haupt, Neubauer, and Thiel. It was to cripple the Pennsylvania Railroad by blowing up its station at Newark, New Jersey, and Horseshoe Bend near Altoona, Pennsylvania; disrupt facilities of the Chesapeake and Ohio Railroads; send New York City's Hell Gate railroad bridge crashing into the East River; destroy the canal and lock complexes at St. Louis, Missouri, and Cincinnati, Ohio; and demolish the water-supply system in greater New York City, concentrating on suburban Westchester County.

The Nazi saboteurs were to make no effort to conceal the fact that they were on a violent rampage in the United States. They were to constantly seek opportunities to blow up public buildings in order to promote panic.

On direct orders from Führer Adolf Hitler no expense was to be spared in Operation Pastorius. When preparing to board the two submarines at the German base at Lorient, France, Lieutenant Kappe had doled out a small fortune of $175,000 (equivalent to about $2 million in the year 2002) to pay bribes to accomplices and for other needs.

Once the sabotage network was established, Walter Kappe himself would slip into the United States as a sort of German supreme commander for boom-and-bang operations. His headquarters would be in Chicago, a city he knew well. He would keep in contact with and issue orders to his scattered bands of saboteurs through coded advertisements in the *Chicago Tribune*, a large circulation newspaper.

Now, on the deserted shores of Long Island and Florida the eight Pastorius saboteurs—four in each team—buried their marine uniforms. They distributed among themselves ingenious sabotage devices: bombs disguised as lumps of coal and wooden blocks, special timing gadgets, TNT carefully packed in excelsior, rolls of electric cable, a wide array of fuses, and incendiary bombs that looked identical to pencils and fountain pens.

Hardly had Team No. 1 landed in the murky fog than George Dasch glanced around and felt a surge of alarm. Coming toward the four intruders was the muted glow of a flashlight, carried by twenty-one-year-old Coast Guardsman John Cullen. Unarmed, he was making a routine beach patrol.

Seaman Second Class Cullen, too, had grown alarmed and stood glued to the spot. In the darkness, he could discern several men talking excitedly—in German. Dasch grabbed the sailor's arm and snapped, "You got a mother and father, haven't you? Wouldn't you like to see them again?" Then the saboteur thrust a wad of currency into the startled Cullen's hand. "Take this and have a good time," Dasch said. "Forget what you've seen here."

Cullen sensed that he had stumbled onto some sinister venture that was far beyond his ability to cope. Step by step he backed off, then whirled and raced away.

Back at the Amagansett Coast Guard station, the excited Cullen roused four of his mates and rapidly told them of his encounter on the fog-shrouded beach. The others were skeptical: no doubt Cullen was pulling a trick to relieve the lonely monotony. Then Cullen showed them the wadded bills—$265 worth—that Dasch had thrust into his hand. Now fully awake, the four Coast Guardsmen armed themselves and, along with Cullen, rushed to the site of the confrontation. There they uncovered the cache of explosives and the German uniforms.

Meanwhile, Dasch and the other three saboteurs caught a Long Island Railroad train to New York City. There they split. Dasch and Burger checked into the Governor Clinton Hotel on West 31st Street, while Heinck and Quirin registered at the Martinique.

Soon after Dasch and Burger reached their hotel room, Dasch said that he planned to notify the FBI of Operation Pastorius. "If you don't agree, I'm going to kill you!" Dasch explained, pointing a pistol at his crony's head. Burger assured the team leader that he had no objection.

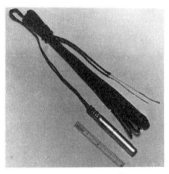

Electric blasting cap with copper wires.

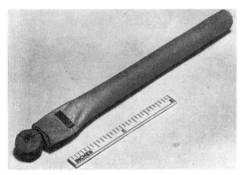

Safety fuse lighter for the ignition of standard safety fuse.

Electric match with screw cap removed—used in conjunction with timing mechanism and battery.

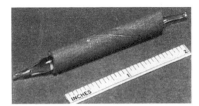

Capsule containing sulphuric acid encased in rubber tubing for protection.

Tools brought ashore by Operation Pastorius saboteurs. (FBI)

Early the next morning Dasch took a train to Washington. At 10:15 A.M. on June 19—one week after Team No. 1 had come ashore—Dasch telephoned FBI headquarters. "My name is George John Dasch, and I have landed in a German submarine and have important information," he stated. "I am in room 351 at the Mayflower Hotel."

Within minutes two G-men arrived and listened in amazement as the former New York City waiter, in the vernacular of the U.S. underworld, sang like a canary. Every two hours, for two days, a fresh stenographer arrived at room 351 to record the incredible story of the Nazi saboteurs who had come to blow up America.

Dasch disclosed the U.S. industrial and transportation targets, described each of the other seven saboteurs in detail, and gave the names and addresses of their likely contacts.

Meanwhile, the seven members of Team No. 1 and Team No. 2 still on the loose scattered to cities across the eastern United States. But fourteen days after the intruders had landed, all had been collared by the FBI.

Five days later, on July 2, President Franklin Roosevelt appointed a military tribunal to hear the case, the first one of its kind in the United States since the assassination of Abraham Lincoln in 1865. During the secret trial, all eight defendants swore that it had never been their intention to commit sabotage and that they had volunteered for the mission as a ploy for getting back to their loved ones in the United States.

All the dark invaders were found guilty, and on August 8 they were sentenced. George Dasch received a term of thirty years in prison, and Ernest Burger was given a life term. At noon the other saboteurs were electrocuted and buried in unmarked graves on a government plot in Washington.[8]

Artillery Confrontation in Oregon

While much of the nation's focus was on Nazi hijinks in the eastern United States, a Japanese submarine, the *I-25*, surfaced about 20,000 yards offshore from Fort Stevens, a complex at the mouth of the Columbia River in Oregon. It was just after darkness had settled in on June 21, 1942.

At its leisure, the submarine's crew fired some twenty rounds up and down the beach, perhaps seeking out Battery Russell, an artillery outfit equipped with ten-inch guns built in 1900. Colonel Carl S. Doney, battery commander, did not order the fire to be returned: His ancient weapons would fire only 16,000 yards. Bright orange flashes would have given away the unit's position.

The sub fired its rounds. The GIs in the battery laid low. The sub left the scene. But after the story of the episode hit the Portland newspapers, people from around the region flocked to the site to look at the "battlefield." There was nothing to see, because the shells had exploded in the sands along the beach.

A few enterprising boys, noting the droves of visitors, hatched a scheme. They located an old cast-iron stove and broke it into small pieces with a sledgehammer. Then they stood along the road leading to the 'battlefield" and sold the items as Japanese shrapnel to eager buyers.

Only after the war would it be found that the attack on Battery Russell was in retaliation for the April raid on Tokyo by Jimmy Doolittle's bombers.[9]

German-American Bund Demolished

"We intend to put the Bund out of business!" Federal Bureau of Investigation Director J. Edgar Hoover told the media.

On July 10, 1942, Hoover had sent squads of G-men to haul in twenty-six leaders of the German-American Bund, including Bundesführer Wilhelm

A year after Pearl Harbor, the FBI apprehended a Nazi sabotage and espionage ring in Detroit. Part of the weapons and explosives uncovered are shown above. (FBI)

Kunze, who had long been under surveillance. Only now had Hoover's agents collected enough solid evidence to bring him to trial.

In early December 1941, at the time of the bombing of Pearl Harbor, Hoover had estimated that there were some 75,000 members nationally. New York City alone had six Bund branches, and there were others in twelve surrounding communities.

There were branches in Chicago, St. Louis, Los Angeles, Philadelphia, Salt Lake City, Boston, Portland (Oregon), Detroit, Seattle, Minneapolis, Kansas City, Milwaukee, Cleveland, and in Georgia and Texas.

Gatherings of Bund chapters had been comic-opera affairs—except for the fact that the underlying goal was to establish a Hitler-directed government in the United States. Men of the *Ordnung Dienst* (the Bund version of German storm troopers) had goose-stepped about as members in the audience showered them with frenzied cheers and shouts of "Heil Hitler!"

Marching in precise military formation, these American storm troopers were clad in grayish-blue tunics, with black cuffs and neckbands, black forage caps with silver braid, black trousers, and boots.

The Bundesführer (supreme leader in the United States) had received his day-to-day orders from the Deutches Ausland Instutut (German Overseas

Institute, the Foreign Section of the Nazi Party under Dr. Ernest Wilhelm Böhle) in Berlin.

Supported by Adolf Hitler's cash register, the German-American Bund had the same structure as that of the Nazi Party in the Third Reich. The United States had three *gaue* (districts), each with its own *gauleiter* (leader).

Trained agents, masquerading as staff members of German consulates in the United States, had provided Bund leaders with advice on espionage, sabotage, and undermining the morale of the U.S. citizens. One of the main functions of the Deutscher Konsum Verband (League of Businessmen), a division of the German-American Bund, had been to mail tens of thousands of hate pieces urging the public to boycott American corporations that did not subscribe to Nazi ideals, as perceived by the Bundesführer.

Bund membership had been climbing steadily when suddenly, in December 1941, the United States was at war. Thousands of Bund members, mostly dupes seeking panaceas for the economic ills of the Great Depression, left the organization. Many volunteered for the U.S. armed forces. Fanatic Bund members went undercover to continue schemes to undermine the U.S. war effort.

Now Kunze and his cohorts were charged with conspiracy to evade the Selective Service Act (draft). They were found guilty in a federal court trial and sentenced to various prison terms.

On the heels of the roundup of the Bund leaders and their underlings, a Washington grand jury indicted twenty-seven other Bund men and women for sedition, charging that they had carried on a "systematic campaign of personal vilification of public officials [including President Roosevelt]" in order to convince "citizens and the military that such public officials are traitorous, corrupt, dishonest, incompetent, and mentally unbalanced."

All except one of these Bund members were convicted and sent to prison.[10]

First Lady Rattles Some Cages

ELEANOR ROOSEVELT WAS UPSET and began rattling some cages in Washington. Why, she demanded to know, did the Navy not have a female component like that of the WAAC in the Army?

Perhaps concerned that it would be labeled antifemale, Congress, in mid-July 1942, authorized the creation of the Women Accepted for Voluntary Emergency Service (WAVES).

In the Navy hierarchy, there were no noticeable demonstrations for the women's branch. One admiral told confidants that instead of women in uniform, he would have preferred "dogs, ducks, or monkeys."

Appointed as director of the WAVES with the rank of lieutenant commander was Mildred McAfee, who had been president of Wellesley College. A native of Parkville, Missouri, she was a graduate of Vassar and received a master's degree from the University of Chicago.

At her first press conference, McAfee was beset by hostility from the all-male reporters. She had to handle such questions as: "Will WAVES sleep in ship bunks with men?" "Will WAVES wear blue panties and brassieres to match their uniforms?"

Undaunted by the taunts of the media and sniping by a few admirals, Commander McAfee rapidly built the new organization, which would consist of one thousand officers and ten thousand enlisted women.

Unlike the WAAC, the WAVES would not be sent overseas.

Not long after the birth of the WAVES, the other seagoing service, the Coast Guard, established the SPARS (short for *Semper Paratus*, that branch's motto). Dorothy C. Stratton, with the rank of lieutenant commander, was appointed director. From the start, the SPARS had a recruiting advantage over the WAVES, although each wore similar uniforms. Pending construction of the SPARS' own facilities, recruits were trained at the ornate Biltmore resort hotel in Palm Beach, Florida.[11]

"I'm Proud of You, Mom!"

ON JULY 17, 1942, ZELMA HANSON and her eighteen-year-old son Richard backed their car out of its garage in suburban Los Angeles and used much of the family's weekly three gallons of gasoline to drive downtown. There they entered a recruiting station and Richard was sworn into the Army. His orders would send him to Fort MacArthur in California.

Mrs. Hanson kissed her son, told him how proud she was of him, and wished him well. Minutes later she joined the WAAC and would be assigned to Fort Des Moines, Iowa. "I'm proud of you, Mom!" the son exclaimed.[12]

Horse Racing Flourishes

FOR MANY MONTHS, James F. Byrnes, chief of the War Mobilization Board, had been casting a jaundiced eye at the sport of horse racing. Banner headlines were screaming about manpower shortages and war-plant absenteeism at the same time newspaper sports pages were telling of soaring attendance at racetracks.

Almost before the echo of bombs falling on Pearl Harbor had faded, Americans, many flushed with money from defense jobs, had plunged into the horses, and racetrack operators were hauling in hefty profits.

Knowing that they had a once-in-a-lifetime bonanza on their hands, racing moguls hired public relations experts to glorify horse racing's brave resolve to help the war effort: by elevating morale on the home front.

Soon the horse-racing nabobs came up with a new tack. The fight against Adolf Hitler and Emperor Hirohito was being helped greatly because, by improving the breed of horses, the U.S. Cavalry was benefiting. When cynics pointed out that most of the cavalry in this war rode in tanks, the public-relations thrust was changed to how racing was aiding the infantry.

After gas rationing began in mid-1942, the sight of racetrack parking lots filled with hundreds of cars—most no doubt loaded with black-market fuel—provided foes of horse racing in wartime with plenty of ammunition.

Media criticism rolled off the racing titans' backs like the proverbial water off a duck, however. Many track owners even thumbed their noses at Uncle Sam. In 1943, the traditional Kentucky Derby was run in Louisville even after the Office of Defense Transportation had urged that the event be suspended for the duration. Another popular track, Narragansett Park, also ignored the ODT request to shut down to save fuel and rubber.

Moguls in the horse-racing field had a billion-dollar business going, and they didn't want the bubble to burst. So when War Mobilization boss James Byrnes ordered all tracks to close down to save vital gasoline and rubber for the armed forces, such a huge outcry was generated that the White House lifted the ban.[13]

Psychological Saboteurs at Work

IN MID-1942, six months after Pearl Harbor, Nazi psychological saboteurs were still actively engaged in undermining the morale of American civilians and members of the armed forces. Much of this propaganda assault was being masterminded at Lake Geneva, Wisconsin, a small, peaceful resort town that billed itself as the "Switzerland of America."

Back in late 1941, only days before Uncle Sam was plunged into global war, the owners and staff of *Scribner's Commentator* moved from New York City to Lake Geneva. Publishers of the slick-page magazine, Douglas M. Stewart and George T. Eggleston, were wealthy entrepreneurs and leaders in the isolationist America First Committee.

This pair of rich New Yorkers had been active in recruiting into America First its most celebrated member, Charles A. Lindbergh—beloved by millions around the world after he had become the first person to fly the Atlantic alone from New York to Europe in 1927.

Lake Geneva became an unofficial headquarters of America First Committee. Another wealthy leader, Janet Ayer Fairbank, the organization's national vice chairman, left Chicago and moved into an ornate mansion at Lake

Geneva. Her house was the site of many conferences when distinguished visitors came to town. These celebrities included two powerful U.S. senators, Gerald P. Nye and Burton K. Wheeler.

Other far less notable persons took up residence in Lake Geneva, although most of them and their activities were probably unknown to national leaders of America First.

Ralph Townsend, who allegedly had been a secret agent for the Japanese, came from his base in San Francisco to Lake Geneva to join the staff of *Scribner's Commentator*. Louise Carus also joined the magazine's editorial department after moving from La Salle, Illinois. She was the daughter of wealthy industrialist Edward H. Carus, at whose palatial home G-men had caught up with and arrested Friedrich Ernest Ferdinand Auhagen a short time before Pearl Harbor.

Prior to his falling into the clutches of dogged FBI agents, Auhagen had been masterminding an intensive and widespread psychological campaign on home-front America. Tall, well-groomed, impeccably mannered, Auhagen had an ideal "front" for his clandestine activities: professor of German literature at prestigious Columbia University in New York City.

In late 1939, Auhagen, a naturalized American who had been a lieutenant in the German Army in World War I, organized the American Fellowship Forum that included on its roster a large number of wealthy, educated men with like-minded ideas.

Auhagen received regular, large sums of money on annual trips to Germany from G. Kurt Johannsen in Hamburg before war broke out; then the Forum was given hefty infusions of funds by Ferdinand A. Kertess, president of the Chemical Marketing Company of New York City.

Auhagen's psychological warfare campaign was closely monitored by Gestapo agents masquerading as diplomats in the United States. Auhagen conferred almost weekly with Friedheim Draeger, who was in charge of espionage-sabotage operations in the New York City area. These *treffs*, as Germans called secret meetings, took place at Draeger's home at 90-50 Fifty-third Avenue, Elmhurst, Long Island. Auhagen also held treffs in the suite he reserved on a permanent basis at the Hotel Royalton in New York City.

Yet another new resident of Lake Geneva was Seward Bishop Collins, a rich New Yorker, who settled in a large estate and began collecting tens of thousands of dollars worth of shortwave radio equipment in his spacious four garages. Collins continued to maintain a bookstore at 231 West 58th Street, New York City, which served as a regular meeting place for Nazi agents.

In August 1941, Douglas M. Stewart and George Eggleston gave birth at Lake Geneva to a newspaper called *The Herald*. Later investigation by federal authorities would disclose that the propaganda sheet was being financed by Charles S. Payson, a New York City multimillionaire.

A deposit slip and foreign draft for sums received by Dr. Friedrich Auhagen from German intelligence in Hamburg. Money was deposited by him to his account at the Corn Exchange Bank in New York City. (FBI)

Meanwhile, some of the shortwave receivers that Seward Collins was storing in his garages were set up in the offices of *The Herald*. Manned day and night, these receivers were kept tuned to Europe and Japan. Official propaganda statements were constantly picked up from Berlin, Rome, and Tokyo, translated, and incorporated into editorials and articles in *The Herald*.

Each issue of the publication was widely distributed free around America. Cost was no obstacle. Special efforts were made to get the propaganda pieces into the hands of servicemen. Knowing that soldiers, sailors, and airmen were often hungry for something to read, Stewart and Eggleston mailed free copies of the magazine to Army bases and Navy facilities, from Alaska to the Panama Canal and from Iceland to Hawaii.

Elsewhere across the land the secret war to damage American morale through print propaganda reinforced the work being done at Lake Geneva. In Muncie, Indiana, Court Asher, publisher of the newspaper *X-ray*, exulted in an editorial: "Pearl Harbor sank more than battle wagons; it sank the hopes of Jewry in this country—and the world forever. Amen and Amen."

In Wichita, Kansas, E. J. Garner, publisher of *Publicity*, informed readers: "With your loyal support the Mongolian Jew controlled Roosevelt dictatorship will be smashed."

In Noblesville, Indiana, William Dudley Pelley wrote in his magazine, *The Galilean*: "Germany is coming to the fore all of a sudden because she represents the best and finest flower of Xanthochroic [fair white] culture."

Soon after America became involved in the war, Gerald L. K. Smith began publishing in Detroit a magazine entitled *The Cross and the Flag*, which violently attacked the U.S. war effort and her allies. Smith was leader of what he called the Committee of One Million. Its goal, he told confidants, was to arm that number of young American men to overthrow the government in Washington and to "bring Franklin Roosevelt to trial."

Senator Robert R. Reynolds of North Carolina, chairman of the Senate Military Affairs Committee, wrote a letter to Smith: "Let me congratulate you with my full heart upon your [magazine]. It hits the bull's eye with every paragraph; it should have its appeal; it speaks the truth."

Naturally, Smith used this glowing letter from one of the most powerful men in Congress to promote subscriptions to *The Cross and the Flag.*

When questioned by Washington journalists about his endorsement of Gerald L. K. Smith's propaganda sheet, Senator Reynolds declared: "I have no apologies to offer for endorsing the program of any individual or group standing for the same things I have stood for many years."

Indeed Reynolds had made no effort to conceal his pro-Nazi views. Three years earlier, on February 5, 1939, the *Voelkischer Beobachter*, Adolf Hitler's official newspaper, had carried an article with the by-line "Senator Robert R. Reynolds of North Carolina."

Reynolds's article was headlined: "Advice to Roosevelt; Stick to Your Knitting." The senator was quoted as saying: "I can see no reason why the youth of [America] should be uniformed to save the so-called democracies of Europe—imperialistic Great Britain and Communist France."

Undoubtedly, the King of Psychological Saboteurs in America was George Sylvester Viereck, editor of *Today's Challenge*, the propaganda newspaper put out by Friedrich Auhagen's American Fellowship Forum. Viereck was born in Munich and came to the United States in the early 1900s. Glib, shrewd, and energetic, a gifted and crafty writer of propaganda pieces, he may have been history's highest-paid psychological saboteur.

Prior to America's entry into the war, Viereck admitted to a congressional committee that he had been pocketing some $3,250 (equivalent to $40,000 in 2002) per month from several different German organizations in the United States. Nearly all of the money had been sent by Berlin.

Viereck's "front" was a correspondent for the *Münchner Nauests Nachrichten*, whose editor was Giselher Wirsing, a confidant of Hitler's Minister of Enlightment (propaganda), Josef Goebbels.

Viereck, who maintained plush apartments in New York City and in Washington, had insinuated his way into the good graces of two like-minded members of Congress, Senator Ernest Lundeen of Minnesota and Representative Hamilton Fish of New York.

Using Fish's room 1424 in the House Office Building for bulk mailing, Viereck launched an enormous propaganda operation. With the congressman's frank (free mailing privileges), Viereck flooded the nation with reprints of anti-Roosevelt editorials, transcripts of radio broadcasts, newspaper and magazine clippings, and anything else that might serve Adolf Hitler's cause.

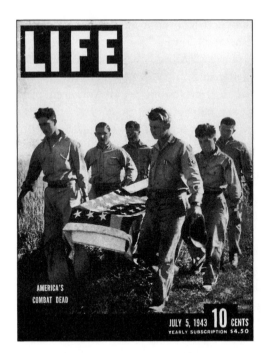

This clever imitation of a highly popular American magazine was created by propaganda artists in Berlin and gained limited distribution on home-front America. The phony picture shows Germans in GI uniforms. This issue featured race riots. (National Archives)

After Pearl Harbor, the Nazi psychological sabotage campaign hardly missed a beat. Only the strategy was changed. The keep-America-out-of-the-war theme was scuttled. In its place was an all-out effort to undermine the people's confidence in the Washington leadership, stir up prejudices against America's allies, foment racial strife and violence, and create artificial antagonisms between business and labor.

Finally, President Roosevelt ordered a crackdown on the raft of psychological saboteurs, who, in peacetime and through the first months of Uncle Sam's going to war, enjoyed impunity.

Even the cagey George Viereck's luck ran out. On March 14, 1942, he was sentenced to a term of two to four years in federal prison. A jury had found that operating a Nazi propaganda mill in the U.S. Capitol was not a legitimate pursuit for a "journalist."

Frail, nervous introverted George Hill, secretary to Congressmen Hamilton Fish, had been duped into doing the actual propaganda mailings for Viereck. He was given a term of two to four years. Fish, who denied any knowledge of the machinations that had taken place under his nose, was never charged.

Among others who heard prison doors slam shut behind them was Ralph Townsend, the suspected spy for Japan and editor of *The Herald* and *Scribner's*

Commentator in Lake Geneva, who was sentenced to eight months to two years for failing to register as an enemy agent.

Even after the conviction of these psychological saboteurs, many propaganda publications continued in business. Then, on July 23, 1942, a federal grand jury in Washington indicted twenty-seven men and one woman on charges of conspiracy to provoke mutiny and disloyalty among members of the armed forces. Listed were thirty publications as vehicles through which the defendants had tried to sabotage morale.

Nearly all of those indicted were found guilty and received varied sentences. Their propaganda sheets went out of business.[14]

Hollywood Superstars
Sign Up to Fight

WITHOUT FANFARE OR MEDIA HYPE, Hollywood superstar Clark Gable quietly slipped into an Army recruiting station in Los Angeles and was sworn in as a private. It was August 12, 1942.

Newspapers got word, and they played up the story. A $7,500-a-week (equivalent of $100,000 in the year 2002) movie idol giving up that salary and going into the service as a $21-a-month private made big headlines.

Hollywood actor Jimmy Stewart is decorated for flying twenty-five combat missions over Europe as a bomber pilot. (U.S. Air Corps)

Soon the overage-in-grade private was enrolled at the Officer Candidate School at Miami Beach, Florida. Twelve weeks later, he donned the bars of a second lieutenant in the Air Corps.

In the months ahead, Gable was in Flying Fortress bombers on missions over Germany to film footage for training gunners. Reichsmarschall Hermann Goering, the rotund leader of the Luftwaffe, reportedly put a large bounty on Gable's head, a reward to any German pilot who would shoot him down.

Also serving in combat with the Air Corps in Europe was another Hollywood superstar, lanky, drawling Jimmy Stewart, who had received an Oscar in 1940.

He had been deferred from the draft because he was underweight (one hundred and forty pounds on a six-foot-two-inch frame). However, Stewart gorged himself with food, put on ten pounds, and barely qualified for acceptance in the Air Corps.

In Europe, Major Stewart would fly twenty-five combat missions as a pilot of a four-engine bomber named *Four Yanks and a Jerk*.[15]

War Hero Meets Joe Kennedy

AFTER HIS RETURN FROM THE PACIFIC in the spring of 1942, newly promoted Lieutenant Commander John Bulkeley, called America's Number-One Hero by the media, had been assigned by the Navy to recruit skippers for PT boats that would be heading for the war zone in greatly increased numbers. In his search, Bulkeley concentrated on Ivy League universities, because a basic requirement for a candidate was that he had had experience in handling small boats. Because most Ivy Leaguers were from wealthy families, they had owned their own craft and had grown up around yacht clubs.

In mid-September 1942, Bulkeley had a brief respite from his cross-county jaunts when he received a telegram signed Joseph P. Kennedy Sr. at his wife's apartment in New York City. Bulkeley and Alice were invited to be Kennedy's guest for lunch the next day at the posh Plaza Hotel.

Joe Kennedy, Bulkeley knew, had been the son of a Boston saloonkeeper and Democratic ward heeler, and he became a self-made multimillionaire in an era where that financial breed was rare.

Although away from home much of the time tending to his extensive business interests around the country and abroad, Kennedy Senior took an intensive interest in his five daughters and four sons, setting up a $1 million trust fund for each when he or she reached the age of twenty-one. The father encouraged—even demanded—that his offspring excel, planned their educations, and closely monitored their romances, of which there would be no shortage among the sons.

Kennedy Senior's oldest son, Joseph P. Jr., and next oldest, John F., were both handsome, poised, energetic, and articulate. They had been ticketed by their father to become world-famous political figures—even president of the United States at an early age, one or the other.

Daddy Joe may have been a little disappointed over John F.'s political potential, for the personable youth had failed to survive even the primaries in an effort to become freshman class president at Harvard.

Now, at the appointed hour—1:00 P.M.—Bulkeley and his wife arrived at Joe Kennedy's large and ornate suite in the Plaza Hotel. To Bulkeley, Kennedy immediately conveyed the impression of a sharp businessman bent on completing a deal. But the host did open a conversation by asking about Bulkeley's trip to the White House a few weeks earlier when President Roosevelt presented the Congressional Medal of Honor to the war hero.

The very mention of Franklin Roosevelt seemed to make Kennedy angry. Because of Kennedy's outspoken remarks that seemed to many to have had a pro-German cast to them while ambassador to England, Roosevelt had fired his old pal. So when lunch was being served, the patriarch of the Kennedy clan launched a long diatribe against Roosevelt.

Then the host got down to the business at hand. He said his son Jack (John F.) was a midshipman (one in training for an officer's commission) at Northwestern University in suburban Chicago. Jack had the potential to be president of the United States, the father declared. So he wanted Jack to get into the "glamorous" PT boat service for the publicity, to get the veterans' vote after the war.

All the while, John Bulkeley sat silently. Then Joe wanted to know if the Navy commander had the clout to get Jack into PT boats. Bulkeley replied that soon he would be at Northwestern recruiting potential skippers, and that Jack would be among those considered.

"If your son can measure up, I will recommend his acceptance," Bulkeley declared.

The lunch turned into a marathon endeavor—the conversation continued until eight o'clock that night. When Daddy Kennedy bid farewell to his guests, he said to Bulkeley: "I hope Jack can be sent to someplace that is not too deadly."

Twenty-five-year-old Jack Kennedy passed muster with flying colors. In his interview with Bulkeley, he came across as eager, dedicated, and energetic. Moreover, he had sailed his own sloop on Cape Cod since he was fifteen years old.

Weeks later, Ensign Kennedy was ready to ship out for the war zone. It would not be to "someplace that is not too deadly," as Joe Kennedy had "suggested." Rather Bulkeley had arranged to send him to one of the hottest locales in the global conflict—the Southwest Pacific.[16]

Wants to Spotlight U.S. Spies

BY MIDSUMMER OF 1942, William "Wild Bill" Donovan, the Medal of Honor recipient from World War I and now chief of the Office of Strategic Services (OSS), had recruited hundreds of agents and was dispatching them all over the globe. Suddenly, he ran into a roadblock. Ruth Shipley, who ran the State Department passport division as though it were her own fiefdom, insisted that Donovan's men travel with their passports clearly marked OSS.

That edict triggered a grim joke at OSS headquarters in Washington: American agents should also go abroad with a sign hanging on their back. It would state, painted in large letters, the word *Spy*.

Heated discussions were held at the highest levels before the State Department became convinced that cloak-and-dagger missions cannot be conducted in the glare of a spotlight. Ruth Shipley's whim was rescinded.[17]

Government Censors Movies

EIGHT MONTHS AFTER Uncle Sam went to war, President Roosevelt grew concerned that the American people were not being imbued with the goals of Washington in the great global conflict. He realized that newspapers and magazines were saturated with "war news" but that these stories did not usually give the hoped-for Washington "angle"—meaning propaganda.

Roosevelt and his wife Eleanor were avid movie fans, and often new Hollywood films were flown to Washington for the First Couple to view at night in the privacy of the White House. Roosevelt, the Great Communicator of the Era, knew that 80 million Americans, many flushed with good-paying jobs in the defense industry, were pouring into sixteen thousand theaters each week.

Armed with this knowledge, the president decided that the seductive qualities of the large silver screen could be "one of our most effective means for informing our citizens of the need for patriotism and unity."

Consequently, in August 1942, a branch of the Office of War Information (OWI) to be known as the Bureau of Motion Pictures (BMP) was established in Washington. BMP's stated function was to work with Hollywood leaders in the production of wartime films.

Publicly, fifty-one-year-old Elmer Davis, a journalist selected by Roosevelt to head the OWI, insisted that his agency's only goal was to "tell the truth." Privately, he confided to aides that the "easiest way to propagandize people is to let a propaganda theme go in through a [movie] when people won't realize they are being propagandized."

Lowell Mellett, a former editor in the Scripps-Howard newspaper chain, ran the Bureau of Motion Pictures from Washington. His number two man, thirty-nine-year-old Nelson Poynter, the publisher of the *St. Petersburg Times* in Florida, was assigned as the hard-nosed foreman to ride herd on the hands at the Hollywood corral.

Mellett and Poynter knew virtually nothing about making movies. Poynter had seldom been to a film in a theater and he was unaware of the names of Hollywood's stars and tycoons. Moreover, Mellett and Poynter were staunch political liberals, as were nearly all of the BMP executives. Most of the Hollywood studio heads, producers, and directors were political conservatives.

Elmer Davis had assured Hollywood filmmakers that Poynter's function was to advise, not censor. However, the BMP movie-reviewing staff, mainly women with liberal views, produced a forty-two-page *Manual for the Motion Picture Industry.*

Hollywood bigwigs were flabbergasted to observe the left-wing thrust of the *Manual.* It stated that Allied victory would promise a New Deal for the entire world, with capitalism regulated by governments and social welfare programs introduced or drastically expanded. Roosevelt had labeled his domestic program the New Deal, which conservatives considered to be socialistic.

King Vidor, a highly successful director with conservative views, was among the first in Hollywood to clash with the BMP. He was developing an epic of the steelmaking industry, *An American Romance.* In Washington, Marjorie Thorson, BMP chief reviewer, was aghast to read in the script that management was praised and union bosses degraded. The storyline focused on a young, penniless immigrant, Steve Dragos, who became a union-busting automobile manufacturer.

"This story is a deluxe automobile edition of Horatio Alger," an irate Thorson declared. "And if Henry Ford himself had written the script, it could scarcely express the Ford [antiunion] philosophy more clearly."

Despite the major "flaws" in the script, BMP felt that it would be beneficial to the war effort to show a movie that depicted that work on an assembly line could be "fulfilling and beneficial." So the agency demanded that Vidor's script be "realigned."

Thorson was especially outraged about the conduct of the immigrant hero, Steve Dragos. When his workers staged a sit-down strike, he brought in armed guards with tear gas to disperse the strikers. "A Nazi tactic pure and simple," Thorson exclaimed.

E. J. Mannix, production chief at the Hollywood studio making *An American Romance,* "yelled and screamed" when the BMP "advisor," Lowell Mellett, handed him Thorson's long list of "desired" script changes. Washington was trying to strong-arm him and King Vidor into making a "New Deal picture," Mannix declared.

Despite their anger, Vidor and Mannix bowed to reality, and they agreed to implement enough script changes to make the images of management and unions compatible with New Deal philosophy.

Throughout the Hollywood hierarchy, it had become apparent that, while the government could not legally censor films, the BMP had the moral clout to achieve that goal. If the movie tycoons were to publicly clash with the BMP, a wartime agency, they would be branded as unpatriotic and risk failures at the box office.

Throughout the war years, Hollywood produced scores of films that had been censored by the noncensors of BMP. Never before or since has a private-enterprise communications medium in the United States been subjected to such ironclad, yet subtle, control by the government. As OWI chief Elmer Davis had predicted would be the case, millions of Americans were "propagandized without realizing they had been propagandized."[18]

Navajo Code-Talkers

AT THE MARINE CORPS TRAINING BASE at San Diego, California, in mid-1942, Colonel James L. Underhill gave an introduction speech to a group of unique recruits that had just arrived. "The rest of us in the Marine Corps are Americans," he declared. "But our Americanism goes back at most no more than three hundred years. Your ancestors appeared on the continent thousands of years ago. Through your ancestors, you were Americans long before your fellow marines were Americans."

Colonel Underhill was speaking to the first group of Navajo Indians that had volunteered to leave their reservation and to contribute a unique talent to marine outfits in combat: passing along messages in a code that the Japanese could never break—the Navajo language. They would eventually be known and admired by marines as code-talkers.

When America had been bombed into war, countless young male Navajos (as with those in other tribes) had to wrestle with their consciences. Most felt, with merit, that the "white man" had taken away their country long ago. So should they fight for the United States?

One Indian mother asked her son who had just enlisted in the Marine Corps, "Why do you have to go to war? It's not your war, it's the white man's war."

"Because, Mother, I'm proud to be an American," the young man replied. "And I'm proud to be a Navajo. We should always be ready when our country needs us."

Early on, the Navajo recruits were given a crash course on operating a radio. Then the men themselves got together to assign Navajo words to the accoutrements of war. Dive-bombers became *ginitsob* (hawk), bombs became *a-ye-shi* (eggs), and observation planes became *ne-as-jah* (owl), among scores of other words that would be used in combat situations.

The Navajo language could not be understood or mimicked by the Japanese; the verb forms were so complex that they could be understood and spoken only by those who had grown up with the language.

Eventually 430 Navajo code-talkers would be involved in all the major battles in the Pacific. Messages sent by radio in their unbreakable code carried information to and from field commanders on Japanese troops deployment, artillery positions, strong points, and observation posts. Most of the code-talkers' activities were highly dangerous, being at or near the front lines—and sometime behind Japanese positions.

A contingent of Navajo marines landed with the assault waves on bloody Iwo Jima in February 1945. Much of the fighting focused on Mount Suribachi, a craggy, 550-foot elevation that dominated the tiny patch of real estate.

After four days of savage fighting, a forty-man marine patrol reached the summit. There Lieutenant Harold Schrier reached into his map case and pulled out a folded American flag that had been given to him earlier by his regimental colonel. Other marines found a long piece of pipe, seemingly a remnant of a rain-catching apparatus. At about 10:30 A.M. four men began fixing the Stars and Stripes to the pole.

At the time, two code-talkers were a short distance from the summit. They sent a message to a command ship offshore: "*Naastsosi Thanzie Dibeh Shida Dahnesta Tkin Shush Wollachee Noasi Lin Achi.*"

On the ship the message was rapidly translated by a Navajo—and a mighty cheer erupted from hundreds of men on board. The message had stated that the American flag was flying atop Mount Suribachi. After the last Japanese had been dug out of caves, Iwo Jima was pronounced secure. It had been a bloody victory: seven thousand marines had been killed and eleven thousand wounded. Four of the American dead were Navajo code-talkers.[19]

Popular Orchestra Disbanded

AMERICA'S MOST POPULAR DANCE BAND, the Glenn Miller orchestra, was performing before a typical packed house in a theater in Boston. The musical ensemble played a beautiful new ballad, "I'll Be Home for Christmas." Many in the audience, with loved ones in the service and far away, wept copiously. It was September 1, 1942.

An Iowan, Miller had been a trombonist and arranger before forming his own band in the late 1930s. Within months the orchestra had skyrocketed to the top in record sales.

Now, near the end of the show in Boston, Miller told the audience that the band would be no more, that he had received a captain's commission in the Air Corps and would be leaving soon for active duty.

What Miller did not say was that he had given up a highly remunerative contract with the Chesterfield cigarettes program on CBS radio, as well as a few million dollars more in other income to volunteer his services to his country.[20]

Gone with the Wind in Chicago

WALTER ASHER, owner of a grocery store in Rolla, Missouri, received a package from something that had the initials OPA. Only later would he learn that OPA stood for a mammoth wartime agency, the Office of Price Administration.

Asher opened the container and was confused by the myriad of bureaucratic gobbledygook. In nearly thirty pages of small type, a booklet described a food-rationing plan conceived by the OPA in Washington to allocate fairly to Americans the most popular foods, such as meat, butter, cheese, sugar, and coffee.

Grocers throughout the nation claimed that the OPA bureaucrats that had concocted the program didn't understand it either. However, there were serious penalties for infractions. "I might go to jail and never know what 'crime' I committed!" a Des Moines grocer complained.

The logistics of the massive rationing program were mind-boggling. Each family in the United States was registered to receive ration books. Some 5600 ration boards, depending largely on volunteers, were established. But there were 60,000 paid employees.

The OPA apparatus consumed 40 million pounds of paper in printing forms, coupons, and instructions, and as many as 5 billion forms were printed and distributed on the home front each year.

Each ration book had stamps with point values for specific foods. Sirloin steaks and pork chops might go for twelve points; pineapple juice for twenty-two points; peaches for eighteen points; cheese for eight points and butter for sixteen points. Consumers paid for the grocery with stamps—plus cash.

At the end of each workday, the grocer—who often ran a mom-and-pop operation—was confronted with an accounting problem that might confound a Harvard business graduate. To replenish his stocks, the grocer had to count the stamps, then send them to his wholesalers, who in turn, had to sort out tens of thousands of stamps into an orderly manner. Then he turned the stamps over to his local bank to get credit for buying more food.

Often the grocery ran out of the gummed sheets on which to stick the stamps. Requests for more of the sheets sometimes got lost in the OPA bureaucracy, causing wholesalers to haul loose stamps to the bank in bushel baskets.

Cuts of meat are marked with ration-point values and OPA ceiling prices at this typical American grocery. (Library of Congress)

On one occasion in Chicago, a violent burst of wind jerked a basket from a wholesaler's hand as he was walking toward a bank. Millions of stamps were scattered over a large portion of the city.[21]

Nasty Bartenders and Redneck Cops

TWENTY-EIGHT-YEAR-OLD Nancy H. Love, daughter of a wealthy Philadelphia physician, was present at a Washington press conference when Secretary of War Henry Stimson announced that she would be head of a new Women's Auxiliary Ferrying Squadron (WAFS). It was September 10, 1942, ten days after First Lady Eleanor Roosevelt suggested in her influential syndicated newspaper column, "My Day," that "our women pilots are a weapon waiting to be used."

WAFS would be volunteers and experienced pilots. As director, Love would set up headquarters at New Castle Air Force Base near Wilmington, Delaware.

At the time of her appointment, Love had been flying for ten years. Since 1936, she and her husband, Robert H. Love, had built a thriving aviation company in Boston, for which she served as one of the pilots. Nancy Love had been a pioneer, having safety-tested aircraft innovations for the U.S. Bureau of Air Commerce.

Soon, eager female pilots, one by one, began arriving at New Castle. They were a varied lot: heiresses (Woolworth's and Luden's cough drops); one who had become the youngest licensed female pilot in the nation at age sixteen; a woman who had been inspired to fly in 1928 after reading an article by Amelia Earhart; and a former barnstormer who had some 3,000 hours of flying experience.

After a forty-day orientation period, Nancy Love's pilots began ferrying aircraft from factories to Army Air Corps bases around the nation.

Only five days after the WAFS had been born, the War Department announced the creation of another Army Air Corps organization, the Women's Flying Training Detachment (WFTD). A day later, its leader, famed aviatrix Jacqueline Cochran, went to work on a paid basis—one dollar a year.

An energetic, tough-minded, competitive, and outspoken woman, she had sent a sharply-worded letter to General Henry "Hap" Arnold, the Air Corp chief, urging creation of an all-female pilots organization—commanded by a woman.

Jacqueline Cochran numbered several Air Corps generals among her friends, and she was on a first-name basis with them. She had started flying in 1932, and was the only woman to enter the McRobertson London Melbourne race in 1934. That same year she became the first woman to compete in the annual cross-country Bendix Trophy race. Much to the chagrin of her male competitors, some of whom would become Air Corps generals, she won the race.

Born in Pensacola, Florida, in 1913, Cochran had pulled herself up from a poverty-stricken early life to become head of her own highly successful national cosmetics firm, established in 1935.

Jackie Cochran put out a call for volunteers for her new outfit. She was swamped with some 25,000 applicants, many of whom tried to beg or connive their way into a cockpit. She chose 1,830 of the most promising candidates, who had to pay their own way to Avenger Field in Texas, the nation's only all-female base.

These recruit trainees for the Women's Flying Training Detachment had experience piloting planes but had not logged nearly as many hours as Nancy Love's WAFS, who already were ferrying aircraft. In the first group of recruits were a Hollywood actress, a Reno blackjack dealer, a stuntwoman from Hollywood, a Chicago stripper, and a Kentucky nurse who made her rounds on horseback. Most noticeable was a member of the Florsheim shoe family who arrived at a nearby hotel with seventeen trunks and a trio of finely coiffured Afghans.

During the first week the women were in training, more than a hundred curious male cadets from the several training schools in the region suddenly developed engine trouble and had to make "forced landings" at Avenger Field.

So the field commander ordered the base closed to all but genuine emergencies. Avenger Field, therefore, became known as Cochran's Convent.

By the early fall of 1942, Nancy Love's WAFS had logged hundreds of thousands of miles ferrying military aircraft around the home front. On one occasion four of the women flew P-51 Mustang fighter planes on an arduous trek from California to a base in Newark, New Jersey. After turning over their aircraft to the authorities, the women decided to cross the Hudson River into New York City for an evening of relaxation. They entered the popular restaurant, Jack Dempsey's, owned by the former world heavyweight boxing champion.

The weather was mild and the pilots were wearing the standard gabardine shirts and slacks. At the bar, they ordered drinks. The bartender glared at them. "No women in slacks," he barked. "But these are our uniforms," they protested. Moments later, they were hustled out of the crowded restaurant.

Halfway down the block, they heard shouts: "Ladies! Ladies!" The manager of Dempsey's was running after them, having been alerted by an angry male Air Corps officer who had watched the episode. "Please come back," the manager pleaded. "We thought you were, er, ah, er, well you're wearing slacks."

He had mistaken them for prostitutes. Hungry and thirsty, they agreed to return, and spent the evening at Dempsey's on the house.

On another occasion, stormy weather caused four female pilots to make an emergency landing at Americus, Georgia. Leaving their aircraft in the hangar, they caught a bus into town to look for a hotel to spend the night. Soon after they began walking through the downtown area, a police car pulled up. Two of Americus's finest got out and ordered the women to come with them to the police station. One cop said sarcastically, "'Ladies in slacks are not allowed on the streets at night around here." He, too, had mistaken the pilots for prostitutes.

The women were locked in a filthy cell. They protested that they were Army pilots in uniform. The police chief was unmoved. That would be merely another charge against them: impersonating military officers.

It was nearly 3:00 A.M. before the women were allowed to make a telephone call. They contacted Nancy Love and related their predicament. She demanded to speak to the police chief. He winced, holding the telephone receiver away from his ear. Ladylike and refined most of the time, Love had acquired a rough vocabulary. She read the riot act to the shaken police chief, impugning his lack of patriotism and charging that she would go directly to President Roosevelt about this outrage.

Minutes later the women were driven back to the airport. After dawn they lifted off in their planes, anxious to put as many miles as possible between themselves and the rednecked policemen in Americus, Georgia.[22]

Plane Bombs Pacific Northwest

IN SEPTEMBER 1942, the Japanese submarine *I-25* was approaching the dark shore of Oregon. Housed in an improvised deck hangar was a light reconnaissance plane. The pilot was not necessarily expected to return from a mission, but the aircraft was equipped with pontoons to make it possible to touch down near the submarine.

A month earlier, the skipper of the *I-25* was in the craft's home port, 9,000 miles from the west coast of America, and he conferred with the former head of the Japanese consulate in Seattle, Washington. The diplomatic official briefed the officers and men of the *I-25* on a scheme to drop incendiary bombs on the thickly forested regions of Oregon and adjoining Washington State, an action designed to ignite roaring blazes.

Now, under the veil of night, the pilot of the submarine-carried airplane took off from the water, headed inland, and dropped two incendiaries near Brookings, Oregon, a short distance north of the California border. Small blazes were ignited, but the U.S. Forest Service rangers rapidly extinguished them before major damage occurred.

For nearly three weeks, the *I-25* cruised along the coast. On September 29, the plane was launched again off the Oregon shore and two more bombs were dropped. A minor fire was put out. The submarine headed back to Japan, with the Americans never knowing that the enemy had started the forest blazes.[23]

Part Four

A Nation in Total War

Covert Project on
Constitution Avenue

NINE MONTHS AFTER AMERICA was jolted into global war, an anonymous group of brigadier generals and colonels was hidden away in the old Munitions Building on Constitution Avenue in Washington, D.C. These officers would never make the headlines, nor even get their names mentioned in newspapers. But on their shoulders rested the fate of Operation Torch, the first major American offensive of the war. It was late August 1942.

The invasion target was French Northwest Africa. No one in Washington entertained any illusion that the task would be easy. Never had a major invasion been mounted from three thousand miles away. There were no textbooks, and no precedents. An untested, partially trained force of some 38,000 soldiers, its vehicles, weapons, ammunition, and supplies would have to be moved to another continent from Hampton Roads, Virginia, near Norfolk.

The convoy, known as the Western Task Force, would have to cross an ocean infested with German U-boats, storm the defended shores, defeat whatever hostile force might be encountered, secure a large beachhead, and prepare to drive hundreds of miles eastward.

There was enormous reason for the secrecy. Should German spies learn of the looming operation, the convoy could meet with a monumental disaster at the hands of waiting U-boat wolf packs.

The officers tucked away in a loft in the Munitions Building were charged with the awesome responsibility of getting the right troops and supplies and weapons to the right place at the right time. There would be 700,000 different items, including 22 million pounds of food and 18 million pounds of clothing. Ten million gallons of gasoline would go ashore in five-gallon containers carried by individual soldiers or would land in bulk by tankers.

Included in the supply list were 508 rat-catchers, 200 alarm clocks, hundreds of stepladders, rubber stamps, steel safes, and cartons of condoms.

Further complicating the gargantuan logistics buildup was the crucial necessity of keeping a tight security lid on the Munitions Building planning. Hundreds of thousands of items would be delivered to ships along the eastern seaboard on cartons marked L-10, or Z-2, or XY, leaving GIs and enemy spies alike puzzled over the contents.

In the knowledge that hostile ears and eyes might be anywhere, security officers in Washington planted rumors that the feverish activity in the Munitions Building was merely for the purpose of moving troops to the British Isles. "Britain" and "Ireland" were code words for Algeria and Morocco, two nations the Allies were to invade.

The planning process was compartmentalized. Some officers knew that a large movement was in the works. Others knew the size but not the destination. Still others knew the targeted locale but not the size of the operation.

Officers hunkered down over desks in tiny rooms never mentioned the words Oran, Casablanca, or Algiers. Even when only two men were in a room, they used code words for those ports, or else they used hand signals for conveying to each other the names of those Northwest Africa cities.

Nothing was left to chance by the Torch planners in Washington. A hundred miles inland, engineer soldiers practiced—often against a stopwatch—loading everything from cans of vegetables to thirty-ton tanks onto every type of freight car existing in America.

Even if saboteurs, secret Nazi weapons, or acts of God should destroy three-fourths of the bridges in the eastern United States, invasion troops and supplies would be transported from the interior to Hampton Roads by preselected alternative routes.

One of the last projects for the Munitions Building planners was the distribution of some one thousand different types of maps. This task had to be carried out under intensely secret conditions. Officers and enlisted men taking part were given no leaves and were more or less under arrest. Maps were shipped to warehouses near Hampton Roads. Watched closely by armed military police, GIs packed the maps into containers for distribution to the proper invasion units, each one having a code marking: 12-R, 8-T, 106-W, and the like.[1]

Patton Calls on the President

COMMANDING THE WESTERN TASK FORCE in Operation Torch, America's first major offensive since the Argonne Forest in World War I, was Major General George S. Patton Jr. Tall, ramrod straight, the fifty-six-year-old Californian was flamboyant in his personal lifestyle, independently wealthy, and possessor of a blue vocabulary that was second to none in the U.S. Army.

The silver-haired Patton had been one of the Army's best-known figures since his days at West Point, where he had been a center of conversation among cadets after he had stood up between targets as his comrades blasted away on the rifle range. "Wanted to know what it feels like to be under fire," young George explained.

Just prior to World War I, Patton had accompanied General John J. "Black Jack" Pershing into Mexico, where the lieutenant expanded his renown by tracking down a notorious Mexican outlaw, killing the bandit in a two-man shootout, and bringing the corpse back to camp strapped over the front fender of an automobile.

In World War I, Patton's Army-wide reputation as a bold fighting man gained further luster. He led a tank brigade in several bloody battles, during which he was wounded.

Now, twenty-four years later, General Patton was preparing to go to war again. Eager to fight but a realist, he scrawled in his diary: "[Torch] will be as desperate a venture as has ever been undertaken by any force in the world's history."

On October 20, three days before the Western Task Force was to sail for Africa, Patton wrote a letter to his wife Beatrice with instructions that it was to be opened "only when and if I am definitely reported dead." To his brother-in-law, Frederick Ayer, the general asked him to "take care of my wife and children should anything happen to me."

Outwardly, Patton was his customarily upbeat self. When he informed Beatrice that he had been invited to make a farewell call on Franklin Roosevelt in the White House, she admonished her husband to remember he was in the presence of the president of the United States and to be careful not to use profanity.

During his visit to Roosevelt in the Oval Office, Patton was at his fire-eating best, but he managed to keep any blue words out of his conversation. However, when taking his leave, the general reassured the president: "Sir, all I want to tell you is this—I will leave the goddamned beaches either a conquering son of a bitch or a corpse!"[2]

Weapons Mysteriously Vanish

D DAY FOR OPERATION TORCH was set for November 8, 1942. At his headquarters in Norfolk House in England, forty-six-year-old Major General Mark W. Clark was deeply worried. His responsibility was coordinating the three task forces that would invade French Northwest Africa, and he was confronted by a monumental problem that threatened to disrupt, or even cancel Torch. Supplies—mountains of them—were mysteriously failing to arrive in England, Torch's main staging base, from New York City.

Entire shiploads of guns, ammunition, spare parts, and other crucial items were simply vanishing. As time neared for the invasion, General Clark learned that one of his assault divisions in England had not received all of its assigned weapons. Frantic investigation disclosed that the weapons were still sitting on New York City docks. Someone had altered the markings on the crates. It was clear that Nazi spies were stalking New York harbor.[3]

A Huge Bounty on Hitler's Head

IN MID-NOVEMBER 1942, soon after American and British forces had stormed ashore in French Northwest Africa, Samuel Harden Church, a wealthy American businessman, was convinced that he knew the key to ending the war in Europe and the Mediterranean. He widely publicized the fact that he would pay a $1 million reward (equivalent to some $12 million in the year 2002) for the capture of Adolf Hitler.

It was specified that the führer had to be taken alive and unharmed. Then the German warlord would be turned over for trial to the League of Nations, an international association of countries, founded after World War I to assure that there would be no future armed conflicts.

Sam Church's brainstorm died when he did in 1943—with Adolf Hitler alive and well in Berlin.[4]

A Tempest in a Teapot

JUST BEFORE CHRISTMAS in 1942, hawkeyed newsmen in Des Moines, Iowa, discovered that Amber D'Georg, a striptease artist in a burlesque show, was actually Kathryn Doris Gregory, who was a WAAC and absent without leave from her camp at Fort Worth, Texas. A tempest in a teapot erupted. Across home-front America, the focus on the war was momentarily set aside while citizens paused to savor the "scandal."

Private Gregory was taken into custody by two military policemen, who had conscientiously carried out their duty by ogling the young woman's nearly nude performance before hauling her away.

While the WAAC was confined to her quarters, groups that were opposed to women being involved in the military had a field day. Some pastors took to the pulpit to complain that the Army was turning WAACs into shameless prostitutes. Others called for the Army to deactivate the WAAC organization and "send the young women home where they belong."

In the case of Private Kathryn Gregory, the Army followed a similar line of reasoning. She was given a less than honorable discharge, mostly, it was reported, to quell the hubbub and get on with the war.[5]

Press Conferences for "Women Only"

EARLY IN JANUARY 1943, First Lady Eleanor Roosevelt pointed out in her syndicated column, "My Day," that there were more than seven hundred correspondents telling the folks back home what was going on in the war. Nearly all of the reporters, the First Lady huffed, were "pure male."

Eleanor backed up her words with actions. Each Monday morning she held a press conference in the White House. As a ploy to impress on media moguls the shortage of women on their staffs, she barred male reporters from her briefings.

Consequently, without fanfare, the wire services, radio networks, magazines, and newspapers quietly beefed up their journalist corps with women.[6]

Secret Plan to Draft Females

ABOUT A YEAR into America's involvement in the war, secret discussions were being held in high places in Washington about a manpower shortage in the armed forces. Lieutenant General Brehon B. Somervell, the Army's supply chief, proposed alleviating the personnel shortfall by drafting 500,000 women each year, using the same selective service apparatus that was bringing men into the armed forces.

Somervell estimated that there were 11 million women available for duty, and he proposed that the Army take 10 percent of them, leaving the remaining pool of females for other essential tasks in and out of the military.

Never had the United States drafted women, and no member of Congress was especially eager to be branded as being in favor of dragooning young women. Behind-the-scenes contacts with leaders in the Senate and House of Representatives convinced Somervell that his revolutionary proposal would be soundly rejected—perhaps unanimously. Women in uniform would continue to be volunteers.[7]

Women in Combat Experiment

GENERAL GEORGE MARSHALL, the Army chief of staff, was mulling over casualty reports from around the world in mid-January 1943. It became clear to him that he would have to try to free more men in noncombat roles to fight. So, in great secrecy, he authorized an experiment in which women would be integrated into male antiaircraft-gun crews.

The field test would be conducted at two batteries protecting Washington, a city Army leaders were concerned might be a target of German bombers. Intelligence reports had indicated that the Nazi scientists were developing a long-range bomber that could hit New York, Washington, and other eastern cities.

There was good reason for the supersecrecy of the experiment. Even though women would not be involved in the actual firing of the ack-ack guns, Marshall feared an uproar on the home front should it leak out that females were involved in what might be regarded as a semicombat type of operation.

Apparently the field test was inconclusive. Or perhaps General Marshall had second thoughts. Whatever the case, the experiment was quietly scuttled.[8]

Jailbreak for a Boyfriend

IN EARLY JANUARY 1943, Ursula Parrott, an established novelist who had been married and divorced five times, managed to get into the news nationwide — but not in praise of her latest book. Rather she had helped her soldier-of-the-week to escape from the Army stockade at Miami Beach, Florida.

After creating a scheme for springing him, Parrott took him home in her car, hid him, then bought civilian clothes for the escapee. The boyfriend tried to get out of the region, was caught, and implicated Parrott.

Before being hauled off to the local pokey, the novelist explained to newsmen: "It was just an impulse."

A judge hearing her case was not impressed by impulses. She received a year in jail.[9]

Megabucks for Jack Benny's Violin

POLICE OFFICERS WERE OUT in force as thousands of people crowded into Gimbel's, a large department store in New York City, not for a major sale but to attend a War Bond rally. These government-issued bonds were to help finance the global conflict, whose cost was astronomical. The bonds were to yield 2.9 percent after a ten-year maturity. It was January 27, 1943.

Magnets for the event were items donated by celebrities, including letters written by George Washington and a Bible owned by Thomas Jefferson.

Famed comedian Jack Benny's violin, a stage prop in countless radio shows, was actually a $75 imitation. Despite it being a fake, Julius Klorfien bought the violin for $1 million (equivalent to some $12 million in the year 2002).

Countless people around the United States were flabbergasted, not only by the fact that a fake musical instrument had been bought for such an outrageous sum, but who in Hades was Julius Klorfien? Few Americans had ever heard of him. He turned out to be the owner of a thriving tobacco business, Garcia Grande cigars.[10]

"Mom, Keep Your Chin Up!"

ALLETA SULLIVAN WAS A TYPICAL American mother with sons in the service. In her bedroom at the family home on Adams Street in Waterloo, Iowa, she

The deaths of the five Sullivan brothers rocked home-front America. From the left: Joe, Frank, Al, Matt, and George. (National Archives)

spent nights in troubled sleep, gripped by anxiety. Unlike most other American mothers, Alleta was unique: she had five sons fighting for the country.

Early in January 1943, Alleta, who was nearing her forty-eighth birthday, was especially fearful. All of her sons were on the cruiser *Juneau*. Since they had departed for training camp almost a year earlier, each had faithfully written to her and their father, Tom. But the letters had stopped coming a few weeks earlier.

Tom was nearing his sixtieth birthday. His had been a hard life. In his teens he had plowed in the fields and later performed hard labor in Colorado mines. In recent years he had been conductor on an Illinois Central freight train.

Tom, too, was almost constantly stricken with pangs of anxiety. Often he took solace in the bottle. Like other parents across the land, both Tom and Alleta tried to hide from each other the agony that gripped them.

In the wake of the sneak Japanese attack on Pearl Harbor, the Sullivan brothers—George, Francis, Joseph, Madison, and Albert—had marched into the Navy recruiting office in Waterloo and volunteered to fight. They vowed to avenge the death of their pal, Bill Ball of Fredericksburg, Iowa, who had been killed on the battleship *Arizona* at Pearl Harbor.

The procedure wasn't all that simple. Before they signed up, the Sullivans told the recruiting officer that they must serve together. That request flew in the face of Navy tradition, a formidable barrier indeed. When brothers were in the same service, they were customarily put on different ships.

"We have always fought for each other," George Sullivan, the oldest brother, explained. "Now we want to continue to fight side by side."

Then there was another roadblock to the mass enlistment. Al was a husband and father of a young son, and the Navy was reluctant to accept recruits with family responsibilities. However, the Navy granted Al an enlistment waiver, and, reluctantly perhaps, agreed to assign the five brothers to the same ship.

When the brothers excitedly informed their mother that they had joined up with Uncle Sam, Alleta slipped into the kitchen so that her boys wouldn't see the tears of pride—and fear—that streamed down her cheeks. Father Tom, a stoic type, outwardly took the news in stride, concealing his own deep worries.

Back in 1937, after three years of drought during which Iowa's corn crops had been ruined, the two older brothers, George and Frank, had joined the Navy.

A friend, John Draude, had enlisted with them. "Like me, the Sullivan boys were hungry," Draude recalled. "We'd all quit school in the tenth grade. I worked shoveling snow for the Illinois Central at twenty-eight cents an hour. George and Frank worked as laborers at a Waterloo slaughterhouse and meat-packing plant for the same wages. The Navy paid better, so we joined."

A day after the five Sullivans signed up, they called on Father Clarence Piontkowski, pastor of the family parish. The brothers had not been the priest's most devoted parishioners. But now, going off to war, they decided they needed all the help they could get.

Later Piontkowski recalled: "I had known the [boys] over a period of seven years or so while they were attending St. Mary's grade school. I found them to be not sensational, but pluggers. Now they said they were going to war together and they would come home together."

That night the Sullivans left for the Waterloo station to catch the train for Des Moines and the induction center. With them was Father Piontkowski, who blessed them as they kneeled in the station. Mother Alleta tried, unsuccessfully, to fight back the tears. Father Tom struggled to maintain his tranquil composure.

Boot camp at the Great Lakes Naval Training Station near Chicago was fast and furious. After four weeks, the Sullivans were shipped out to the Brooklyn Navy Yard, where they were assigned to the new cruiser *Juneau.*

Although the Sullivan boys continued to write their parents, they were not permitted to disclose the location or destination of their ship. Nine months after enlisting, the five sailors and their shipmates on the *Juneau* crossed the international date line as they steamed westward across the Pacific.

On August 8, 1942, home-front America, accustomed to one military disaster after another in the Pacific, had been elated by radio news bulletins. Under Major General Alexander A. Vandegrift, the 1st Marine Division had stormed ashore on a ninety-mile-long hellhole of thick, steaming jungles and swamps called Guadalcanal.

Civilians scrambled for encyclopedias that might give some clue about Guadalcanal. About all they learned was that the island was a throwback to the Stone Age, totally unimpeded by progress.

In Waterloo, Tom and Alleta Sullivan kept tab on the fighting at Guadalcanal. Alleta was convinced—call it a mother's intuition—that her five sons were taking part in that operation. But she had no way of knowing that on the night of November 12–13, 1942, thirteen U.S. warships had been engaged in a bitter fight with a Japanese armada. At dawn, only six U.S. vessels were able to steam away under their own power.

Early in the morning of January 11, 1943, Tom Sullivan slipped quietly out of bed and dressed. Knowing that Alleta was distraught over the absence of mail from her sons, he told her to remain in bed and that he would cook his own breakfast before getting aboard a freight train bound for Dubuque, Iowa, with a heavy cargo of war accoutrements.

Downstairs in the kitchen, Tom was fussing with a coffee pot when he heard car doors slam in front of the house. Peeking out the front window, he saw three men in Navy dress uniforms coming up the sidewalk. Tom was puzzled. He knew that the Navy sent telegrams delivered by Western Union boys in the event of deaths and wounds.

Tom opened the door and the three men entered. The lieutenant commander introduced himself as Truman Jones, head of Iowa's recruiting operation in Des Moines. The others were a Navy doctor and a chief petty officer. Tom asked them to be seated and went upstairs to tell Alleta about the visitors. She threw on a bathrobe and slippers, and awakened daughter Genevieve, and Katherine Mary, the wife of youngest son Al.

As the three women came down the stairs, they were gripped by fear. There could be only one reason for the Navy to send three men to the house.

After introductions, Commander Jones, choking with emotion, said, "I'm afraid I'm bringing you very bad news."

A hush fell over the room. Tom, Alleta, and the two young women were ashenfaced. Finally, Alleta asked in a shaky voice: "Which one was it?"

More moments of silence as Jones swallowed hard. In a quiet tone he replied: "I'm sorry. All five of your sons."

The family was in shock. All sat quietly. Genevieve and Katherine Mary were near collapse.

Commander Jones and his two men looked on helplessly. In moments, Tom Sullivan, despite his grief, said gently to his wife, "My train's leaving in a half hour. Should I go?"

Alleta knew the freight train was loaded with war materials. If the cargo didn't reach the fighting men in time, it might mean that other boys would die, that other mothers might have to face such grief.

"It's all right, Tom," she replied. "It's the right thing to do. Our boys would want you to go."

Tom reached for his dinner pail, put on a heavy coat and muffler as a hedge against the bitter Iowa cold, kissed Alleta, and left the house.

On the short walk to the train station, Tom passed the playground in the neighborhood where, years earlier, he had watched his boys cavort. With his gloved hand, he brushed away tears.

Meanwhile, back at the rambling old family home on Adams Street, the three women sat weeping, trying to console one another. Maybe the boys will turn up alive, they told one another.

Only much later would the family on Adams Street learn what had happened to the *Juneau*. On the moonless night of November 12, the cruiser had been standing watch over transports that were unloading badly needed men and supplies on Guadalcanal where 20,000 Japanese were resisting tenaciously.

When radar detected the approach of a large flight of Japanese bombers, the unloading was halted and the *Juneau* soon found itself under attack from the air. Lieutenant Roger W. O'Neill, a medical officer on the ship, would recall: "A near-miss by a bomb seemed to lift the *Juneau* out of the water. Our ship was strafed repeatedly. We recovered some of the Japanese slugs and were keeping them as souvenirs."

But *Juneau*'s luck soon ran out. A torpedo exploded in a port fire room that killed seventeen men and caused the ship to list. By morning the *Juneau* was ten feet down by the bow, but her crew began nursing her to safety.

Near midnight, the Japanese submarine *I-26* fired three torpedoes at the *San Francisco*. The lethal fish missed the heavy cruiser but struck the *Juneau*. Men on other ships were awestruck by the force of the explosion. Only a pall of thick smoke hovered over where the "Mighty J" and her seven hundred men, including five named Sullivan, had been. No survivors were spotted.

News of the *Juneau* disaster and the deaths of the five Sullivan brother swept across America like a tidal wave, in newsreels, magazines, newspapers, and on radio. Their deaths seemed to galvanize the home front into recognizing that much blood and grief would have to be expended before victory in a global war could be achieved.

Letters and condolences from Americans poured into the house at 98 Adams Street. Each weekday a truck from the Waterloo post office would arrive to deliver a new batch of messages.

In the deluge of mail was a letter handwritten by a man who lived at 1600 Pennsylvania Avenue in Washington. Although he never mentioned the fact, he, too, knew the agony of parents in wartime: he and his wife had four sons in uniform. The message read, in part:

> As commander in chief of the Army and Navy, I want you to know that the entire nation shares in your sorrow. We who remain to carry on the fight will maintain a courageous spirit, in the knowledge that your sons' sacrifice was not in vain.

As one of your sons wrote, "We will make a team together that can't be beat." It is this spirit which in the end will triumph.

—Franklin D. Roosevelt

Meanwhile, newsreel camera crews descended upon Waterloo and set up shop in the Sullivans' snow-covered yard. Despite broken hearts and grief that would haunt them the remainder of their lives, Tom and Alleta felt it was their duty to appear before the cameras.

Alleta, still in shock, her face swollen and eyes reddened, faced the cameras and said: "I know now what my five boys meant when they wrote me all the time, 'Mom, keep your chin up!' All I can say to you mothers here in America is to keep your chins up, too. Our five boys did not die in vain."

The deaths of the Sullivan brothers came to symbolize the devotion and sacrifices of all men of the armed forces and their families during the war. These typical young men spurred the home front into even greater effort to bring the global conflict to a successful conclusion.[11]

Firm Gets Big Payoff

EXCEPT FOR ISOLATED STRAGGLERS, the last Japanese soldier had been killed or evacuated from bloody Guadalcanal by February 7, 1943, six months to the day since the marines had landed. It had been a costly victory. War is never totally one-sided. Including the five Sullivan brothers, the Navy had some forty-nine hundred casualties on and around Guadalcanal. Nearly eighteen hundred marines and soldiers were killed in securing the primitive island.

On home-front America, millions of people, each in his or her own way, celebrated the first victory over the Japanese army that had been heading hell-bent to invade Australia. Perhaps none rejoiced more than the executives at Lever Brothers, the huge soap-manufacturing corporation.

In an it-could-only-happen-in-America action, the U.S. government shelled out $7 million (equivalent to $90 million in the year 2002) to Lever Brothers for war damage to the coconut groves the firm owned on Guadalcanal.[12]

A Glamorous Nazi Agent

WHILE LARGE NUMBERS of American mothers were enduring agony over the loss of sons, there were other American women trying to sell out their country.

Burton Huffberg (not his real name) had made good money as an employee at the Ford plant in Detroit before being drafted into the Navy in early 1943. Tall, handsome, and well built, the twenty-six-year-old Huffberg was an ideal employee in the huge factory that was producing mountains of weapons for the armed forces.

Assigned to Navy duty at Sheepshead Bay in Brooklyn in June, Huffberg carried out his assignment with all the vigor he had shown as a civilian employee. But there the similarity ended. Huffberg was a Nazi spy, and his mission was to collect information on ships and convoys sailing from New York harbor.

Huffberg, in fact, had been a spy for more than a year. At the Ford plant, he had been approached by a Nazi undercover agent working there and offered good-sized sums of money for merely pilfering drawings of war equipment. Huffberg accepted, and his bank account grew steadily.

Huffberg had been recruited into a Nazi spy ring that had been operating in Detroit with considerable success since late 1941. The brains and motivating force behind the network was Grace Buchanan-Dineen, a glamorous beauty. Well bred and a graduate of exclusive Vassar College in Poughkeepsie, New York, she was also an "alumna" of a spy school known as the Academy in Hamburg, Germany.

After Huffberg entered the Navy, he continued his role as a spy for the Mata Hari of Detroit by merely changing his focus from industrial espionage to harbor surveillance. Information obtained at New York harbor was shuttled by coded letters to Buchanan-Dineen, and she rushed it along to her Nazi controllers in Hamburg.

At about the same time that Huffberg had been sent to Sheepshead Bay, the Federal Bureau of Investigation uncovered clues that indicated an organized spy ring was operating in the Motor City, and G-men were infiltrated into the Ford plant under the guise of being genuine employees.

Information was soon developed that Grace Buchanan-Dineen was the unlikely chief spymistress and that her gang had been paying big money to obtain secret blueprints of tanks and airplane engines.

In late 1943, the FBI swooped down on the Nazi gang, arresting Buchanan-Dineen, Huffberg, and other members of the network. Facing the electric chair for wartime espionage, the wealthy Vassar grad sang like a canary. At her trial in early March 1944, she pleaded guilty and received a twelve-year term in prison.

A short time later, Huffberg went to trial, wearing his Navy uniform (he was presumed innocent until proven guilty). He, too, faced the electric chair. Soon after the trial opened, he began going through a series of strange gyrations. On the witness stand, he gave nonsensical replies to the prosecutor's questions.

Psychiatrists were brought in to examine Huffberg. After weeks of questioning, they concluded that he was "mentally unbalanced" and the case against him was dismissed.

But was this seemingly bright young man truly "crazy"? Many press observers doubted it. Rather, the resolution of his case may have been a means for getting him off the hook because he had provided the FBI with an abundance of information that enabled a deep dent to be put in the Nazi espionage apparatus in the United States.[13]

Marine Commander's Dilemma

GENERAL THOMAS HOLCOMB, commandant of the Marine Corps, was skewered on the horns of a dilemma. Men wearing the famous globe-and-anchor insignia were trained to fight, and Holcomb feared that the introduction of women into the organization would create confusion, dissension, and major morale problems.

Yet, after the marines had taken heavy casualties in the Pacific during the latter part of 1942, he knew that beefed-up manpower would be needed on the long and bloody road to Tokyo. So he asked Secretary of the Navy Frank Knox to provide the Corps with as many women as possible to be used in noncombat roles, thus releasing a greater number of men for essential combat duty.

Knox approved Holcomb's request, and plans were developed to establish the Marine Corps Women's Reserve (MCWR) in February 1943. Forty-seven-year-old Ruth C. Streeter was given the rank of major and appointed director. Enthusiastic and energetic, Streeter held both private and commercial pilot licenses. More than any of the directors of the women's components, she had firsthand knowledge of what the war was all about: three of her four grown offspring were in the service, one in the Army and two in the Navy.[14]

A Patriotic Heroine's Long Ordeal

IN THE MIDWEST CITY OF COLUMBIA, MISSOURI, Anna Froman Hetzler had spent the past few days in anxious concern. She knew that her daughter, thirty-five-year-old Jane Froman, was to fly to Lisbon, Portugal, in a Pan American Airways Clipper, a large amphibian aircraft. Like countless other mothers across the United States with an offspring going overseas and into a war zone, she prayed for her daughter's safety.

Jane Froman was beautiful and talented, a star in Hollywood movies, on the Broadway stage, and on nationwide radio networks. Public opinion polls rated her as America's most popular female singer. Now she was going on a tour of Europe to entertain American servicemen and servicewomen.

Late in the afternoon, Anna, who was on the faculty at Christian College (later Columbia College), responded to a knock on the door at her home. It was

Jane Froman, America's most popular songstress, underwent more than thirty operations after miraculously surviving an airplane crash on the way to entertain American troops. (Courtesy of Columbia College)

February 24, 1943. A Western Union boy handed her a telegram. She felt faint, knowing that the next of kin were notified of overseas casualties in this manner.

With trembling hands, Anna opened the yellow envelope and read the message from Washington: "Your daughter Jane Froman has been seriously injured . . . " The terse message did not disclose that the songstress was in a Lisbon hospital and hovering on the brink of death.

Jane, in fact, was lucky to have survived. Before leaving New York, she and another entertainer, Tamara Swan, had been assigned seats next to each another in the largest compartment. They remained in these seats for the most of the flight but, as the Clipper neared Lisbon, the two women switched places.

When the airplane glided down for what promised to be a routine landing on the Tagus River, it suddenly plunged into the water with tremendous impact. Swan, who was in the seat assigned to Froman, was killed instantly.

Jane's mink coat, blouse, shoes and stockings were ripped off. She suffered a broken right arm, a compound fracture of the right leg, a left leg nearly severed below the knee, three broken ribs, and a rash of cuts and bruises. Countless tiny bits of metal and wood from the Clipper were embedded in her body.

Froman was one of thirteen survivors afloat in the turgid water with night descending upon Lisbon. Another who escaped instant death was John Curtis Burn, the copilot, who had been hurled near the songstress. Although he had received a fractured spine and a skull fracture, he somehow made his way to Jane and kept her head above water by clinging to a piece of the wreckage.

It was a strange rendezvous, there in the darkness and the icy water. In shock and numbness, they carried on a casual conversation. Burn said that he had been a fan of Jane's for years, but had never expected to meet her adrift in a river.

Despite the idle chatter, both knew they were goners unless rescuers arrived soon. Some forty-five minutes after the crash, a launch fished the couple out of the water, and they were rushed to a Lisbon hospital.

John Burn recalled: "Jane was by far the worst hurt of the survivors, but she didn't whimper in the water or afterward. In the hospital, she kept telling the nurses to take care of the other survivors. All during the first night, when she was suffering so severely, she kept sending people to see how I was getting along."

Jane had made her Broadway debut in the hit musical *Ziegfield Follies* of 1934 with Fanny Brice and a young hoofer named Buddy Ebsen. Meanwhile, she had her first smash record, singing "I Only Have Eyes for You" in her deep, resonant voice. By now, Jane was a national celebrity and was hauling in $1,000 weekly, an imposing salary in the Great Depression era.

In the spring of 1935, Froman took a train to Hollywood where she made her first movie, *Stars Over Broadway*, with Pat O'Brien, one of Tinsel Town's most gifted actors, and noted singer James Melton. Three years later, she did her second Hollywood flick, *Radio City Revels*, and in 1940, she was back on Broadway, starring in *Keep Off the Grass* with comedian Jimmy Durante.

Meanwhile, one of Jane's most ardent fans was President Franklin Roosevelt. On five occasions, she was invited to the White House to entertain guests and to warble the President's special request, "It Ain't Necessarily So."

With her White House connection, it was logical that she was among the one hundred foremost entertainers to be invited to participate in USO shows for servicemen and women when the United States went to war. Jane wired her acceptance in less than an hour, fully aware that the commitment to her country would deprive her of many highly paid show business performances.

Fifteen months after the United States was bombed into the global conflict at Pearl Harbor, Jane Froman, broken badly in body and in spirit after the Pan American Clipper's plunge into the Tagus River, was in a Lisbon hospital and being rolled into an operating room. Her last conscious plea was for the Portuguese doctors not to amputate her nearly severed left leg. They didn't.

At the same time, John Burn, the Clipper copilot who had saved Froman's life by keeping her afloat in the Tagus until rescued, also was undergoing extensive surgery for his multiple injuries. While recuperating in the weeks ahead, Jane and John became good friends.

A month after the Clipper crash, Jane had a visitor, Stanton Griffis, a multimillionaire New York businessman who had heard her sing on Broadway and the NBC radio network. He was chairman of the board of Madison Square Garden (the site of countless major sports events), owner of Brentano's nationwide book chain, and a top executive of Paramount Pictures in Hollywood.

Griffis was purportedly touring Lisbon and other neutral capitals to explore the business situation. Actually, he was a spy for the Office of Strategic

Services (OSS), the U.S. cloak-and-dagger apparatus. Three months earlier, he had been in Scandinavia, where, despite the fact that he was under surveillance by the Gestapo, Griffis organized Allied spy networks in Finland and Sweden.

Now, in the Portuguese hospital, Stanton Griffis was shocked at Jane Froman's condition. She was feeble; her face was milk-white, and she had shrunk to about ninety pounds. As soon as he arrived back in the United States aboard a Clipper a few days later, he set wheels to turning in Washington to get the singer back to New York for sophisticated medical treatment.

Jane's mangled body precluded her flying on a Clipper. She would have to be in a ship where she could stretch out. The only oceangoing accommodation that could be located for her was a berth on a small Portuguese freighter, the *Serapa Pinto*. Chances were excellent that she would never arrive in New York. Either she would die in the Atlantic enroute, or the freighter would be torpedoed by one of the scores of German U-boats (submarines) lurking along the sea-lanes between Europe and New York.

The snail-like *Serapa Pinto* did have to dodge one torpedo, but it finally steamed into New York harbor late in April 1943, two months after the Tagus River episode. An ambulance carried Jane to Doctors Hospital.

A few days later, Jane's mother Anna visited the medical center. She struggled to conceal her horror over the daughter's appearance—emaciated, face drawn and pale.

Jane smiled and joked weakly, "Well, Mom, it's better than going on a diet!"

But it was no joke; Jane had lost forty-two pounds in eight weeks. Yet her determination was evident. "I'm going to keep both of my legs," she told her mother, "no matter how hard it may be!"

In the weeks ahead, the entertainer underwent a series of operations, including a bone graft on the mangled leg. She was never given assurances that the leg could be saved. "We'll do our best," the doctors had said.

Six months after the accident, Jane decided to go back to work, even though she was still a semi-invalid. Doctors felt that work would be good therapy, and enormous medical bills were piling up. Incredibly, neither the U.S. government nor Pan American Airways would pay a penny of her hospital expenses.

Lou Walters, a Broadway producer, signed Froman to a contract to appear in the musical *Artists and Models*. The show was planned and partly rehearsed in her room at Doctors Hospital.

Artists and Models opened at the Broadway Theater amidst the customary hoopla. For each performance, Froman was carried from the hospital to the theater, wearing a thirty-five-pound body cast. During each show, stagehands, behind a closed curtain, carried her on and off the stage twenty-two times.

In show business terminology, *Artist and Models* was a turkey. It closed after six weeks in the wake of scaldings by media critics. Froman came out of the disaster with her reputation intact, however. A critic praised her by describing the musical as *One Artist and Some Models*.

After more agonizing weeks and four more operations in the hospital, Jane accepted offers to perform in several of Manhattan's plush nightclubs. Not wanting to appear using crutches, she devised a mobile, electrically powered piano driven by her accompanist. As the apparatus moved slowly around the floor, she was able to stand and sing.

Just after the war in Europe concluded in early May 1945, Jane startled her mother by blurting out, "I'm going overseas again for the USO." Anna couldn't believe her ears. Her daughter was still on crutches with several more operations to go. Why, Anna asked, when there were so many able-bodied entertainers available?

"I'll sing in the military hospitals all over Europe," Jane replied. "It'll be better for the wounded soldiers than speeches on fortitude and patience. When they see a young woman has been able to make up for a crippled leg and other injuries, it will give them hope."

Jane flew overseas, traveled 30,000 miles, and gave ninety-five shows in three and a half months while on crutches. It was an enormous burden as she toured France, Germany, Luxembourg, Austria, and Czechoslovakia. Only when it was discovered that she had dislocated a bone in her spine did she agree to take the ocean liner *Queen Elizabeth* back to the United States.

In December, the Newspaperman's Annual Page-One Ball named Froman the Most Courageous Entertainer of 1945. Although a heavy snow blanketed New York City, she went to the gala from her hospital, sang one song with the orchestra leader and composer Duke Ellington, and received the award to a thunderous ovation.

Jane returned to the hospital in an ambulance. In the months ahead, she would endure nineteen more operations.[15]

A Platinum Smuggler's Demise

ONE DAY IN MARCH 1943, a Federal Bureau of Investigation undercover agent in Quito, Ecuador, sent a long communication to the agency's chief, J. Edgar Hoover, in Washington. It told about possible platinum smuggling by a man named Harold Ebury.

Probing by G-men in the United States disclosed that Ebury lived in luxury in his California home near the smooth greens of the Monterey Peninsula Country Club. It was found that, from his home, he was orchestrating a massive platinum smuggling apparatus in South America, an operation that was aiding Germany.

Two years earlier, President Roosevelt had directed Hoover to launch a covert action to wipe out a widespread German espionage operation in South

America after it had become clear that major cities on that continent were being used as staging grounds for slipping spies and saboteurs into the United States.

Information on American defense and industrial efforts was being funneled through South America by clandestine radio stations to German espionage posts in Cologne and Hamburg. It was while secret FBI monitoring stations in South America were eavesdropping on German spies that Harold Ebury's platinum smuggling was uncovered.

Only five nations in the world produce platinum in quantity. The German war juggernaut had a serious need for platinum, and the Nazis reached out to Colombia to obtain the precious commodity. Colombia was the only one of the platinum-producing nations not at war with the Third Reich in 1943.

By agreement with the Colombian government, the United States was supposed to receive all the country's platinum. Much of Colombia's platinum came from the big dredges of the Choco Pacifico Company and this haul was purchased by the United States. But the second major source was some 30,000 natives who panned the metal from streams and sold it to the highest bidder. Controlling the native production was the key to keeping platinum from Germany.

In Washington, meanwhile, G-men learned from British intelligence that Ebury, a Briton, was a suspected smuggler. So FBI agents in South America dug into Ebury's transactions and found that platinum was being smuggled from Colombia to Ecuador and then on to Argentina, an allegedly neutral nation whose leaders were sympathetic to Nazi Germany.

FBI sleuths followed a trail that led to a tailor's shop in Buenos Aires, and the firm's frightened owner disclosed that he had received a cablegram from Ebury in California, stating that he would arrive soon by way of Quito.

On July 17, 1943, FBI agents closed in on Ebury at his palatial home on the Monterey Peninsula. The suspect greeted the visitors warmly and invited them into his large living room. He talked at length about his world travels, and, yes, he was going to Quito soon—to establish an import-export business.

As the G-men continued to hammer him with questions, it seemed to be clear to Ebury that the FBI knew a great deal about his operations. Finally, he smiled and said evenly, "Yes, gentlemen, I smuggled platinum to Buenos Aires twice." But he denied that any of his platinum was being sent to German agents for shipment to the Third Reich and said that his action was not criminal in nature.

Despite his protests that he was but a simple businessman trying to make a few legitimate bucks, Ebury was indicted. In a California court, he again stressed his innocence, but he pleaded guilty to censorship violations, confessing that he had used codes in his letters to South American contacts.

Ebury was sentenced to eighteen months in prison. No doubt the FBI was happy. It could not prove that the platinum had reached Germany by way of Ebury's operations, but now the smuggler would be ensconced behind bars in a California prison and unable to carry out covert operations.[16]

"Get Going! Time Is Short!"

IN EARLY 1943, a captain in a U.S. infantry company fighting against the Germans in North Africa was asked by a war correspondent how he planned to take a barren elevation that was heavily defended. "I'm going to let the taxpayers take that hill!" he replied. Soon two battalions of artillery plastered the German force with shells, and the objective was captured by the GIs without the loss of a man.

That isolated incident reflected the goal of President Franklin Roosevelt to amass the most gargantuan panoply of war machines, equipment, and ammunition ever known to spare American life and limb as much as possible. Only a month after Pearl Harbor, he had challenged the nation to produce within two years 125,000 airplanes, 85,000 tanks, and 25 million deadweight tons of shipping.

In Berlin, Adolf Hitler scoffed at Roosevelt's goals. Propaganda for his home front, the führer sneered.

Despite the skepticism of Hitler—and many American industrial leaders—a near-miracle was unfolding on home-front America. A sleeping production giant was awakening. This massive surge was being energized by Donald Nelson, chairman of the War Production Board, who had been executive vice president of Sears, Roebuck and Company until asked to take his current post by Roosevelt soon after Uncle Sam went to war.

Management and employees alike found themselves absorbed in jobs about which they had known nothing only a few short months earlier. A company that produced canned fruit began to build parts for merchant ships. A grower of ferns learned to manufacture parachutes. A plant that had built machinery for processing cotton began making rifles. A large automobile dealer turned to creating airplane engine parts. Mosquito netting became the product of a bedspread factory. A manufacturer of pencils started producing bomb components. A soft-drink firm went into the business of loading shells with explosives.

Under the pressure of converting to wartime production, inevitable snarls surfaced. Just when a manufacturer thought he had mastered the myriad of problems involved in producing a particular war item, an Army, Navy, or Air Corps officer would burst into his plant and demand a change of design, necessitated by battle experience. Production plans tediously developed over many weeks had to be scrapped. New plans had to be created. All the time the officers were calling out: "Hurry! Hurry!"

Donald Nelson and his aides were saddled with the eternal manufacturing question: What to make first, when, where, and how much? Tens of thousands of separate parts had to be produced to go into tanks, planes, ships, guns, radar, and radios. These components were built in hundreds of plants. Each part had to be available in the right amount at the right time and at the right place. To be seriously wrong at any point could mean disaster on the battle-field, at sea, or in the air.

Early on Nelson met with one hundred and fifty of the nation's foremost industrial leaders. The production chief's appeal was simple: "*Get going! Time is short!*"

The tycoons complained about the inordinate length of time it took to get a signed contract from the government. So Nelson took a drastic step: on his own volition, he told them to charge ahead without waiting for written contracts and that he would see that they got paid adequately. Such were wartime expediencies.

The tycoons were delighted to comply. They promptly put their plants to work building vitally needed weapons and equipment—contract or no contract.

Along the way there were groans and moans—even screams—from industry as it tried to team up with government to drive war production ahead. An almost magical transformation of American industry evolved. Huge new plants dotted every section of the country. The traditionally agricultural South became heavily industrialized. A new, enormous synthetic rubber industry was created.

If ever there was a production genius, his name had to be Henry John Kaiser. He implemented assembly-line methods that competitors were convinced would not work and became history's greatest shipbuilder. Most amazing was the fact that Kaiser had no previous experience in that industry.

Kaiser, a Sprout Brook, New York, native, who had dropped out of school at thirteen years of age to go to work, used his past experience in building huge Hoover Dam, which supplied electric power to Los Angeles, to learn how to mass-produce large individual units.

With his enormous drive and know-how, Kaiser was able to reduce construction time of Liberty cargo ships from two hundred and eighty days in the previous war to twenty-two days. At one point he was launching one Liberty ship a day, and would eventually produce nearly fifteen hundred vessels, including an escort aircraft carrier each week.

Prior to the Japanese sneak attack, pioneer automobile manufacturer Henry Ford had been opposed to U.S. involvement in "any foreign wars." Nearing eighty years of age at the time America went to war, the man who had developed the mass production of Model T automobiles, sold at a price the average citizen could afford, promptly announced that he would build a plant that would turn out one bomber each hour.

Despite the awe with which most U.S. manufacturing leaders held the grammar school dropout, they laughed at his goal. Can't be done, was the chorus.

Henry Ford had his architects and designers develop a plan for the largest assembly line that history had known. It would be built at Willow Run, near Detroit, and Ford planned to use the same technique that he had created for building automobiles. However, the elderly man, who was not inhibited by a shortage of idiosyncrasies, rapidly ran into difficulties.

The Willow Run plant would be a mile long, but Ford, a staunch Republican, discovered that part of the building would be in a township controlled by Democrats. Consequently, he ordered a new design in which the entire facility would be in "Republican territory," even if it meant the assembly line would not run in a straight course, as was originally contemplated.

With the legend's son, Henry Ford II, being the driving force behind the mammoth project, the company overcame daunting obstacles and the automaker's eccentricities, and four-engine B-24 Liberator bombers began pouring off the assembly line at Willow Run.

Elsewhere, Chrysler Corporation went from producing automobiles to building and operating the nation's largest tank factory. Eventually 25,507 tanks would roll out of the Chrysler arsenal.

Packard's performance in turning out in record time the complicated Merlin aircraft engine was another powerful blow struck against German and Japanese warlords. General Motors also converted operations with remarkable speed and built thousands of Oerlikon antiaircraft guns.

Andrew Jackson Higgins Jr., like Henry Kaiser, was a self-taught production genius, who, it was said, drank a bottle of whiskey a day. Brimming with energy, Higgins built a tiny industry in the New Orleans region to one with a workforce of more than 30,000. In the Deep South and under wartime pressure, his team, as he called it, was integrated—blacks, whites, women, and men.

Higgins Industry's main product was small craft in which assault troops rode ashore in scores of invasions around the world. They were known as Higgins boats. After hitting a beach, the front would flop down, and the soldiers would dash out. Then the Navy enlisted man steering the boat would back it off the beach and return to the mother ship offshore for more soldiers and weapons.

Andy Higgins had a knack for inspiring his employees to even greater effort. In the rest rooms of his factories, he put photographs of Adolf Hitler, Benito Mussolini, and Emperor Hirohito sitting on toilets. A caption in large type above the pictures stated: "Come on in, brother. Take it easy. Every time you loaf here helps us plenty." Hanging over the Higgins assembly lines were huge banners: "The Worker Who Relaxes Is Helping the Axis."

So crucial were Higgins boats to the war effort that planning for each invasion hinged around the availability of a sufficient number of these small craft. When one Anglo-American invasion had to be postponed to allow time to assemble more landing craft, British Prime Minister Winston Churchill declared: "It seems like the destiny of two great nations revolves around something called a Higgins boat!"

Higgins was involved in producing a wide variety of the accoutrements of war, including larger craft known as LCTs (landing craft, tanks) and LCVPs (landing craft, vehicles/personnel). Also rolling out of Higgins's plants were PT (patrol torpedo) boats that would write a glorious chapter in U.S. naval lore,

C-116 airplanes, water purifiers, newfangled helicopters, smoke generators, explosives, and portable bridges.[17]

Women Flock to War Plants

As the war continued and the shortage of workers in defense industries grew acute, the War Production Board focused on techniques for augmenting the force of able-bodied white men. The federal agency sent out literature encouraging employers to hire "Negroes, the handicapped, women, China-men, and Spaniards (Hispanics)."

Factories on the home front began to develop a diversified workforce, including more than 3 million women, most of whom probably would not have taken jobs had there not been a war.

Rosie the Riveter was a composite created to inspire women to go to work in defense plants. Supposedly she was based on a genuine aircraft worker, Rosina Bonavits, who, with a coworker, attached some thirty-three hundred rivets on the wing of a Grumman Avenger airplane in only six hours. That feat received wide play in the media and became the subject of a wartime movie, *Rosie the Riveter.*

Although women flocked into factories, there was an equal number hesitant about taking a job. Consequently, an advertising campaign was launched to urge females to go to work when they had never had a job outside of the home. The thrust of the campaign was to convince women that it was patriotic and also proper to accept employment that previously might have been considered "socially undesirable."

Orchestrating the program to recruit women was the Bureau of Campaigns, a division of the Office of War Information. Ken Dyke, a former marketing chief at NBC radio and advertising director of Colgate-Palmolive, was head of the bureau.

Dyke and his staff coordinated government policy by means of a monthly *War Guide for Advertisers*, which told of objectives and promotional techniques, and provided drafts of ad layouts. So important was the recruitment of female workers that the Treasury Department issued a ruling that permitted defense contractors to deduct publicity costs from taxable income.

One magazine advertisement had a puzzled woman stating: "But I've never worked before! What kind of war job could I do?" Then the ad answered her question.

Another ad pictured a woman war worker and the headline: "My husband's in the Army. I'm in a shipyard. We're in the war together!" A "shock ad" demanded to know of females: "Will it take a bomb to break up your bridge game? Get out and drive a truck, load a freight car, or operate a fork-lift!"

A *former waitress worked as a sealer at Kaiser Shipyards, Richmond, California, to help build cargo vessels. (National Archives)*

Ads for Crosley refrigerators hailed the "resourcefulness and ingenuity of American women," and an ad for Eureka vacuum cleaners proclaimed, "You're a Good Soldier, Mrs. America!"

Bibb Manufacturing pictured men and women in lockstep "marching with determination toward victory," and Arvin Manufacturing declared that "women are working shoulder to shoulder with men." An Armco ad featured a pretty young female truck driver: "I got a job when Paul went across. I'm hauling the stuff they fight with!"

Many ads were designed to promote the theme that women were physically capable of performing strenuous tasks. A major utility firm's ad pictured a dainty female operating a huge machine. The text stated: "Five-feet-one from her 4A slippers to her spun-gold hair. She loves flower hats, smooth orchestras — and being kissed by a boy who's now [fighting in] North Africa. How can 110 pounds of beauty boss 147,000 pounds of steel? Through the modern magic of electric power."[18]

Recruiting the Blind and the Deaf

ALTHOUGH AMERICAN WOMEN of all ages were going to work in unprecedented numbers, there remained a critical need for even more employees. So the War Production Board reached an agreement with the government of Mexico in which 100,000 laborers came across the Rio Grande River and took jobs in defense plants. Thousands of American teenagers lied about their ages and went to work in armaments factories; supervisors turned a blind eye to the falsifications.

In their search for "draft-proof" workers, labor recruiters for aircraft plants in the Los Angeles region called at government old soldiers' homes and gave jobs to Spanish-American war veterans sorting nuts and bolts. An organized recruitment of the nation's physically handicapped resulted in blind people being given jobs packing film in darkrooms or sorting tiny parts.

Unhampered by the constant din around them, deaf people toiled as riveters or in similar noisy tasks. Epileptics, too, went to work; most of them held jobs for the first time. They labored in pairs so that, if one had a seizure, the other could help out.

The War Manpower Commission even gave the green light for defense plants to hire certain people with mental impairments. In one such case on Long Island, New York, a woman believed that she was Queen Elizabeth. As long as she was addressed as "Your Majesty" and spoken to in a manner befitting her lofty regal status, she performed in superior style at her machine.[19]

Offer to a Striptease Artist

GYPSY ROSE LEE, America's most popular striptease artist, was performing in a stage play of sorts, *Star and Garter*, in New York City. She was packing in the male customers for each performance, except on Sundays. New York officials frowned on women removing their clothes in public on the Sabbath.

One afternoon Gypsy Rose received a telephone call from an old friend, Barney Oldfield, who had worked for *Variety* (the show-biz newspaper) and was now an Army captain and public relations officer in the 82nd Airborne Division. He was calling from Fort Benning, Georgia. It was February 1943.

Oldfield, who had been a press agent for a young Hollywood actor named Ronald Reagan and a promising child actress named Elizabeth Taylor, explained to the burlesque queen that the post commander wanted to sell a large number of War Bonds to soldiers at an Easter Sunday breakfast. Would she be present as the star attraction?

A day earlier, Captain Oldfield had been sent to meet with representatives of the post commander to plan for the affair. Oldfield explained that persuading soldiers to come to a breakfast during which they would be asked to shell out money for War Bonds did not promise to be a rousing success.

Consequently, Oldfield told the planners that he would telephone Gypsy Rose Lee and ask her to fly to Benning after her late-night performance on a Saturday. "With Gypsy Rose present, I feel confident that our boys will suddenly take an eager interest in helping finance the war," he declared.

Before the artist appeared on stage, Oldfield continued, she would remove all of her clothes and be covered with War Bonds attached by transparent tape. The higher-priced bonds would be strategically placed on her anatomy. Then the members of the audience would be asked to bid on the bonds. As each was sold, the bond would be removed from Gypsy Rose's body, eventually leaving her wearing lipstick and earrings.

The officers present at the conference were enthusiastic. The contrivance was worthy of a nimble-minded Hollywood press agent. So Oldfield put in his call to New York City. Gypsy Rose was delighted to have the chance to join in the war effort, and she promptly accepted the invitation.

Word that the famous striptease queen would be present spread around Benning like wildfire. It seemed certain that the post gym would not be large enough to hold the crowd of GIs eager to help finance the war.

Planning progressed until about a week before the extravaganza when the post commander learned of the star attraction. "A striptease artist performing at an Easter morning breakfast!" he roared. The affair was cancelled immediately.

It was Captain Oldfield's lot to telephone Gypsy Rose and inform her that she would have to boost the war effort in some other manner. Oldfield told a friend: "Then I went out and crawled under the nearest flat rock!"[20]

The FBI Arrests "Good Old Ernie"

FROM SEA TO SHINING SEA on home-front America, earnest and dedicated volunteer civilian defense air-raid wardens of all ages and economic status dashed around enforcing blackouts, while spotters, armed with high-powered binoculars, stood on the roofs of buildings and scanned the friendly skies for hostile aircraft. Most of the volunteers were often on duty in pouring rains, subfreezing temperatures, and even in a hurricane that pounded the Atlantic coast.

On occasion, however, the eager-beaver air-raid wardens exasperated professionals. Recalled a New York City police captain: "They did some wonderful things, but it was just by the grace of God that none of them were hurt. Sometimes they were too enthusiastic. During one blackout, a switch got stuck at Coney Island, and the volunteer wardens tried to fix it themselves instead of calling for professional help right away. It was sure nice of them to try, but they didn't know what they were doing and almost blew up Coney Island."

Not one of the million and a half wardens ever saw an enemy airplane. But most citizens felt reassured to know that these conscientious civilians were standing guard.

One of the air-raid wardens was fifty-eight-year-old Ernest Lehmitz. "Good old Ernie" was regarded by his neighbors on Staten Island, a New York City borough, as a kindhearted gentleman and a superpatriot who dearly loved his country.

Ernie really took his volunteer task seriously and would bawl out people for not masking lights. And he tenderly nurtured the neighborhood's largest backyard victory garden in response to President Franklin Roosevelt's urgent appeal for citizens to raise their own vegetables.

One morning late in June 1943, the Staten Island neighborhood was shocked. Three agents of the Federal Bureau of Investigation arrived at 123 Oxford Place and led good old Ernie Lehmitz away in handcuffs. His friends refused to believe that this tall, lean, stoop-shouldered grandfather and super-patriot was a spy for Adolf Hitler.

Neighbors, of course, had been unaware that FBI agents had been on Lehmitz's tail for weeks. He bore no resemblance to the stereotype of a spy dashing about with a bomb in one hand and a stolen top-secret blueprint in the other. There was no glamour in his life, no beautiful women accomplices. He wore ill-fitting suits and old-fashioned rubbers on his feet, and for his dangerous work he received a paltry forty dollars monthly from the Abwehr, Nazi Germany's intelligence service.

After his apprehension, Lehmitz was taken to FBI headquarters in Foley Square. At first he was indignant over his arrest. But when the G-men confronted him with a mass of evidence that had been collected, Lehmitz broke down and signed a confession that he was a German spy.

Lehmitz was clearly devastated to learn that the FBI knew of his background in such depth. He had first come to the United States in 1908 as a clerk in the German consulate in New York City. During what came to be known as World War I, he had served as a spy for the German kaiser, but later became a naturalized citizen.

While visiting Germany in 1939, Lehmitz had been recruited by the Abwehr, and after training as a coast watcher in Hamburg he returned to the United States in 1941. His mission was to snoop out information on ship sailings and convoys in New York harbor. His role as a volunteer air-raid warden served as a perfect cover for his treachery.

To carry out his espionage mission, Lehmitz got a job as a handyman at a waterfront saloon frequented by merchant seamen. He sent his reports to a Hamburg branch of the Abwehr through a mail drop in Lisbon, Portugal; sleuths learned that Lehmitz had been signing his letters "Fred Lewis" or "Red Sloane."

In September 1943, Lehmitz, whose spying had no doubt resulted in the deaths of countless merchant seamen, was tried for wartime espionage in federal court in Brooklyn. He was sentenced to a term of thirty years in prison.[21]

America's Least-Known Boomtown

IN MID-1943, folks in eastern Tennessee knew that something big was taking place in and around what had been the sleepy little town of Oak Ridge. But as far as the rest of the United States was concerned, Oak Ridge didn't exist. Only a tiny group of federal officials and scientists were aware that Oak Ridge would become one of the most important communities that history has known.

Back in June 1942, at the urging of a group of America's foremost scientists, President Roosevelt secretly gave the green light to develop a revolutionary device of gargantuan destructive power that would be known as an atomic bomb. The colossal experiment was code-named Manhattan Project. (The Germans, too, were working to develop an atomic bomb.)

Soon a band of federal officials quietly descended upon the Oak Ridge region and purchased fifty-two thousand acres of land. On this site, a huge laboratory would be built in a crash program.

Oak Ridge had been selected for the atomic laboratories because of the abundance of water and electric power in that region. But mainly, its strategic location in hills and valleys, in a sparsely populated region, would help mask the true nature of the project. About a thousand families had to be moved to clear the area. They were told that a factory to build goods for the home front was going to be constructed.

Soon Oak Ridge became a boomtown as hundreds of engineers and construction workers moved in. Everything was supersecret. By 1943, Oak Ridge had about fifty thousand residents, becoming the fifth largest town in Tennessee.

The Manhattan Project had AAA priority—the highest. Brigadier General Leslie R. Groves, a forty-six-year-old West Pointer who had recently completed building the huge Pentagon outside Washington, took command of the operation. What followed was an only-in-America miracle. The nation was embarking on the most prodigious scientific-industrial-military enterprise ever conceived.

Groves' task boggled the mind. Without known tools, blueprints, or materials, he would try to transform an invisible compound of equations, theory, and scientific faith into a practical military weapon.

The hulking Groves, who had longed for a combat command in Europe after the Pentagon job, was purposely chosen for the Manhattan Project because he was hard-nosed and, in pursuit of a goal, was not picky about whose toes he stepped on. He "drafted" industrial magnates and PhDs like so many army privates, lectured them, or shouted at them on occasion. He upstaged Congress, trusted absolutely no one, and coaxed incredible sums of money from the U.S. Treasury without being able to disclose for what he was using the funds.

Groves was especially strict on security. He would scold famous scientists for any real or perceived violation of secrecy. Mail was censored, telephone calls monitored, scientists shadowed after they left the laboratory.

Because a large number of funerals in the boomtown of Oak Ridge might tip off lurking spies that something big was going on, there were no new mortuaries in the city. In the research laboratory area, the garbage and trash-collection companies hired only illiterates so that if they found classified material, they would not be able to read it.

As far as most of the outside world was concerned, wartime, bustling Oak Ridge would be a noncity. Security was so tight that no German or Japanese agent would ever know about the crucial installation.[22]

"Hello, America! Berlin Calling!"

HOME-FRONT AMERICA WAS SHOCKED on July 26, 1943, to hear stories on radio and read them in newspapers that six United States citizens were indicted *in absentia* by a grand jury in Washington, D.C., on charges of wartime treason, which called for the death penalty. The six Americans had been broadcasting German propaganda to America on shortwave radio.

Those charged by the U.S. Justice Department were Jane Anderson, Robert Best, Fred Kaltenbach, Constance Drexel, Douglas Chandler, and Edward Delaney. They had been living in the Third Reich or had arrived there shortly after war erupted in Europe in September 1939. They were accused of being commentators on the Die Deutschen Überseesender (German Overseas Stations), which was located in Berlin and had twenty-three powerful transmitters scattered around Germany.

Eight newscasts were beamed each day, at hourly intervals, to the United States, where hundreds of thousands of citizens had shortwave radio receivers. Paul Josef Goebbels, the diminutive, brainy, Nazi propaganda chief, had recruited the six Americans to replace the German commentators. Goebbels thought the propaganda would be more believable if spoken in "American English" by genuine Americans.

Most of the broadcasts began with an upbeat voice calling out: "Hello, America! Berlin calling!"

In charge of the North American zone of the German radio network was Kurt von Boeckmann, who held a law degree from Heidelberg and had served as a captain in the German Army during World War I. He began his radio career as an advisor for a Bavarian radio station and became its *Intendant* (chief executive) a few years later. In 1933, he was appointed to his current post.

Von Boeckmann was a mysterious figure. When Adolf Hitler sent his legions plunging into neighboring Poland to ignite what would become a global conflict, the broadcaster requested prompt retirement. Later reports would surface that he was a key figure in the Schwarze Kapelle (Black Orchestra), a secret movement headed by prominent German military, government, and civic officials, whose goal was to get rid of the führer. The request was denied.

Knowing that the Geheime Staatzpolizei (Gestapo) would be watching his every move and gesture, von Boeckmann went about his work with vigor. Perhaps the best of his American recruits was Frederick W. Kaltenbach, who was born in Dubuque, Iowa, the son of an immigrant German butcher.

In 1920 Kaltenbach received a BA degree from Iowa State Teacher's College, then took an MA at the University of Chicago before accepting a job as a school principal in his hometown of Dubuque. Soon after Adolf Hitler had seized total power in Germany in 1932, Kaltenbach visited the Third Reich and was greatly impressed with the promise of National Socialism (Nazism).

Only a few weeks after his return to Dubuque, the school board fired him for organizing a Hitler Youth kind of club on the high school campus. That event resulted in his going to Germany to obtain his doctorate. There he married a young German woman, and in 1939, he began making his first shortwave broadcasts to the United States, using the name Fred W. Kauffenbach.

The cultured Kaltenbach loaded his propaganda broadcasts with potshots at Allied leaders, referring to the American president as "Emperor Roosevelt I, who aspires to be the Lord of the Universe." Compared with Roosevelt, "Benedict Arnold was a mere piker. All he did was to betray a fort to the Red Coats [British]. Roosevelt has betrayed the whole country," Kaltenbach exclaimed.

Jane Anderson, who had been born in Atlanta, Georgia, came to Berlin in early 1941 with a journalistic background. During World War I, she had made a name for herself as a daring reporter covering the Western Front for the London *Daily Mail.*

In the early 1930s, Jane married a wealthy Spanish aristocrat, the Marquis Alvarez de Cienfuegos, an act that gave her the royal title of marquesa. With the outbreak of the Spanish Civil War in 1936, she again served as a correspondent for the *Daily Mail.* She was captured by Spanish government forces, charged with spying for the Nationalists of General Francisco Franco, and was held in a dirty Madrid prison for six weeks.

Anderson managed to slip a message to the U.S. embassy, which intervened and secured her release, with the provision that she promptly leave Spain.

Anderson hurried to Paris to be reunited with her husband, then she left for the United States to launch a lecture tour that focused against Communism. She described in detail the horrors of her jail time under the Communists. Americans adored her. She was proclaimed by the *Catholic Digest* as the "world's greatest orator against Godless Communism." *Time* quoted the noted Monsignor (later Bishop) Fulton Sheen as describing her as a "living martyr."

After her lecture tour in 1939, Anderson returned to Europe, where she was recruited by Josef Goebbels, who had noted in his diary that she had been a "big sensation in New York." In her first broadcast to the United States, she compared Adolf Hitler to Moses: "He has reached to the stars, and the Lord's will would prevail."

Not all listeners on home-front America were enthralled with Anderson's propaganda broadcasts. One New York City newspaper declared: "If her microphone hysteria is a clue to her personality, she is probably mentally unhinged."

Be that as it may, Anderson's broadcasts became even shriller after Adolf Hitler declared war on the United States in early December 1941. "So the American people have gone to war to save [Josef] Stalin and the Jewish international bankers," she exclaimed. She charged that Roosevelt was in constant contact with the "Red Antichrist" [Stalin], who "is beating children black and blue for their religion."

*William L. Shirer (standing), for many prewar months a reporter
stationed in Berlin, is listening to a propaganda broadcast from
Germany at a New York City studio. Fluent in German, Shirer
would go on the air minutes later to "debunk" the Nazi broadcast
for American listeners. (National Archives)*

In March 1942, Anderson was setting her American audience straight on
the reported German food shortage by describing her visit to a posh Berlin
restaurant: "On silver platters were sweets and cookies, a delicacy I am very
fond of. My friend ordered great goblets filled with champagne, into which he
put shots of cognac to make it more lively. Sweets, cookies, and champagne!
Not bad!"

British propaganda experts rubbed their hands in glee. Anderson's bac-
chanalian bombast was translated from "American English" into German and
radioed back to the Third Reich, where the *Herrenvolk* (people) were feeling
food pinches and most knew champagne as only a hazy memory.

The impact of the turnaround broadcast was considerable, Allied agents
in Germany reported. People were furious that some privileged persons, such
as Anderson and Nazi leaders, were gorging themselves while the plain people
were scrounging.

Jane Anderson disappeared from the airwaves.

William L. Shirer, a prominent American journalist who covered the
Berlin beat in the years before the United States got involved in the global conflict, described Edward Delaney, another of the broadcasters, as being a "very
mild fellow" but one consumed with a "diseased hatred for Jews."

Delaney was born in Olney, Illinois, to Irish immigrants; he spent most of his youth in Glenview, a suburb of Chicago, and launched a career on the stage, traveling the world with a road company.

After the stock market crash of 1929, Delaney was jobless. When he was invited to Berlin in August 1939, after his anti-Jewish views were noted by the German embassy in Washington, he was offered a job countering anti-Nazi propaganda overseas. He began broadcasting to the United States using the name E. D. Ward.

In one broadcast Delaney told Americans that there was a plan afoot to install the Duke of Windsor [the abdicated king of England] as first viceroy in Washington, "a sort of assistant to President Roosevelt—or would Roosevelt be subordinated to him?"

No doubt the most inept of the indicted six was Constance Drexel. William Shirer said of her: "The Nazis hired her principally because she was the only woman in [Berlin] willing to sell her American accent to them."

Born in Darmstadt, Germany, Drexel's parents brought her to Roslindale, Massachusetts, when she was an infant. After attending several schools in the United States, she eventually obtained her degree from the prestigious Sorbonne in Paris. Constance returned to America in 1920 and, for the next two decades, she worked for several newspapers.

In May 1939, Constance quit her job and left for Germany, telling friends she wanted to visit relatives. A year later, she began broadcasting to America on German radio, which introduced her as "the famous American journalist" and as a "Philadelphia socialite and heiress."

It was not long before Drexel fell from grace, and top Nazis began avoiding her. She had pulled a monumental *faux pas* while attending a reception for Party leaders. On being introduced to a beautiful young German woman, Constance blurted: "Oh, you are the girlfriend of Adolf Hitler!"

The crowd around the two women melted away. Everyone in the Nazi hierarchy knew that Eva Braun was the führer's long-time romantic interest.

The blue blood among the indicted six was Douglas A. Chandler, who was born in Chicago and made a stab at being a freelance newspaper columnist after World War I. A few years later, he hit it big, being married to a Pittsburgh heiress, Laura Jay Wurtz. She was the great granddaughter of John Jay, the first chief justice of the U.S. Supreme Court, and the daughter of a wealthy inventor, Alexander Jay Wurtz.

In the early 1930s, Chandler, mainly through his prestige connections, got a job as assistant city editor of the Baltimore *Sunday American*. In the months ahead, Chandler became convinced that a "Jewish conspiracy" was trying to take over the United States. So he and Laura moved to Europe, living like nomads (rich ones) in several countries before settling down in a small town in the Black Forest of Germany.

After roving Europe for several years as a stringer (freelance operator) for a popular American magazine, *National Geographic*, Chandler was in Berlin when he met an executive of the German radio propaganda broadcasting organization, who signed him on as a commentator for the North American zone.

In January 1942, a month after Hitler declared war on the United States, Chandler began making fifteen-minute broadcasts several times a week. He was the highest paid commentator in the North American zone stable. His shrill commentaries followed the customary Nazi clichés, his prime target being President Roosevelt and his administration.

In one broadcast, Chandler nominated Roosevelt for the "Meddle Medal," for implementing "Jewish plans for world domination." Another: "By all means, let Pearl Harbor be avenged, but not upon the Japanese, who have been forced into this struggle, but upon the real author of this war, the Jews."

Robert Best may have been the professional journalist of those indicted by the Washington grand jury. Born in Sumter, South Carolina, the son of a Methodist preacher, he graduated from the prestigious Columbia University School of Journalism in New York City. Soon he obtained a job with the Berlin Bureau of United Press, but only as a stringer.

During the years leading up to World War II, Best became more bitter as his colleagues were promoted and he remained a stringer. He decided that he had become a victim of "Jewish interests."

After Pearl Harbor, when American correspondents were being ejected from the Third Reich, Best wrote Berlin and asked to stay so he could play a role in the "construction of a new [Nazi] federation in Europe." He not only gained approval to remain, but he was hired as a radio commentator for the North American zone.

On April 10, 1942, Best went on the air as "Mr. Guess Who," and six weeks later, when he felt he had grabbed an audience in the United States, he disclosed his true identity. This new voice was the most shrill and emotionally fierce of any of the American propagandists, and he fired an ongoing babble denouncing "Jews and Jewed-up gentiles" in the United States.

Best also commented on current topics on the far-flung battlefields. When Allied forces invaded Normandy on June 6, 1944, he cautioned listeners in America that "now will begin a flow of death for the USA. . . ."

No doubt the American traitors broadcasting Nazi propaganda to the United States must have been convinced that Germany would win the war. They had to be aware that every word they spoke on the radio was being recorded by monitoring stations on the eastern seaboard of the United States and in England, and that, if Hitler lost, they would be held accountable for their actions.

After the war ended in Europe, a roundup of the American Nazi propagandists was launched:

Edward Delaney was brought to the United States in 1947 and told a jury that he was being prosecuted for speaking out against the Soviets. The jury agreed, and the indictment was dismissed.

Constance Drexel faced a U.S. federal court in 1948, and the judge dismissed the indictment on the grounds her remarks were only "cultural."

Fred Kaltenbach never was brought to trial. He had been captured by the Soviets and died suddenly—and mysteriously—in late 1945.

Douglas Chandler was found guilty of treason in 1948 and sentenced to life in prison. In 1963, President John F. Kennedy commuted the remainder of his sentence.

Jane Anderson was arrested in Austria in 1947. In view of her Spanish citizenship, the United States declined to prosecute her.

Robert Best, in a trial in Boston in 1947, was given a life term in prison.[23]

A Picture Stuns the Nation

ALL AROUND THE WORLD in 1943, momentous events were unfolding as the tide of war began to inexorably tilt toward the Allies. After the Italians suffered a major disaster in losing the Mediterranean island of Sicily, mild-mannered King Victor Emmanuel III summarily fired Benito Mussolini, who had been a virtual dictator for twenty-one years. On September 8, Italy surrendered and joined the Allies in the war against Germany.

Countless newspapers on home-front America trumpeted the identical theme: one down (Italy) and two to go (Germany and Japan).

At the same time, the mighty German army had suffered devastating defeats at Stalingrad and elsewhere to the Soviets. In the Pacific, General Douglas MacArthur's forces in the Southwest Pacific and Admiral Chester W. Nimitz's largely Marine Corps outfits in the Central Pacific were leapfrogging toward Tokyo.

In Washington, Elmer Davis, head of the Office of War Information (OWI), took note of accumulated evidence that the people of America were starting to believe that the war was about over and growing complacent and overconfident. Absenteeism in war plants had accelerated in recent weeks.

An OWI-sponsored poll gave warning to President Roosevelt that the public had gained the impression that "soldiers fight, that some of them get hurt but they ride away smiling in ambulances, and that none of them get badly wounded or spill any blood."

Since America's entry into the global conflict, it had been the policy of the Roosevelt administration to shield the home front from gruesome photographs taken in battle. Combat cameramen could and did take pictures they chose, but censors confiscated any that showed dead or severely wounded GIs.

This happens every **3 minutes**

STAY ON THE JOB AND *GET IT OVER*

Not until America had been in the war for two years would Washington permit the release of pictures of dead Americans. (Author's collection)

Thousands of these forbidden photos were locked up in a War Department vault known to insiders as the Chamber of Horrors.

Now Roosevelt gave the green light to the OWI to release harsher photographs for publication. The idea was to prepare home-front America for the huge GI casualties yet to come, provide a powerful antidote to rising war-plant absenteeism, and curb excessive grumbling by citizens over minor inconveniences.

Consequently, in September 1943, shockwaves struck home-front America when *Life* magazine published a picture of three GIs sprawled in death on a beach in New Guinea. These images had been carefully selected so as not to disclose any blood or mutilations.

An OWI analysis disclosed that the released photograph produced the desired effect, "bringing the realities of war closer to home." Absenteeism was greatly reduced, War Bond sales soared, and scrap drives took on a new vigor.[24]

A Tragedy in St. Louis

THOUSANDS OF EXCITED ONLOOKERS packed sun-drenched Lambert Field, the busy airport in St. Louis, Missouri, to watch a demonstration of a CG-4A glider,

Glider loaded with political and civic leaders plunges earthward before thousands of onlookers at Lambert Field. (St. Louis Globe-Democrat)

the sixty-fifth one built by the local Robertson Aircraft Company. It was August 1, 1943.

Also present was an array of dignitaries who had been invited to take a ride as a means of expressing St. Louis's support for the four regional firms building gliders.

Called by admirers the "most ugly beast that ever flew," the CG-4A would be the workhorse of glider forces during the conflict. It was 48 feet long and had a wing span of 83.6 feet. So unique was its design that it could carry a payload of 4,060 pounds—620 more pounds than the glider's empty weight.

Among eight guest passengers waiting to board the glider was St. Louis Mayor William Dee Becker, who, typically, was chomping on a cigar. He had arranged for a large banner that read "Buy War Bonds" to be attached to the tail of the craft. Now Becker was furious. The car that was to have brought the banner was nowhere to be seen (it had gotten stuck in heavy traffic).

Louise Becker, the mayor's vivacious wife, was also angry. Unbeknownst to her husband, she had received an invitation from the president of Robertson Aircraft a few days earlier, inviting her to go along on the flight. Arriving at Lambert Field, she was politely informed by an Air Corps officer that the regulations forbid civilian women from flying in military aircraft.

Among the others following Mayor Becker into the glider were Henry L. Muller, presiding judge of the St. Louis County Court (the governing body of the jurisdiction); Thomas N. Dysart, president of the St. Louis Chamber of Commerce; and William B. Robertson, head of Robertson Aircraft.

As the pilot and copilot prepared to begin the flight, Becker glanced outside to see wife Louise. He shrugged, meaning there was nothing he could do about leaving her on the ground.

There was a roar of engines as a C-47 transport plane ran down the runway with the glider in tow and lifted off. At three thousand feet, the C-47 circled back over the airport, where onlookers were squinting into the bright sunlight. Then the pilot of the plane hit the release lever, the cable between the two aircraft fell away routinely, and the glider soared gracefully for a short distance.

Suddenly, a sharp noise—many on the ground thought it was a clap of thunder. Then the right wing ripped away and shot upward. The glider began to plunge downward. A voice among the multitude shouted: "My God, they'll all be killed!"

Seconds later with a mighty thud the CG-4A smashed into the ground. Everyone on board died instantly. A hush fell over the stupefied spectators.

News of the disaster left St. Louis in shock. Almost to a person, the citizens were convinced that the crash had been the dirty work of German and Japanese agents. But FBI investigators ruled that the disaster had been caused by a wing lift strut-to-fuselage fitting. That piece had been manufactured by the Gardner Metal Products Company of St. Louis, a subcontractor for Robertson. Ironically, in peacetime, Gardner built coffins.[25]

"Legal Kidnapping" by Soviet Thugs

AT DAWN ON SEPTEMBER 5, 1943, two policemen were walking their beat along the San Francisco docks when they spotted five men beating a struggling captive, who was then hauled aboard the Russian freighter *Leonid Krasin*. Because the Soviet Union was an ally of the United States, the policemen could only watch helplessly.

Soviet diplomats had total freedom of movement throughout the nation, a privilege not granted American diplomats in the Soviet Union. Although the Federal Bureau of Investigation knew that Soviet diplomats were linked to espionage operations in the United States, little could be done to thwart what had often been an arrogant disregard for the nation's laws.

A report on the San Francisco kidnapping was given to the FBI, which already had much information on the participants. The victim was Alexander S. Egorov, a young Russian seaman, who had jumped ship a year earlier and hid out on a chicken farm in Oregon. At that time, the Soviet consulate in San Francisco reported the episode, and the U.S. Immigration Service tracked Egorov down.

The escapee told immigration agents that he had jumped ship because the Soviet police had murdered his father and thrown his mother into a concentration camp. Immigration authorities allowed Egorov to leave San Francisco aboard a Norwegian ship, but when the vessel docked in Oregon, he fled again.

Soviet secret agents got on Egorov's trail. For some reason, the fugitive returned to the San Francisco docks, where he was strong-armed onto the *Leonid Krasin.*

FBI chief J. Edgar Hoover ordered an investigation of the kidnapping, but the State Department, apparently fearful of ruffling Soviet feathers, declared that the FBI did not have jurisdiction in the case. Two days after Egorov was shanghaied in violation of U.S. law, the FBI withdrew and an official of the Immigration Service boarded the freighter in San Francisco. Egorov was brought to a wardroom to be interviewed by the U.S. official. Wearing trousers and an undershirt, the youth's injuries from the beating were quite visible. He was clearly frightened and in great fear for his life. He said that he did not want to leave the United States, and begged the Immigration official to take him from the ship.

During the tense confrontation, the distraught youth pointed to one of the men who had beaten him severely and dragged him aboard the *Leonid Krasin.* He was Yakov Lomakin, the consul general at the Soviet consulate in San Francisco.

Lomakin broke into the conversation to claim that he, personally, already had signed the captive aboard as a crew member, and that the U.S. government had no business involving itself with the personnel of Soviet freighters.

When the immigration official departed, Egorov burst out in sobs knowing that he would be sailing to certain death. Early the next day, the *Leonid Krasin* set a course for the Soviet Union.[26]

Spy Nabbed a Second Time

GUENTHER GUSTAVE MARIA RUMRICH was only thirty-one years of age in 1943, but he was regarded by the Federal Bureau of Investigation as one of the slickest spies operating in the United States in recent times. A year before Pearl Harbor, Rumrich had been tried on espionage charges after having been captured by the FBI and was given a tap on the wrist—two years in prison.

Rumrich, a slim, soft-spoken man, had been released from prison in 1941 after serving a few months—and he immediately resumed his espionage career, which was paying him handsomely in funds from Adolf Hitler's Third Reich.

Rumrich was born in Chicago, Illinois, where his father, Alphonse, was secretary of the Austria-Hungarian consulate. When Guenther was two years old his father was transferred to a post in Bremen, Germany, where the boy grew up in war-torn Europe.

At the age of eighteen, Guenther could not find a job. Then he learned that due to his birth in Chicago, he was an American citizen, so he decided to seek his fortune in the United States.

Guenther Rumrich was the slickest and most productive Nazi spy, and the only one convicted twice. (FBI)

Arriving in New York City with a few dollars in his pocket and only several words of English in his vocabulary, he obtained a job as an office boy, but soon proved to be a misfit and was fired. Desperate, he joined the U.S. Army, but in six months he got his fill of military life and deserted.

A curious mixture of shiftlessness, arrogance, and brains, Rumrich was apprehended, court-martialed, and sentenced to six months. In two months he was released and rejoined the Army.

For the next three years he apparently had carried out his duties satisfactorily and was even promoted to sergeant. However, he was detected stealing money from a post hospital, and he deserted again and settled in New York City. There he took a job washing dishes at the Spic and Span restaurant, at 42nd Street and Eighth Avenue, for two dollars per week.

Soon the apparent misfit found his true niche. He wrote a letter to a high-ranking intelligence officer in Germany offering his services as a spy, and months later he was accepted and given the code name Crown.

Rumrich began holding meetings at the Café Hindenburg in the Yorkville section of Manhattan with Nazi agents who crossed the Atlantic masquerading as employees of ocean liners. From these operatives Rumrich received his "shopping lists" from his German controllers in Hamburg.

Rumrich plunged into his job with vigor and ingenuity. Posing as a U.S. Army officer, he telephoned an Army hospital and obtained statistics on the prevalence of venereal disease, which he used as the basis for an accurate estimate on the strength of the military units served by the hospital.

On another occasion Rumrich wrote a letter to a high-ranking Army officer in an effort to get the officer to bring to a New York City hotel complete mobilization and coastal defense plans. Rumrich and an associate plotted to assault the colonel and take the plans from him, but the scheme fell through when the targeted officer became suspicious.

Rumrich's downfall came when he attempted to obtain thirty-five blank American passports at the New York City branch of the State Department's Passport Division, located in the Sub-Treasury Building, at Wall and Pine Streets. In applying for the documents, the spy gave his name as Edwin Weston, and said he was the undersecretary of state. Suspicious, the passport official discovered that there was no one by that name in the State Department. Rumrich was arrested.

Although Rumrich's innovative espionage plots went awry on occasion, he had succeeded in stealing a large number of U.S. military secrets. His *modus operandi* was to stroll around army posts and naval bases (America was still at peace) and engage in friendly conversations with officers, during which the Nazi agent was provided much secret information.

Since being freed from prison in 1941, Rumrich resumed his espionage career. He got a job at the Kaiser Shipyards in Richmond, California, where vessels were being built on almost a conveyor-type basis.

Using the alias Joseph De Bors, Rumrich next obtained a job on a ship that made regular runs between San Diego and Alaska, stopping at major ports on the West Coast. Presumably, he had been slipping his observations on these key locales in the war effort to his controllers in Germany. By now, America was fighting Germany.

Rumrich finally tripped himself up when he applied for a Coast Guard pass at Richmond, California, and the FBI was called in. Although he had been conducting widespread espionage for nearly three years after his release from prison, only one government charge could be pinned on him: fraud for using an alias to try to obtain a Coast Guard pass.

After a brief trial in Oakland, California, Rumrich was sentenced to two years in prison.[27]

Scoundrels in the War Effort

WHILE YOUNG AMERICAN MEN were fighting and dying on far-flung battle-fields, in the air, and on the sea, there were weasels entrenched in home-front America. Among those in that category was Amerigo Antonelli and his henchmen, who knowingly manufactured and shipped defective grenades to squeeze out more profit from war contracts. When some GI died in battle because of a faulty grenade, it may well have been one produced by Antonelli.

His firm was called the Antonelli Fireworks Company and was based in Spencerport, New York. For the five years prior to Pearl Harbor, the owner's reported income was some $2,000 per year. After receiving contracts to build grenades and incendiary bombs, Antonelli's salary skyrocketed to $26,000 annually (equivalent to some $300,000 in 2002) plus profits.

Government inspectors had trouble with Antonelli and his foremen from the beginning. When defective grenades were detected by employees, they were supposed to be put into boxes so as not to become mixed with the good ones. But these faulty grenades ended up in the boxes already approved by the inspectors.

Finally, the FBI was brought into the plant. Agents interviewed scores of employees, and many of them swore they had been given orders by Antonelli or his foremen to put only three charges of powder into grenades instead of the necessary four charges.

One young woman told a G-man that she had been instructed: "The hell with what the grenades are like, get out more grenades!" Another employee told of spilled powder being swept up from the floor and then poured into the grenades, dirt and all.

Amerigo Antonelli and several of his foremen were arrested, tried, and convicted of defrauding the government. Although their perfidy had no doubt resulted in the deaths of an unknown number of fighting men, they were let off with taps on the wrist. Antonelli was sentenced to two years in prison and fined $5,000, and the Antonelli Fireworks Company was fined $10,000. Before the war would end, Antonelli would be free to enjoy the remainder of the money his fraud had brought to him.

In the same putrid category as the Antonelli crowd were the officials of the Collyer Insulated Wire Company in Rhode Island. They had cooked up a scheme to foist defective electrical wire on the armed forces, wire that would be used on ships and by the ground forces.

During a routine inspection at the Collyer plant, FBI agents became suspicious when they noticed clues indicating that switches had been removed and the wiring changed on panels on which voltmeters were installed. There also were signs that switches had been removed from an electrical circuit on which galvanometers (instruments used in testing the wire and cable) were operated.

The G-men rapidly found the reason for these unusual changes—a rapid effort to conceal fraud. Some company officials had been using electrical sleight-of-hand to fool the inspectors. By changing the wiring and using an extra switch, the culprits could send 500 volts through a cable and make the voltmeter read 2,000 volts. Therefore, the inspector would approve the cable as being capable of withstanding a 2,000-volt charge. Similar sleight-of-hand techniques were utilized to alter the galvanometer readings.

The FBI agents found that the Collyer representatives were testing the same sample of good wire several times as a method for getting tags of approval for defective reels of wire. The bad reels would be hidden and later the approval tags would be switched to the wire that had been unable to pass examination by inspectors.

In the face of a mountain of evidence collected by the FBI, five officials and employees of Collyer Insulated Wire Company pleaded guilty to charges of fraud against the government. Actually, these miscreants had perpetrated fraud against America's fighting men. If a battalion commander suddenly lost contact with his units during a crucial fight on the battlefield, thereby putting the entire outfit in jeopardy, it could be that the defective wire came from Collyer Insulated Wire Company.

Amazingly, none of the guilty men was sent to prison. All escaped with fines of only $2,500 to $5,000.[28]

"Bomb Japan Out of Existence"

IN EARLY OCTOBER 1943, the *Washington Times Herald* loosed a blockbuster that rocked home-front America. Plastered across its front page was an accurate story of Japanese army atrocities in the Pacific. For various reasons, the government had been keeping a muzzle on this horrible component of the bloody conflict against Japan. But keeping a secret in Washington is akin to trying to hide a rising sun from a rooster.

The *Time Herald* story was sketchy. Clearly, someone in position to have access to the report, written by Air Corps Lieutenant William "Ed" Dyess, had leaked bits and pieces to a reporter. Dyess had been confined to a Japanese prison camp in the Philippines, escaped to Australia, flew to Washington, and dictated his story of Japanese atrocities perpetrated in what came to be known as the Bataan Death March.

After his return, Dyess was promoted several grades to lieutenant colonel, then put in a deep freeze to keep him away from media types. A decision had been made at the highest level—presumably by President Roosevelt—to hide Dyess's account.

In weeks ahead, heavy pressure was mounted for the Roosevelt administration to release full details of the report. In Texas, the officer's father was seething with anger, making scathing remarks about "pencil-pushing generals in Washington who would faint if they smelled gunpowder."

On January 28, 1944, newspapers across the land published banner head-lines and stories giving complete details of the Dyess document. More than five thousand Americans had died of starvation and torture at the hands of the Japanese after having been captured on Bataan and Corregidor in early 1942.

Home-front America was stupefied by the news. On the Senate floor in Washington, Missouri Senator Bennett Champ Clark thundered a demand to "bomb Japan out of existence." Georgia Senator Richard B. Russell loudly called for hanging Emperor Hirohito as a major war criminal. Many other members of Congress expressed similar sentiments.

From Portland, Oregon, to Portland, Maine, the battle cry "Remember Pearl Harbor" was no longer merely a slogan. Now Americans were demanding that Japan be wiped off the map.[29]

War Hero Bounced from Air Corps

FOR MORE THAN A YEAR, Air Corps Staff Sergeant Clifford Wherley had been risking his life almost daily as a turret gunner in a Marauder bomber. After flying twenty-one combat missions in North Africa, Sicily, and Italy, he had earned the Air Medal with three oak-leaf clusters.

Suddenly, he was ordered to return to the United States immediately. Over his vigorous protests, he was given an honorable discharge and sent home. It had been discovered that the sergeant was still barely sixteen years of age.[30]

An Overseer of GI Morals

TOWARD THE CLOSE OF 1943, millions of American servicemen were stationed around the world. Because the real item was usually unavailable, the GIs substituted pictures of statuesque beauties clipped from newspapers and magazines. They plastered barracks, Quonset huts, even the insides of helmets with these pictures. Without doubt, the two most popular ones were Hollywood movie sirens Rita Hayworth in a flimsy nightgown and Betty Grable in a swimsuit.

Almost as popular with the homesick GIs were the sultry paintings of curvaceous young women dressed in diaphanous costumes that appeared each month in *Esquire* magazine. None of these paintings revealed any more than could have been seen at any American swimming pool. But in early 1944, Postmaster Frank C. Walker decided that these images of sexy ladies tended to corrupt the morals of America's clean-cut young servicemen.

Walker appointed himself as a sort of Overseer of GI Morals and banned *Esquire* from the mail. Thus he firmly established himself among servicemen as the most despised human, ranking slightly behind Adolf Hitler.

One sailor expressed the indignation of the uniformed masses when he wrote to his senator: "Who in the hell got the bright idea of banning pictures. I, for one, have more than fifteen of them, and none of them seem to demoralize me in the least. What will these ignorant specimens back in the States think up next? I wish these high-browed monkeys could spend a year overseas without a magazine to look at."

In Washington, top-level officials quietly quelled the global protest by rescinding the *Esquire* ban, thereby abolishing the implied post of Overseer of GI Morals that Postmaster Walker had assumed.[31]

A WAVE tends to a top-secret marvel that decoded intercepted coded German messages in Europe. This scene was at the Nebraska Avenue station in Washington, D.C. (National Security Agency)

Top-Secret Projects Opened to Women

ALTHOUGH WACS and Army and Navy nurses were on active duty in many parts of the world as 1943 drew to a close, the law prohibited WAVES, SPARS, and Women Marines from duty stints outside the United States. Yet these thousands of females were making significant contributions to the war effort on the home front.

At Cherry Point, North Carolina, 80 percent of the control-tower operations at the Marine Air Station were handled by women marines. WAVES serving in naval aviation taught instrument flying, aircraft gunnery, and celestial navigation.

WAVE officers and SPAR officers, nearly all of them university graduates, were involved in finance, chemical warfare, and aerological engineering. At Norfolk, they helped install sophisticated radar on aircraft carriers and other warships.

For the first time, top-secret projects were opened to military women. Both the Navy and the Coast Guard utilized females in Long-Range Aid to Navigation (LORAN) stations, and WAVES were involved in a night-fighter training course. At a hidden communications center in Washington, D.C., WAVE officers spent countless hours staring at electronic screens, watching for "blips." It was boring, seemingly senseless work; the women had never been told the reasons for their job. When they were finally informed that each blip represented a U.S. ship being sunk, the task took on meaning and morale soared.

WAVE Lieutenant Mary Osborne was assigned to a supersecret Naval Intelligence facility in Washington. Her job had its roots back to mid-1939, just before England went to war with Nazi Germany. British scientists had cracked the Enigma code, which was used by the German armed forces and diplomats to send wireless messages. Adolf Hitler and other leaders were convinced that the code was unbreakable.

Throughout the war, the British intercepted the German messages and gave the code name Ultra to all intelligence gathered from Enigma. British Prime Minister Winston Churchill had agreed to share the Ultra information with the United States, so Mary Osborne and her WAVE colleagues were receiving this information by wireless from England for transmittal to government and military leaders in Washington.[32]

Roosevelt: Chloroform Drew Pearson

ON HIS WEEKLY BROADCAST from New York City, muckraking columnist Drew Pearson ignited an uproar on home-front America. He gave a garbled and highly exaggerated account of how Lieutenant General George S. Patton Jr., a hero in the United States after his brilliant victories in North Africa, had slapped an enlisted man, a court-martial offense. It was November 12, 1943.

Back on August 10, Patton had visited the 93rd Evacuation Hospital in Sicily and became enraged to find a nonbattle casualty. "It's my nerves, sir," the weeping GI muttered. "I can't stand any more shelling."

Patton, widely known for his short fuse, exploded, calling the soldier a "yellow bastard" and slapping him with a glove. "There's no such thing as battle fatigue," Patton screamed. "Only goddamned cowards!"

Reportedly a nurse in the 93rd Evac told her boyfriend, a captain in public affairs, about the episode and he passed it along to correspondents assigned to Patton's Seventh Army.

Collectively, the reporters in the Mediterranean agreed to sit on the explosive story for the time being. But they sent Demaree Bess of the *Saturday Evening Post*, Merrill Mueller of NBC radio, and Quentin Reynolds of *Collier's* to call on General Dwight Eisenhower.

Eisenhower told the three journalists that he had severely reprimanded Patton, had relieved him of command of the Seventh Army, and suggested that he apologize to the troops for his unacceptable behavior. His only goal, Eisenhower explained, was to retain Patton, his boldest combat leader, for the battles that lay ahead in Europe.

Based on Eisenhower's actions, all correspondents decided to keep mum, and the episode remained unknown on home-front America until Drew Pearson's broadcast.

Taking their cue from Pearson, newspapers around the United States erupted in a barrage of blaring headlines. The *New York Sun* ran a three-column, page-one picture of a scowling Patton under the headline: STRUCK SOLDIER. Vicious editorials were rampant.

In Congress, members fell over one another in their eagerness to take the floor and denounce Patton. A few demanded that he be stripped of his rank and thrown out of the Army.

While the Patton controversy was swirling, President Roosevelt declined public comment. But he made it known to confidants how he felt about Drew Pearson: "I'm all for chloroforming him!"[33]

An Ace German Operative

IN LATE JANUARY 1944, a German spy operating a shortwave radio station outside New York City flashed a message to his controllers in Hamburg, Germany. From an "unimpeachable source," the covert agent stated, he had learned that the Americans were planning to launch an invasion of the Kurils, a chain of Japanese governed islands stretching from Hokkaido, Japan, northeast for a few hundred miles.

As the German spy knew would be the case, Hamburg relayed the information to intelligence officers in Tokyo. Actually, the message was a hoax. The German was working for the Federal Bureau of Investigation, which had given him the code name of ND98.

An element of a large American armada that was forming for an invasion would make a feint at the Kurils, but the true target was Kwajalein, a strongly defended atoll in the Marshall Islands in the central Pacific Ocean.

Back in mid-1941, ND98, who had been operating an import-export firm in Germany, was summoned to the Abwehr office in Hamburg. A stern Nazi official told him that he was going to go undercover for the Third Reich in South America, where a widespread German espionage network was entrenched. He was told to set up a radio transmitter and was handed the code names of three people who would send him information concerning war production from the United States.

Two weeks later, ND98 arrived in Montevideo, Uruguay. When he was certain that Nazi agents weren't tailing him, he arranged to meet with a U.S. State Department official and offered his services.

Several days later, the German advised his bosses in Hamburg: "Unable to establish radio station. Am going to United States where I will be able to operate more freely. Will contact you."

Flying into New York City, ND98 was met by two FBI agents and escorted to a nearby hideout where he made radio contact with Hamburg on February 20, 1942.

Soon ND98 started feeding high-grade intelligence to Germany—information painstakingly prepared by FBI operatives and screened or furnished by the Joint Security Council that operated under the direction of the Joint Chiefs of Staff in Washington.

More than a year later, in August 1943, officials at the Hamburg post complained that while ND98's intelligence had been good, it was quite expensive. Presumably Hamburg had been getting heat from Berlin to trim its budget. By now the Nazis had paid him some $34,000 (equivalent to about $400,000 in 2002), which was handed over to the Alien Property Custodian.

ND98's FBI handlers decided to be outraged. So he sent a message: "Sorry you regard information as too expensive. If not satisfactory, will be glad to withdraw."

As the FBI had anticipated, Hamburg immediately assured their ace operative that not only was his production highly satisfactory, but he would soon receive a $20,000 bonus.

ND98 acknowledged receipt of the hefty bonus with the message about the phony Kurils invasion.

Later the Joint Chiefs of Staff told FBI Director J. Edgar Hoover that the fake intelligence received in Tokyo from Hamburg had contributed to the success of the invasion of the Marshall Islands in February 1944.[34]

Part Five

On the Road to Victory

Hoodwinking Hitler from New York

DURING THE EARLY MONTHS OF 1944, thousands of families on home-front America were gripped with anxiety on knowing that loved ones were in England or bound for that destination. Except for an elderly monk who had been living alone for fifty years in a cave high in the mountains of Tibet, the entire world knew that the Allies were mustering a powerful force in the British Isles to cross the English Channel and strike against Nazi-occupied Europe.

Allied Supreme Commander Dwight Eisenhower wrote from London to a general in the Pentagon: "This will not be just another battle. All our chips will be on the table!"

British Major General Frederick Morgan, the architect of the original operation against Normandy, told Allied commanders: "If the Germans obtain as much as forty-eight hours warning of [our plan], the chances of success are small. And longer warning spells certain disaster."

In London, the cleverest brains in the Allied camp were orchestrating a master deception scheme code-named Fortitude South. It was designed to keep Adolf Hitler and his generals in the dark about the time and locale of *der Grossinvasion.*

Cornerstone of the plan was a fictitious U.S. Army group, supposedly commanded by General George Patton, who had been brought to England from the Mediterranean in recent weeks. In Berlin, the Oberkommando der Wehrmacht (High Command) regarded Patton as the Allies' boldest battle leader, so he seemed to be the obvious choice to command the cross-Channel assault.

Patton's fake force of one million men would assemble in southeastern England, only twenty miles across the Channel from the region in France known as the Pas de Calais. The deception goal was to coerce German intelligence into concluding that the Allies would strike there. Actually, the true landing beaches would be two hundred miles to the southwest in Normandy.

Fortitude South became an elaborate deception on a massive scale. Movie-set designers from Shepperton Studios were called in, and they supplied the fictitious Patton army group with landing craft, tanks, artillery, trucks, and artillery pieces—all of inflatable rubber.

Meanwhile, the air over southeastern England crackled with a flood of bogus radio messages that were passed back and forth between nonexistent command posts and headquarters. All of this heavy radio traffic (generated by a signals battalion) was closely monitored by the Germans along the Pas de Calais.

In the United States, FBI chief J. Edgar Hoover and his agents were playing a key role in Fortitude South. It evolved after G-men had taken into custody a Dutch native, Walter Koehler. He claimed that German intelligence officers had sent him to America to gather information on Allied plans for the looming invasion. However, the spy said he had had a change of heart and now was eager to be an agent for the United States.

Koehler turned over to the FBI agents the secret code given to him before he left Germany and the radio over which he was to send messages to Hamburg. Hoover assigned Koehler the code name Albert van Loop.

Making certain that the fifty-two-year-old Dutchman did not betray the FBI, he was kept under guard in a fleabag hotel in Manhattan. At the same time, a pair of G-men who spoke the German language were working from a small, secluded house on Long Island, not far from Manhattan, and established radio contact with Hamburg, using van Loop's secret ciphers.

A selected group of FBI men created ongoing scripts for van Loop's reports to Hamburg (there would be a hundred and twenty-two of them). The messages were a careful blend of truths on insignificant matters, half-truths, and outright lies.

One day van Loop (that is, the FBI imposters) informed his German controllers that he had obtained a job as a night desk clerk in a Manhattan hotel, which had been taken over by the U.S. Army to lodge officers bound for England. Curiously, Hamburg never asked the identity of the hotel, which existed only in the fertile minds of the FBI agents stage-managing the fraud against Adolf Hitler.

In the weeks ahead, van Loop radioed Hamburg with troop convoy sailings (all of them phony). From the nonexistent Army officers staying briefly in the hotel, he passed along the designations of the phantom units that were going to join General Patton's dummy Army Group in southeast England.[1]

A Spy in Allied Headquarters?

LATE IN MAY 1944 employees at a Chicago post office accidentally opened a badly wrapped package and discovered a collection of official-looking documents of a kind that they had never seen. Most puzzling was that the word "Bigot" was stamped in large red letters on each piece.

A postal official rushed the package and its documents to Sixth Army headquarters in Chicago, where a general and three colonels inspected them. They, too, were mystified by the Bigot designation. Only much later would they learn that security officers in England used Bigot to signify that a person or an office had been cleared to be told the projected date and locale of the Normandy invasion.

Despite their confusion over the word Bigot, the Sixth Army officers knew that the documents disclosed the landing beaches, the strength of the various assault units, and the approximate date of Overlord, code name for the invasion.

Army intelligence agents and the FBI promptly launched a probe of what appeared to be a frightening security breach. It seemed as though the Germans had a spy right in the London building in which planning for the invasion was being conducted. Tension increased when the FBI and the Army agents found that the address, on Division Street, was in a neighborhood that was home to hundreds of German immigrants. The female addressee was questioned, and she identified the handwriting on the package as that of her brother, an Army sergeant assigned to General Eisenhower's headquarters. The sergeant and his sister were of German ancestry—but so were eleven million other loyal Americans.

In London, meantime, the sergeant was grilled intensely. Time after time he gave the same answer. He had been working constant fourteen-hour days and was near exhaustion and worried about his sister, who was ill, in Chicago. The Bigot documents were supposed to have been sent to the Division of Transportation in Washington, so he must have written his sister's Division Street address without realizing he was making a mistake. His tired mind had confused the two Division addresses.

An investigation of the sergeant's background disclosed only that he had been a loyal American and a dedicated soldier. But there were eight post office employees and at least four officers at Sixth Army headquarters who knew the D Day secrets. The FBI sternly warned each of them that any loose talk could result in tragic consequences for their country. Then a tail was put on each postal employee until after D Day.

A court-martial was recommended for the sergeant, but no action was taken. However, he was kept under constant surveillance, his telephone was tapped (as was his sister's in the United States), and he was not allowed to leave his quarters until after the invasion.

The weird episode was not over, for there were security officers in Washington who were convinced that the leakage had not been accidental, that it was in some manner connected with the *Chicago Tribune*, a large-circulation newspaper based in the same city in which the sergeant's sister lived.

Owned and published by Robert H. McCormick, a bitter foe of President Roosevelt and his New Deal domestic program, the *Tribune* had been held with deep suspicion by the Pentagon (and millions of Americans with loved ones in the Pacific) six months earlier when it had printed top-secret information that the Allies had broken the Japanese code. Cracking the code meant that the American commanders were able to learn in advance about Japanese plans and intentions, thereby saving thousands of lives and vastly increasing chances for U.S. victories.

Official suspicion against the *Tribune* would surface again when it was discovered that, with D Day for Normandy drawing close and correspondents in England barred from leaving the country for security reasons, an editor of the Chicago newspaper had been caught trying to sneak out of the country in a U.S. transport plane.

Despite intensive probing by the FBI and military intelligence officers, no connection between the Chicago post office episode and the *Tribune* was ever established.[2]

Two Broadcast Rivals Called Up

DAVID SARNOFF, head of the National Broadcasting Company (NBC), arrived at his office high in a skyscraper at 30 Rockefeller Plaza in New York City and was handed an urgent message from the War Department. He had held a commission in the Army Reserve for many years, and now the fifty-two-year-old tycoon was being ordered to active duty for ninety days. It was early March 1944.

Sarnoff, whose penniless parents had emigrated from Russia when he was a boy, was mystified by the secrecy of his call-up. There was no mention of his assignment. All he knew was that he was to proceed to London on the first available airplane.

Colonel Sarnoff reached London on March 20 and was billeted at Claridge's, the city's most prestigious hotel. No doubt he was surprised to learn that his long-time archrival, William S. Paley, also a reserve colonel, was already in London. Paley was head of the Columbia Broadcasting Company (CBS).

Twenty-four hours after his arrival, Sarnoff learned the nature of his special mission. It had a unique twist. After twenty years of broadcast rivalry, he and Bill Paley were to work as a team to organize and coordinate the maze of wireless circuits that would be required to flash the news of D Day to home-front America and the world.[3]

Tributes to a Fallen Female Pilot

EARLY ON THE MORNING OF April 3, 1944, twenty-three-year-old Evelyn Sharp, burdened with flight gear, strolled toward the twin-engine P-38 "Lightning" fighter plane at an air base near Harrisburg, Pennsylvania. She was to ferry the sleek aircraft to an Air Corps base in the southwest.

Like other female pilots, Sharp was now known as a WASP. Earlier, the War Department had combined the female components of the Army Air Corps

WASPs in Texas plan cross-country flight. (National Archives)

into one organization. The new formation would be called the Women's Airforce Service Pilots (WASP) under Jacqueline Cochran, who had been head of the Women's Flying Training Detachment.

Evelyn, an orphan, had been adopted by the Sharp family of Ord, a small town in Nebraska. As an energetic teenager, she had taught many children in the town to swim and to ride horses. At fourteen, Evelyn embarked on a love affair with airplanes, and before she turned eighteen, she had earned a pilot's license.

The vivacious youngster became a heroine of sorts when she had flown in Ord's first sack of airmail letters. Later she thrilled the townspeople by doing acrobatic stunts, and she taught several young Ord men, now serving in combat, how to fly.

Now, outside Harrisburg, Evelyn, who was regarded as the most skilled pilot in her WASP group, climbed into the cockpit of the P-38 and lifted off. Within seconds one of the engines died, and the plane plummeted toward the ground. The pilot died instantly.

Although Evelyn Sharp and the other one hundred WASPs had been ferrying warplanes for millions of miles around the United States the women were not bona fide members of the military. She did not qualify for Army death benefits. So the WASPs at their ferrying base near New Castle, Delaware, took up a collection and sent Evelyn's family in Ord more than $200 to help with the funeral expenses.

Betty Gilles, the squadron commander at New Castle, wanted a uniformed WASP at the final rites, so the women pilots pooled their money to buy a railroad ticket for Nancy Batson to accompany Evelyn's body to Ord. An undertaker met the train and helped remove the coffin.

Late that afternoon, the coffin was wheeled into a room at the funeral home. While Nancy sat nearby with a heavy heart, the Sharp family grieved over the open casket of their once beautiful daughter. Steadily, townspeople poured into the funeral home, most of them crying profusely.

Spotting her uniform (which WASPs had to pay for themselves), a man asked Nancy if he could drape the casket with an American flag. That remark struck a chord of anger with her. None of the WASPs flew with insurance or benefits—and received no official honors if they were killed. Now this fine young woman who died for her country was going to be buried anonymously, as far as the Army was concerned. "Of course," Nancy finally told the man. She should be interred just like the military heroine she was.

On the following morning, the town of Ord turned out en masse for the two-and-a-half hour funeral, time mainly occupied with eulogies. Near the close of the service, the mayor of Ord announced to the congregation that the town airport would now be called the Evelyn Sharp Field.

After the funeral, the hundreds of townspeople moved on to the cemetery. Scores of men and women, eyes brimming with tears, came up to Nancy and told her how proud they were of Evelyn and all the women serving their country as ferrying pilots.

Evelyn's casket was lowered slowly into the ground as a bugler played taps. Only then did Nancy, her official duties concluded, break down in a torrent of tears.[4]

Cheers for a Lady

ALTHOUGH WOMEN PILOTS had been ferrying airplanes for hundreds of thousands of miles across the United States for nearly two years, they were still largely unknown to many Air Corps officers operating flying fields around the nation. Carole Fillmore lifted off from the West Coast to deliver a P-51 fighter plane to Newark, New Jersey. She decided to fly the southern route, and near the end of the first day, she radioed the tower at Athens, Georgia, for landing instructions. No answer. Again she called. Still no response. Now she was circling the airport and asking for radio check.

Then the angry male voice blurted into Carole's earphones: "Will the woman who is calling please stay off the air; we're trying to bring in a P-51."

The veil of dusk was starting to cloak the region. Carole looked around for another P-51, but saw none. So she again asked for clearance to land.

Now the male voice was furious. "Will the [bleeping] woman who is clogging up the radio waves get off the [bleeping] air!" he shouted. "We're trying to make contact with a P-51!"

After flying all the way from Long Beach, California, Carole was near exhaustion—and her patience had run out. "For your information," she bellowed into her mike, "the lady is *in* the P-51!"

Without waiting for a reply, Carole zoomed in toward the runway and landed at a speed in excess of one hundred miles per hour.

As Carole taxied toward the tower, a large number of cadets poured out of a building to get a look at the sleek fighter plane they hoped to be flying one day over Europe or in the Pacific. Coming to a halt, the pilot threw back the canopy, removed her helmet, and the breeze ruffled her long blond hair.

The phalanx of young men ground to a halt. One of the cadets shouted, "Good God, it's a girl!"

A few moments of silence. Then, as Carole stood on a wing, the cadets burst out in cheers and whistles, waving their caps wildly.[5]

D Day Anxieties and Prayers

CURIOUSLY, IT WAS NOT the hundreds of Allied correspondents in London who broke the blockbuster news for which home-front America and the free world had been breathlessly anticipating: the invasion of Adolf Hitler's Festung Europa (Fortress Europe) had been launched. Breaking the story was the German news agency, Transocean. It was early morning on June 6, 1944.

In New York City, the Associated Press picked up the Berlin flash and sent it to media clients across America, just past 2:00 A.M. (eastern standard time). Radio stations interrupted regular programming to air the bulletin.

Broadcast commentators across the nation leaped to stress that there had been no official announcement from the headquarters of Allied Supreme Commander Dwight Eisenhower, and they cautioned that the Berlin announcement could be a Nazi trick to cause the large underground in France, Belgium, and the Netherlands to rise prematurely, thus exposing it for destruction by the German army.

At precisely the same time in London, Colonel William Paley, the head of the CBS network in the United States, was pacing his office. In recent days, a message had been recorded by General Eisenhower, and it was Paley's job to flash the brief statement to home-front America and elsewhere when Allied troops were ashore in Normandy.

Now Paley was nervously waiting for a specified officer to telephone him and give the single code word "Topflight," which meant the Eisenhower message could be broadcast.

At mid-morning, the telephone on Paley's desk jangled urgently. The colonel felt his heart skip a beat. Clearing his throat, he answered as calmly as

(*Philadelphia Inquirer*)

possible, "Yes?" After a split-second pause, the voice on the other end said, "Testing."

Paley slammed down the receiver. His nerves grew tauter. About three minutes later, the telephone rang again. Paley heard the voice say, "Testing."

Paley was angry. Minutes later, it happened a third time. The colonel exploded, telling the caller that if he made one more "testing" call, he would "knock your bleeping head off." Don't phone again unless it was the real thing, Paley shouted.

Within three minutes came yet another call: *"Topflight!"*

General Eisenhower's recorded voice began swirling around the world, confirmation that the mightiest invasion that history has known had been launched.

Eyewitness reports from correspondents started flowing over American airwaves by 9:10 A.M. (eastern standard time). These accounts were vague and repetitive. Big guns on warships sending shells onto the beaches and inland. Much smoke. Warplanes strafing and dropping bombs. Nothing specific. Allied Supreme Headquarters had put a tight muzzle on information about units involved to keep the Germans guessing. Nor was the locale of the invasion permitted to be told, other than "northern France."

As daylight of D Day seeped over a fearful and anxiety-ridden home-front America, tens of thousands of parents, wives, and girlfriends of servicemen known to have been in England nervously awaited more news. Casualties? Not a single word came over the radio.

In large cities and small, Americans crowded into churches and synagogues to pray for loved ones—and for the success of the invasion. President Roosevelt came on the air to unify the nation in prayer:

Almighty God. Our sons, pride of our nation, this day have set upon a mighty endeavor. Lead them straight and true. Give strength to their arms, stoutness to their hearts, steadfastness in their faith.

These men are lately drawn from the ways of peace. They fight to end conquest. They fight to liberate. They yearn but for the end of the battle, for their return to their homes.

Some will never return. Embrace these, Father, and receive them, Thy heroic servants, into Thy kingdom.

And, O Lord, give us faith. Give us faith in Thee, faith in our sons, faith in each other. Thy will be done, Almighty God. Amen.

That morning in Philadelphia, Mayor Bernard Samuel and a large number of dignitaries and citizens gathered around the Liberty Bell, a treasured relic of the early days of American independence. It had been rung on July 8, 1776, to call citizens together to announce the adoption of the Declaration of Independence. Weighing more than two thousand pounds, the bell was now struck with a wooden mallet by Mayor Samuel, its tone spread throughout the nation by radio networks.

That early-morning ceremony triggered the ringing of thousands of church bells in large cities and tiny ones. It was not a celebration, but a grim call for unity and a sense of national purpose.

In Marietta, Georgia, police cars with sirens screeching raced about in the predawn darkness of D Day frightening the sleeping citizens who thought the town was being bombed.

In Clayton, Alabama, the town's lone fire truck, jammed with volunteers, charged up and down the streets clanging the vehicle's bell.

In Columbus, Ohio, Mayor James Rhodes arranged to have air-raid sirens and factory whistles sounded as a call to prayer at 7:30 that night. When the cacophony of sound erupted, cars, buses, trucks, and streetcars halted where they were and people got out to join pedestrians in prayer.

In St. Louis, the historic Old Cathedral near the Mississippi River was packed with worshippers; many had loved ones in Europe.

In Chattanooga, long lines of donors waited patiently at the Red Cross blood center.

In Mount Vernon, Illinois, twenty members of a Cub Scout pack, each carrying an American flag, marched along the downtown streets.

Only sixteen people filed for divorce in Reno, Nevada, a remarkable reduction in the customary one hundred and seventy-five on a normal weekday.

New York City had been one of the nation's most thriving locales since the war had begun. Known as the city that never sleeps, it had lived up to that reputation handsomely. Bars, theaters, and hotels were jammed day and night. Now, on this historic day, America's largest city virtually shut down.

Macy's department store closed at noon. Yet throngs gathered around the building because a loudspeaker had been set up to bring war news over the radio. Gimbel's, Macy's longtime competitor, locked its doors and sent its employees home.

Fashionable Lord & Taylor never opened its doors. The head of the firm, Walter Hoving, had sent the three thousand employees home to pray. "The invasion has begun," Hoving announced. "Our only thought can be of the men who are fighting in it."

Times Square in Manhattan had been a haven for servicemen on leave, many in search of female companions, so the square was usually crowded with prostitutes eager to do their patriotic bit for the war effort. Now, on D Day, these "working ladies" provided their talents to men in the armed forces at a greatly reduced fee.

Even many taxi drivers in Manhattan were stricken with pangs of patriotism on this occasion and refused to cheat on the fares for passengers in uniform.

Elsewhere, sixty-four-year-old Robert McCormick, owner and publisher of the influential *Chicago Tribune*, spent most of the day hunkered down in his posh office suite high in Tribune Towers, a downtown landmark. Never accused of being overly compassionate, the crusty McCormick was worried. His ace war correspondent, John "Beaver" Thompson, was scheduled to go ashore with the first assault waves.

During the Allied invasion of North Africa a year and a half earlier, Thompson had jumped with the U.S. 509th Parachute Infantry Battalion, becoming the first American correspondent to make a combat leap. As time neared for D Day in Normandy, he planned to bail out with paratroopers again.

However, Thompson received an urgent telegram from his boss, McCormick: "No more jumping out of airplanes into battle. It's too dangerous. We don't want to lose you."

So instead of parachuting into Normandy, the thirty-four-year-old Thompson went in with the first amphibious assault waves at Omaha. It was not until three and a half hours after landing that large numbers of GIs had clawed, scratched, and fought their way to the top of the bluffs. A colossal debacle, one that could have jeopardized the entire invasion, had been averted by a hair's breadth.

The triumph at blood-soaked Omaha had a gargantuan price tag—some 2,450 Americans dead, wounded, or drowned. When Beaver Thompson was able to send his story to the *Tribune*, he included a note to Bertie McCormick: "Dear Boss, you were right—Omaha Beach was *very* safe!"[6]

A Virginia Town Is Jolted

IN THE SMALL TOWN of Bedford, Virginia, on D Day morning, an especially somber mood hovered. Hundreds of families had sons, brothers, uncles, nephews, husbands, or boyfriends in the 29th Infantry Division, a National Guard outfit that had been called to federal duty after Pearl Harbor.

The 29th had sailed for Great Britain in September 1942 aboard the converted British luxury liner *Queen Mary*. So there was no doubt in the minds of Bedford citizens on this historic day: many of their loved ones were involved in the savage battles for French beaches.

To keep the Germans confused about Allied strategy and plans, casualties were kept secret. A month after the landings, Bedford received a colossal jolt. The Pentagon disclosed that fourteen families in the town had loved ones killed on Omaha Beach on D Day. More deaths of Bedford men would follow when the savage fighting moved inland.[7]

Calamity at Port Chicago

FORTY MILES NORTHEAST of San Francisco, Port Chicago was the site of a huge ammunition depot to which black and white sailors were assigned as stevedores to load ships bound for the Pacific battlefront. On July 17, 1944, the men were putting nearly a million tons of incendiary and fragmentation bombs onto the *Quinault Victory* and *E. A. Bryan* when a gargantuan blast erupted.

The monstrous explosion killed 323 sailors, 202 being black, and destroyed five ships, a locomotive, and sixteen boxcars loaded with munitions—and the town of Port Chicago. Damage occurred in twelve other towns as far away as seventy-five miles.

It was one of the most destructive disasters in maritime history. An official investigation reported that the precise cause of the holocaust would never be known. But civilians in the Port Chicago region felt that they knew the cause—saboteurs in the employ of Tokyo and Berlin.

A month after the explosion, hundreds of the Navy stevedores were ordered to report for duty at a nearby ammunition depot outside the town of Vallejo. Three hundred and thirty black sailors refused the transfer. The Navy commander, Admiral Carleton Wright, threatened to have them arrested, court-martialed, and shot for mutiny. Fifty of the strikers still refused to accept the transfer order.

One of the resistants, Joseph Small, was called into his office by the admiral. "Small, you are the leader of this bunch," the officer declared. "If you don't go to work, I'm going to have you shot!" The young sailor replied angrily: "You bald-headed old [bleep], go ahead and shoot!"

The fifty resistants were put on trial on October 24, and after an hour and a half's deliberation, the panel of officers found the defendants guilty of mutiny. They were sentenced to fifteen years in prison and given dishonorable discharges. In January 1946, most of the black sailors were released from prison.[8]

Secret Project in a Movie Studio

DURING THE SUMMER OF 1944, most Americans were anxiously following developments in Europe after Allied forces established a solid bridgehead in Normandy. Others on home-front America, however, had loved ones in the Pacific where a savage battle was raging in Saipan, a small island located sixteen hundred miles southeast of Tokyo.

In the final tally after Saipan was pronounced secure by the U.S. commanders, 23,000 Japanese had been killed and American marines and soldiers had suffered some 3,500 dead and several thousand wounded.

America's youth had paid a horrendous price for a tiny patch of desolate real estate. But Saipan was to serve as a base for huge B-29 Superfortresses to strike at Tokyo and other targets in Japan.

Meanwhile, far from Saipan, in Culver City, a suburb of Los Angeles, Captain Ronald W. Reagan was deeply involved in a top-secret project to train B-29 crews for raids on Japan. On a movie sound stage, special-effects men had built a detailed mock-up of Tokyo. Above the display was rigged a crane and camera mount.

From a perch above the miniature Tokyo, the special-effects men photographed various locales to show how the targets would look to bombardiers from different altitudes and speeds under varying weather conditions.

Captain Reagan, a Hollywood actor in peacetime and a future president of the United States, served as narrator for the training films, guiding pilots to their Tokyo targets.

Later, General Henry H. "Hap" Arnold, leader of the Army Air Corps, credited the special-effects project as being "a highly useful tool" for briefing Superfortress crews.[9]

WASPs Test New B-29

AT EGLIN FIELD, FLORIDA, in the fall of 1944, flight tests for the huge new B-29 Superfortresses were launched under the most intense secrecy. These were the planes that would bomb Tokyo and other cities in Japan. A B-29 had a wingspan forty feet wider, was twenty-five feet longer, and was twice as heavy as the B-24 Liberators and the B-17 Flying Fortresses that pilots had been accustomed to using.

Men would fly the B-29s in the Pacific and suffer the casualties. But two women, members of Jacqueline Cochran's WASPs, would test the B-29.

Male pilots had been dubious about flying a Superfortress because of the plane's immense bulk and a rash of the engine fires that had broken out after the planes had been hastily manufactured. Consequently, Colonel Paul W. Tibbets Jr. recruited two WASPs, Dorothy Johnson and Dora Daugherty, both in their early twenties. Tibbets did not inform them of the engine fires.

After several days of intensive training and briefings at Eglin Field, the two WASPs climbed into a Superfortress. On its nose was a tribute to the test pilots; Tibbets had technicians paint the name *Lady Bird*. Then the B-29 lifted off routinely for a long flight to a bomber base at Alamogordo, New Mexico.

Tibbets, it would be said, intended to demonstrate to doubting male pilots that "even women" could handle the bulky bomber.

For a week, Daugherty and Johnson flew male pilots and crewman around the southwestern United States. The B-29 designers apparently had worked out the kinks, and no fires broke out in the engines.

When the two WASPs flew back to Eglin Field, Colonel Tibbets seemed to have accomplished his unspoken goal. In light of future developments, Johnson and Daugherty were convinced that they had played a role in bringing victory in the Pacific.[10]

The Fable of Fala

With the approach of fall 1944, Franklin Roosevelt confounded the ghosts of America's Founding Fathers and his Republican foes by announcing that he would seek reelection for the third time in November. It was clear to most observers in Washington that Roosevelt was in poor health. But his personal physician, Vice Admiral Ross T. McIntire, pronounced the incumbent "fit for duty."

Roosevelt's opponent would be Republican Thomas E. Dewey, who had made a big name as a racket-busting special prosecutor in New York City before being elected governor of the state in 1943.

As a warm-up to the campaign, Dewey's supporters spent a great amount of time trying to ridicule Roosevelt by turning the spotlight on his Scottish terrier, Fala, who was the world's most publicized dog.

Fala was what journalists call "good copy." When his master was present for the launching of a battleship, Fala sat at his side. Press photographers snapped more pictures of the black Scotty than they did of the president.

When world leaders, such as British Prime Minister Winston Churchill, called at the White House, they always asked about Fala and insisted on seeing the cocky little dog. When Fala once got into a noisy hassle with a female Scotty, it was front-page news.

This flood of publicity about the White House pet was bound to generate rumors. None was more ridiculous than the one claiming that Roosevelt, during his travels, had absentmindedly left Fala on some island. The story never named the place. When the president returned to Washington, so went the fable, he immediately dispatched a warship to pick up the canine, at great expense to the American taxpayers.

There had not been an iota of truth in the story. But Roosevelt, the consummate politician, used it to turn the tables on Dewey's campaign. At a rally carried nationwide by a radio hookup, the president brought up Fala and the rescue by a mythical warship. A gifted storyteller, he had his listeners guffawing by reciting invented details of the Great Rescue of Fala from a nonexistent island.[11]

Roosevelt's Foe Keeps a Secret

ALTHOUGH GENERAL GEORGE MARSHALL, the Army chief of staff in Washington, kept a neutral stance in the bitter 1944 presidential campaign between the incumbent, Franklin Roosevelt, and his Republican challenger, Thomas Dewey, he watched developments closely to see how they might affect the war effort. It was said that Marshall had always been so intent on remaining detached from partisan politics that he would not vote for fear that his stance might leak to the media.

One morning Marshall received shocking news. A culprit in the Navy or State Department had smuggled supersecret information to Dewey about Magic, code name for the interception and translation of Japanese messages. American cryptologists had broken the Japanese code four years earlier.

General Marshall feared that Dewey might disclose the existence of Magic, causing the Japanese to change codes. That would have destroyed a huge American strategic advantage, cost thousands of American lives, and prolonged the bloodbath in the Pacific.

Marshall found himself skewered on the horns of a dilemma. If he failed to contact Dewey and explain the crucial value of Magic, he would be derelict in his duty. If he approached the Republican nominee, the general would be charged with injecting himself in the presidential campaign to curry favor with Roosevelt.

After consulting with Admiral Ernest King, the Navy chief, Marshall decided to send a Pentagon intelligence officer, in civilian clothes, to deliver to Dewey a top-secret letter explaining Magic. The two men met secretly in a hotel room in Tulsa.

Dewey, a seasoned old pro, suspected the scenario was a scheme hatched by the cagey Roosevelt to silence the Republican. Dewey snapped at the Pentagon emissary, "He knew what was happening before Pearl Harbor and instead of being reelected, he ought to be impeached."

On election night, Missouri Senator Harry Truman, Roosevelt's selection to be his vice president, and several cronies from Truman's artillery battery in World War I, gathered in a suite in Kansas City's Muehlebach Hotel. Truman played the piano, there was much elbow lifting, and ears were tuned to election reports on the radio.

It was a long night. Clearly, the election was close. Then, at 3:45 A.M., Governor Dewey conceded. He had never as much as hinted that the secret Japanese code had been cracked by the Americans prior to Pearl Harbor.[12]

A Father-and-Daughter Spy Team

IN THE AUTUMN OF 1944, tiny Harpers Ferry, West Virginia, was a peaceful oasis seemingly far removed from any connection to the slaughter abroad. A few months earlier, one of its residents, sixty-one-year-old soft-spoken Simon Koedel, had left his home on Riverside Drive in New York City to escape the big-city turmoil, he told neighbors.

Left behind in New York was his twenty-six-year-old foster daughter, Marie Hedwig Koedel, who liked the bright lights of New York and refused to flee to a "hick town" in the wilds of West Virginia. Attractive Marie made a living as a clerk in a clothing store.

Harpers Ferry is situated on the Potomac River, fifty-five miles northwest of Washington. The town had been made famous by John Brown's raid in 1859, just before the Civil War erupted. Brown led a group to seize a Union Army arsenal at Harpers Ferry, but he and eighteen of his followers were captured and later tried and hanged.

Soon after Koedel's arrival, with most of Harpers Ferry's young men gone to war, he got a job as projectionist in a movie theatre. A friendly type, he made friends, but generally kept to himself.

Just before dawn on October 23, 1944, Koedel was deep in slumber at his rooming house when he was awakened by sharp rapping on the door. Answering the summons, he was confronted by two strangers. One flashed a badge and said, "FBI."

Neighbors in Harpers Ferry were stunned to learn that this outwardly gentle man, who was masquerading as a theater projectionist, had been one of the most productive Nazi spies in the United States.

Born in Germany, Koedel had come to the New World in time to serve three years in the U.S. Army in World War I. In 1935, he returned to Germany on a visit and, excited over what he considered to be the bright promise of

Bustling New York harbor was the focus for the father-and-daughter spy team, Simon and Marie Koedel. (New York Port Authority)

Nazism, offered his services as a spy to Admiral Wilhelm Canaris, chief of the Abwehr, the intelligence agency.

Koedel was given an exhaustive course on espionage in Hamburg, then told to return to New York City as a "sleeper" and await a call to go into action. It would be in early 1940, four years later, when the summons to duty came. The lean, gaunt, humorless "sleeper" was being activated as Abwehr Agent A-2011. He was given a commission as a captain and was soon promoted to major because of his innovative and highly productive spying activities.

Koedel sought and was granted membership in the American Ordnance Association, a lobby for a strong national defense. Often he strolled brazenly up to the gates of plants, flashed his Ordnance Association card, and was admitted. Sometimes officials took him on a guided tour of what should have been a top-secret facility.

Once he tried this ploy at the Chemical Warfare Center at Edgewood Arsenal, Maryland, where the strictest security measures were employed. There the Army tested its newest hush-hush weapons. Guards would not permit Koedel to enter.

Returning to his drab flat on Riverside Drive, Koedel promptly telephoned an official at the Ordnance Association office in Washington and feigned deep indignation over the treatment he had received at the Chemical Warfare Center.

The association official contacted a high officer in the War Department and demanded to know why this distinguished chemical engineer (he knew nothing about chemistry), army veteran, and loyal booster of a strong national defense was being barred from Edgewood Arsenal. "You would think Mr. Koedel was a spy!" the executive complained.

Within hours an officer in the War Department read the riot act to the Edgewood Arsenal commander, and Koedel entered the facility and was given a guided tour. Two weeks later, Abwehr officers in Berlin were reading Agent A-2011's report on what he had seen and been told at the secret arsenal.

These espionage triumphs had been conducted while the United States was not at war. So the most serious penalty Koedel could have received if unmasked was a prison sentence.

In the meantime, Marie Koedel, the daughter, had been playing a highly active espionage role. She covered her waterfront "beat" in New York City almost daily, sauntering into dingy saloons in dresses that left little to the imagination and casting flirtatious glances at the merchant seamen. Soon one or more of the men would join her.

Loose-tongued from booze and seeking to impress the willowy brunette, the seamen told her about departure dates of convoys, their routes, ship armaments, cargoes, and other maritime secrets. Based on Marie's information and his own connivances, A-2011 kept detailed convoy reports flowing to the Third Reich, from where the data were relayed to U-boat commanders prowling the Atlantic Ocean sea-lanes.

After Koedel's arrest, Marie Koedel was picked up in New York City by FBI agents. Tried in federal court in Brooklyn, Simon Koedel was sentenced to fifteen years in prison. Marie, whose spying had no doubt resulted in the deaths of many merchant sailors, received a term of only seven and a half years.[13]

Stumbling into a World Series

IN ST. LOUIS IN EARLY SEPTEMBER 1944, Sportsman's Park, a stadium rich in baseball lore, was decked out in colorful bunting for the opening of the annual World Series. The teams that had stumbled into the annual fall classic, the St. Louis Browns in the American League and the St. Louis Cardinals in the National League, were so inept that Warren Brown, a sports writer, predicted: "I don't believe *either* team can win."

Soon after Pearl Harbor, President Franklin Roosevelt had felt that major-league baseball would have a positive and morale-boosting role in the momentous years that lay ahead before victory over Japan and Germany was secured. So he had written to Judge Kennesaw Mountain Landis, the baseball commissioner: "I honestly feel that it would be best for the country to keep baseball going."

Unique even among wartime major-league baseball players was one-armed Pete Gray, who played for the St. Louis Browns. (Author's collection)

And baseball did "keep going"—but barely. By World Series time 1944, more than three hundred major-league players were wearing military uniforms. They included most of the genuine superstars. Detroit slugger Hank Greenberg had been the first big-name player to sign up soon after America went to war. He volunteered as a private in the Army Air Corps, was commissioned, and saw duty with a B-29 bomber outfit in China as a captain.

"Jolting Joe" DiMaggio, who led the New York Yankees to World Series titles several times and established a record (that still stands) of hitting safely in fifty-six consecutive games, turned in his pin-striped baseball uniform for Army Air Corps khaki and eventually became a staff sergeant serving in Hawaii.

Boston Red Sox slugger Ted Williams, known as the Splendid Splinter because of his gangling build, joined the marines, became a fighter pilot and a captain, seeing heavy action in the Pacific.

"Rapid Robert" Feller, who set strikeout records while pitching for the Cleveland Indians, was a gunner on the battleship *Alabama*. Warren Spahn, a classy lefty who hurled for the then Boston Braves, received a Purple Heart and a Bronze Star for an heroic action. Spahn was the only major-league baseball player during the war to receive a battlefield commission.

Wartime major-league baseball consisted largely of washed up veterans (like forty-two-year-old Jimmy Foxx who had hit more than five hundred home runs in his prime), players with lesser skills, and rejects of the past. Symbolizing the game's patchwork quilt was Pete Gray.

Gray had lost his right arm at age six in an accident. Yet, like countless small boys, he dreamed of one day becoming a major-league baseball player. As gently as possible, his father tried to discourage such thoughts or Pete's spirit would be crushed. Perhaps Pete might get into bowling or tennis, the father had hinted.

Undaunted, the boy pursued his dream. Off in a pasture where he could not be seen, he would spend hours tossing walnuts into the air just above his head, then swinging his broomstick "bat" at the kernel as it came back to the ground. With considerable merit, he felt that if he could gain the knack of connecting with a small nut using a thin broomstick, one day he could hit a much larger baseball with a much larger bat. Soon he became skilled in hitting walnuts.

In his teens and on into manhood, Gray played amateur baseball, and in the wartime year of 1944, he started the season as an outfielder with the professional Memphis team in the Southern Association.

Gray had developed techniques that were not necessary for other players. In the outfield, he caught the ball with his gloved hand, placed the ball against his chest, let it roll out of his glove and up his wrist as he tucked the glove under the stub of his right arm, then drew his left arm back across his chest until the ball rolled into his hand. He had practiced this lightning-like maneuver for countless hours, and could fire the ball back to the infield as rapidly as other players.

Major-league scouts couldn't believe that a player with only one arm could hit at this level of competition, and they flocked to Memphis to watch Pete play. The attitude of the scouts soon changed, however, when Gray hit a remarkable .333 (one hit in three times at bat) that year. Anything above a .300 batting average is considered to be excellent.

On opening day of the 1945 season, an awed Pete Gray, wearing the uniform of the St. Louis Browns, stepped onto the diamond at Sportsman's Park. He had signed a contract with a major-league team: his boyhood dream had come true.

At this level of competition, even with mainly wartime-caliber players on the teams, the rookie found pitchers were difficult to hit consistently. In seventy-seven games, Pete sparkled in the outfield and his powerful arm threw out numerous runners trying to take an extra base, but he hit only .218.

Only Pete's family knew a secret: early in the war he had tried to volunteer for the Army in any capacity, but was politely rejected.[14]

A Riot Erupts in New York City

MANHATTAN WAS COLD AND BLEAK on the morning of October 12, 1944, when a ruckus broke out in Times Square. Some thirty thousand frenzied bobby-soxers stormed the Paramount Theater box office, but only three thousand tickets were available to see and hear a frail crooner with rumpled brown hair named Francis Albert Sinatra.

The crush of mainly teenaged girls snarled traffic, causing a strident cacophony of honking horns and loudly cursing drivers. The mass of flesh trampled luckless passersby and plunged through storefront windows. A force of seven hundred riot police was hastily rushed in to try and restore a semblance of order.

Inside the cavernous Paramount, Frank Sinatra was greeted by squeals of delight from the three thousand girls, most of whom had stayed on the cold sidewalk all night to get tickets. Trumpeted by press agents as the King of Swoon and the Voice that Thrills Millions, Sinatra started singing. His sparkling blue eyes searched the faces in front of him, causing each bobby-soxer to believe that he was vocally romancing her alone. Adolescent voices screamed in ecstasy.

In what may have been an orchestrated promotion by Sinatra's clever press agents, scores of schoolgirls swooned as the Voice crooned the velvety words of a popular ballad, "All or Nothing at All." Curiously, ushers happened to be armed with smelling salts and had stretchers to carry "swooners" out of the Paramount—as newspaper cameras clicked.

Twenty-eight-year-old Frank Sinatra was a new phenomenon on the American scene. No other singer, not even the fabled Bing Crosby, had ever inspired such wild adulation.

Adults and most press people were mystified by the hoopla. *Newsweek* magazine huffed: "As a visible male object of adulation, Sinatra is baffling."

In an era when the accepted image of a manly American was a brawny soldier in muddy combat fatigues wreaking havoc on the Germans or Japanese, Sinatra did seem to be an unlikely idol. Five feet ten inches tall and weighing only one hundred and thirty-five pounds, the singer seemed to be in danger of collapsing from malnutrition.

Various psychiatrists tried to explain the phenomenon. "Mass hypnotism," said one. "Mass frustrated love," guessed another. "Mammary hyperesthesia," stated yet another, referring to Sinatra's wispy build, a maternal "urge to feed the hungry."

Newspaper and magazine columnists had different analyses. With most young men in the service, Frank was the only male around. One critic said of the Sinatra cult: "They're imbecilic, moronic, screaming-meemie kids."

Be as it may, the Voice was pulling down a whopping $10,000 (equivalent to some $120,000 in 2002) for each performance at the Paramount. This fee for an hour of singing on stage was more than an entire company of GI infantrymen battling the Germans along the Siegfried Line was being paid per month.

Singer Frank Sinatra received more money for a one-hour gig at New York City's Paramount Theater than an infantry company fighting in Europe was paid for an entire month. (CBS)

There were two thousand Sinatra fan clubs across the nation. He was receiving more than five thousand letters a week from girls and women, many asking for a date. Sinatra was not overburdened with humility. "I'm riding high, kid," he told a reporter for the *New York Times*.

Many American adults were outraged by the Sinatra-mania. George Chatfield, the New York City education commissioner, threatened to file charges against the Voice for encouraging truancy because thousands of teenaged girls were skipping school to attend his concerts. A member of Congress took to the floor to declare that the primary reasons for juvenile delinquency in the United States were the Lone Ranger and Frank Sinatra.

Much of the adult loathing of Sinatra had its roots in an affronted patriotism. It seemed grossly unfair to many that brave boys usually much younger than the singer were being killed and maimed fighting the Germans and Japanese while a skinny entertainer was earning millions of dollars and the adulation of America's teenage girls.

Failure to serve in uniform was not Sinatra's fault, however. Several times he was called in to take Army physical examinations, while hordes of weeping bobby-soxers protested this outrage in front of the induction center. Each time he was reclassified 4-F because of a punctured eardrum.

The Army newspaper, *Stars and Stripes*, summed up the view of most American servicemen and civilian adults: "Mice make women faint, too."[15]

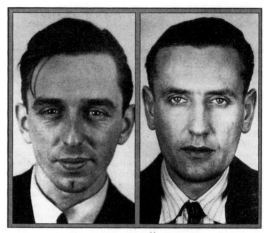

FBI agents in New York City arrested Nazi spies
William Colepaugh (left) and Erich Gimpel only one
month after they emerged from a U-boat near Bar
Harbor, Maine. (FBI)

Dark Intruders Sneak Ashore

NEAR DAWN ON THE BITTERLY COLD MORNING of November 29, 1944, the long-range German submarine, *U-1230*, skippered by Lieutenant Hans Hilbig, was threading its way around the shoals into Frenchman Bay, a body of deep water protruding ten miles into the rugged coast of Maine near the fashionable resort of Bar Harbor. On board were two Nazi spies, Erich Gimpel and William C. Colepaugh. The two men were embarking on Unternehmen Elster (Operation Magpie), a desperate espionage mission to the United States.

Both men had met for the first time and been trained at A-Schule Westen (Agent School West), located on a secluded estate named Park Zorgvliet, between The Hague and suburban Scheveningen in the Netherlands.

Colepaugh, twenty-six years of age, was born and reared in Niantic, Connecticut, on the Long Island Sound and had been a member of the U.S. Navy Reserve when he became dazzled by Adolf Hitler's promise of a new world order. Colepaugh had made his way to Lisbon, Portugal, as a merchant sailor, then went by land into Germany just before Pearl Harbor.

Gimpel had been born in Merseburg, a small town ninety miles southwest of Berlin. He had been recruited by the Reich Central Security Office to work as a secret agent.

At the A-Schule Westen, Gimpel and Colepaugh were instructed to ferret out technical information on ship construction, rocket experiments, and aircraft production. The key to the cipher they were to use in their radioed reports to Germany was the American advertising slogan: "Lucky Strike cigarettes—they're toasted!" They were to achieve these goals by exploiting America's democracy and gleaning information from newspapers, magazines, technical journals, radio newscasts, and books. It was important, the two spies were told, that this intelligence reach the Third Reich quickly through radio transmissions.

When their espionage course was completed, Gimpel and Colepaugh each was given a Colt pistol, a tiny compass, a Leica camera, a Krahl wristwatch, a bottle of secret ink, powder for developing invisible-ink messages, and instructions for building a radio.

Upon arriving at the Baltic port of Kiel where they were to board Lieutenant Hilbig's *U-1230*, the two spies were furnished phony papers. Gimpel's papers identified him as Edward George Green, born in Bridgeport, Connecticut. They consisted of a birth certificate, a Selective Service registration card showing him registered at Local Board 18 in Boston, and a Massachusetts driver's license. Colepaugh's false documents were virtually the same and were made out in the name of William Charles Caldwell, born in New Haven, Connecticut.

Now, on November 29, Gimpel and Colepaugh climbed from Hilbig's submarine into a rubber raft off bleak Crabtree Point, Maine, and were paddled ashore by two sailors. Along with their espionage accoutrements, the spies carried $60,000 (equivalent to about $700,000 in the year 2002) in a briefcase. A blinding snowstorm was raging as the two men stumbled onto land, but neither had thought to bring along a topcoat or hat.

The Nazi agents bent their heads to the howling wind and trudged inland until they reached a dirt road. Hardly had they begun walking along it than they were caught in the headlights of a car driven slowly by eighteen-year-old Harvard M. Hodgkins, a high school senior who was returning to his nearby home. His father Dana was a deputy sheriff of Hancock County.

Gimpel and Colepaugh continued through snowy woods for about five miles until they reached U.S. Highway 1, where they flagged down a passing taxi. The driver agreed to take them the thirty-two miles to Bangor, Maine, for six dollars. At the Bangor station, the spies caught a train to Portland, Maine, and from there took another train to Boston.

Meanwhile, Deputy Sheriff Hodgkins had returned from a hunting trip and was told by his son of the two lightly dressed strangers in the blizzard. The elder Hodgkins promptly notified the FBI field office in Boston, and agents were rushed to Crabtree Point to launch an investigation.

After spending a night in Boston, Gimpel and Colepaugh entrained for New York on the morning of December 1. Upon arrival at Grand Central Station, they checked a suitcase holding their spying accoutrements and taxied across town to Pennsylvania Station, where they put their cash-filled briefcase in a locker. Then they checked into the Kenmore Hall Hotel at 145 East 23rd Street.

They urgently needed to find an apartment to serve as a shortwave radio studio, and on December 8 they rented a place on the top floor of a townhouse at 39 Beekman Place. "Caldwell" and "Green"—they were using their aliases—

left the townhouse early each morning and returned late in the evening, as though they were legitimate businessmen.

Gimpel and Colepaugh's enthusiasm for spying began to waver. Forgotten was their mission of digging up technical information. Instead they began wining and dining in plush restaurants and taking in the latest Broadway stage shows. They were sprinkling Hitler's money around as though it were going out of style. Colepaugh, especially, was on a money-spending binge. When not picking up girls, he was buying expensive suits at a Roger Kent store.

On the night of December 21, Colepaugh waited outside a Robert Reed store in Rockefeller Center while Gimpel was buying a topcoat and a suit to replace his German-made "American" clothing. When Gimpel came out, his companion had vanished.

Colepaugh had taken the subway to the plush St. Moritz Hotel on Central Park, where he spent two nights. Then he went to see an old high school pal, who lived in the borough of Queens. He told his friend that he was a Nazi spy and the nature of his mission. However, he said that he had a change of heart. So with Colepaugh's approval, his friend called the FBI.

Colepaugh was eager to talk. He told the G-men what Gimpel looked like, that his alias was Edward Green, and that he often bought newspapers at a stand in Times Square.

On the night of December 30, Times Square was cold and windswept. Just before 9:00 P.M., two G-men staked out a newsstand and saw a man resembling Gimpel's description approaching. They pounced on and handcuffed him. The sleuths found $10,574 in cash in his pockets and $4,100 more in his hotel room.

Colepaugh and Gimpel were charged with espionage and tried by a military court at Governor's Island in New York harbor. They were found guilty, and on February 14, 1945, were sentenced to be executed. Later the verdict was reduced to life in prison. After the war, the two spies were released and sent back to Germany.[16]

Robot Bombs Threaten East Coast

DURING THE FBI'S INTERROGATION of the two Operation Magpie spies, alarming information surfaced. Before leaving America, they said, their controllers in the German intelligence service had told them that a flotilla of U-boats would follow them. These submarines, the spies swore they had been informed, were outfitted with special rocket-firing devices that would enable the skippers to bombard New York City and Washington from beyond the horizon.

Because William Colepaugh and Erich Gimpel had nothing to gain by disclosing this information, the FBI and the Office of Naval Intelligence (ONI) took the ominous threat seriously. Evidence was uncovered that indicated these U-boat "special devices" could launch Adolf Hitler's *Vergeltungswaffe* (vengeance weapons) against America's East Coast.

These weapons had long been known to the British and Americans as buzz bombs, and since June 1944 they had been raining on London and other locales in England, causing thousands of deaths and injuries and widespread destruction.

Called the V-1 by the Germans, the buzz bomb was a pilotless aircraft with speeds up to 440 miles per hour, far faster than any Allied fighter could fly. A timing device caused the engine to shut off over a target, and the craft would plunge earthward, exploding with the impact of a 4,000-pound blockbuster bomb.

No doubt the FBI and Navy investigators envisioned the devilish devices' engines going dead over Washington and crashing into the White House or the Capitol.

Along the eastern seaboard, a network of high-frequency direction finders—electronic sleuths from which no U-boat could evade—disclosed that German radio traffic had rapidly increased in the North Atlantic. Although this evidence was inconclusive, Navy Intelligence took this development as a signal that U-boats were preparing a Pearl Harbor-type sneak attack on New York City and Washington.

On the bleak and frigid morning of January 8, 1945, a bevy of media reporters hovered around Admiral Jonas Ingram, commander of the Eastern Sea Frontier, in a wardroom aboard a warship in New York harbor. The journalists had been promised an "historic press conference."

Ingram, a heavyset, flat-nosed old salt who had gained national recognition as football coach at the Naval Academy, was one of the service's most outspoken and colorful characters. Seated at the end of a long table, Ingram said, "Gentlemen we have reason to assume that the [bleeping] Nazis are getting ready to launch a strategic attack on New York City and Washington by robot bombs!"

Reporters are seldom astonished. They now issued gasps of amazement.

"I am here to tell you that [robot bomb] attack is not only possible, but probable as well, and that the East Coast is likely to be buzz-bombed within the next thirty to sixty days." Ingram paused and stared at his wide-eyed listeners, then added grimly: "The thing to do is not to get excited about it. The explosions may knock out a high building or two, might create a fire hazard, and most certainly would cause casualties. But the [buzz bombs] cannot seriously affect the progress of the war."

The gruff admiral added: "It may be only two or twelve buzz bombs, but they may come before we can stop them. So I'm springing the cat from the bag to let the Huns [Germans] know that we are ready for them!"

Admiral Ingram's blunt and terrifying warning was broadcast from coast to coast and splashed across newspapers. A blaring headline in the *New York Times* screamed:

ROBOT BOMBS ATTACKS HERE HELD POSSIBLE

After sixty days had passed and there were no buzz-bomb strikes, citizens, especially those in New York City and Washington, began to breathe easier.

Had the Germans really been capable of launching these buzz-bomb attacks some four thousand miles from the nearest U-boat bases? Had Ingram's public warning that the armed forces were on the alert for such an attack caused the Kriegsmarine (German Navy) to call off the project?[17]

The Führer Staggers America

AS CHRISTMAS SEASON 1944 APPROACHED, heady optimism that the war in Europe was as good as over was rampant on home-front America. Taking their cues from the rose-colored views held by Allied commanders in France, editorial writers comfortably perched in their ivory towers assured readers that Germany was on the brink of collapse.

The Germans seemed to be hanging on by their fingernails. Powerful American, British, Canadian, and French forces were deployed along the western frontier of the Third Reich, awaiting the signal to launch a full-blooded offensive that would nail down the Nazi coffin.

Based on the flow of euphoric stories in American media, there was even much talk across the nation that "the boys will be home for Christmas."

Draft boards were instructed to cut back greatly on the number of inductees, and the War Department reduced orders for the manufacture of weapons. The Pentagon had completed plans for transferring scores of units in Europe to the Pacific for an invasion of Japan.

President Franklin Roosevelt continued to broadcast his highly popular fireside chats that always began with "My Friends . . ." His talks were rife with guarded optimism that the war against Germany was nearing a conclusion.

White-haired, bespectacled Bernard M. Baruch, a Washington fixture for decades and unpaid confidant of Roosevelt, was among those in the capital wearing rose-colored glasses. Described by one White House official as "a royal pain in the ass," Baruch nevertheless was highly regarded by the president and had entrée to the Oval Office at any time.

Baruch's experience in wartime economics dated back to World War I when he had been head of the War Industries Board. However, he refused to accept any similar post in the current conflict because, it was said, Henry Ford, the automobile tycoon, had accused him of being a key figure in a Jewish conspiracy to take over control of the economy of the world.

Because businessmen were flooding Washington with demands to know when they could resume producing civilian goods now that the war in Europe was virtually over, Bernie Baruch prepared a report for the president on industrial reconversion. In the document, the advisor urged the government to hurry in its preparations to start producing civilian goods, so as to avoid serious unemployment when Germany collapsed.

Most civilians were still beset with shortages of coffee, sugar, meat, gasoline, and tires. And they could not always locate a favorite whiskey, cigarette, or candy bar. Now, it seemed, these "hardships" would soon evaporate.

On the morning of December 17, citizens across the land were scanning their Sunday newspapers, anxious to hear if Germany had collapsed. Apparently the European front was quiet; for one of the few times since the Normandy invasion six months earlier, the Pacific fighting monopolized the front pages. Stated a big, bold headline in the *St. Louis Post-Dispatch:*

AMERICANS CAPTURE AIRFIELDS ON MINDORO

The *Chicago Tribune* told readers in large letters:

GI'S ADVANCE IN PHILIPPINES

Buried inside scores of newspapers were short items with small headlines that told of minor German probing attacks on the Western Front, which were beaten back.

There was plenty of news—blockbuster news—however. But the Allied high command in Europe had installed a news blackout. Twenty-four hours earlier, at dawn on December 16, tens of thousands of Adolf Hitler's assault troops and hundreds of low-slung panzers, paced by bands of German soldiers driving captured American vehicles and wearing GI uniforms taken from prisoners, had launched a massive offensive in the Ardennes forest of Belgium and Luxembourg. Later called the Battle of the Bulge, the gigantic attack was the führer's final roll of the dice to snatch victory from the jaws of defeat.

From General Eisenhower on down to a private manning a machine gun at an outpost, the Americans had been taken by total surprise. German spearheads smashed through thin and disorganized U.S. positions and plunged deep into Belgium.

In Washington, the White House was in a state of shock. This simply could not be taking place in the bitterly cold and snow-covered Ardennes forest. Hadn't the Pentagon believed that Germany was on the verge of collapse?

Harry Hopkins, President Roosevelt's closest and most trusted civilian advisor, rushed to see J. Edgar Hoover, the Federal Bureau of Investigation chief. The hard-driving, high-strung Hopkins breathlessly informed Hoover of an amazing Nazi plot to murder Roosevelt while official America was focusing on the slaughter taking place in the Ardennes.

The gaunt, stoop-shouldered Hopkins said he had authentic information from confidential intelligence sources in London that there was a plan to kill President Roosevelt.

At this time, there were nearly 425,000 German prisoners of war in the United States, and some 75 of them were escaping each month (most were soon recaptured). According to Hopkins's source, the attempt to murder Roosevelt would be made while thousands of German POWs created enormous turmoil and confusion by a mass escape.

When informed of the plot, Roosevelt scoffed at the idea that a group of hard-core Nazi fanatics, no doubt garbed in civilian clothes, would storm the White House. But Mike Riley, the veteran, astute chief of the White House Secret Service detail, refused to take the threat lightly.

Riley secured the services of an Army unit and beefed up security around the president, who joked about the "rumpus." When his long-time, middle-aged secretary, Grace Tully, came to work one morning, the president, flashing his trademark lopsided grin, quipped: "Well, Grace, did Mike Riley's boys frisk you?"

In Europe meanwhile, American correspondents were furious. Because of the embargo on information about the German offensive, they had to sit on one of the war's biggest stories. A half-million GIs were battling an equal number of German soldiers in a death struggle with no holds barred.

Despite the official news blackout, bits and pieces of information seeped back to home-front America: something was amiss on the Western Front. Concern would have turned to panic had civilians been privy to a notation scrawled in his diary by the customarily upbeat General George Patton: "We can still lose this war!"

Three days after the Germans struck in the Ardennes, the news blackout was lifted—perhaps through the direct order of President Roosevelt. Blaring headlines and bulletins on the radio staggered a complacent home front. Loved ones of Americans battling for their lives in the heavy snows and sub-zero climate in Belgium hurried to churches to pray.

At the same time in the Pentagon outside Washington, Secretary of War Henry Stimson and Army Chief of Staff George Marshall were grimly discussing the unthinkable: What if Adolf Hitler pulled off the enormous gamble and his forces soundly defeated and administered a bloodbath to the Americans?

Always a realist, Marshall declared: "If Germany beats us, we will have to recast our view of the entire war. We will have to take up defensive positions in Europe." Next, he made a startling observation: "Then the people of the United States would have to decide whether they want to continue the war enough to raise large new armies."

Marshall and Stimson knew that "raising new armies" would mean the drafting of hundreds of thousands of men who were exempt because they were fathers, above the current draft age, or had physical handicaps. It was conceivable that should the Americans suffer enormous losses, the home front might rebel against feeding more men into the European meat grinder.

After six weeks of savagery in the Ardennes, the Nazi army limped back into the Siegfried Line, a barrier along the western border of the Third Reich. Adolf Hitler's final gamble had been costly: 120,000 casualties. More than 90,000 Americans had been killed, wounded, or captured.[18]

Back Home for Christmas

Snow was blanketing the affluent New York City suburb of Greenwich, Connecticut, in mid-December 1944. In recent weeks, two residents, Prescott and Dorothy Bush, had gone through the torments of the damned after the Pentagon notified them that one of their four sons, Navy Lieutenant George Herbert Walker Bush, was missing in action in the Pacific.

Prescott Bush was the managing partner of the Wall Street firm of Brown Brothers, Harriman and Company, an international banking house. So George Bush had grown up surrounded by wealth and influence. He attended Phillips Academy in Andover, Massachusetts, where he captained the basketball and soccer teams, played varsity baseball (a left-handed first baseman), and served as president of his senior class.

Young Bush had a slot open for him at Yale University, but he enlisted in the Navy and took flight training at Corpus Christi, Texas, after which he was commissioned. Late in 1943, Bush was assigned to the new aircraft carrier *San Jacinto* as a member of Torpedo Bomber Squadron VT51 and at the time was the youngest pilot in the Navy.

Bush engaged in heavy fighting in the Pacific. As a pilot in a torpedo squadron, his was one of the most hazardous flight jobs in the Navy. His luck finally ran out and he was shot down but survived in a small raft for several days before he was spotted and rescued by a ship. Hungry, thirsting for water, bedraggled, clothes soaked, he offered up a prayer of thanks.

On Christmas Eve 1944, there was a knock on the door of the Prescott and Dorothy Bush mansion in Greenwich. When it was opened, there stood a grinning Lieutenant George Herbert Walker Bush, a future president of the United States.[19]

Episode on a Florida Bus

A black soldier, who had served in North Africa, Sicily, and Italy, climbed aboard a bus in Tampa, Florida, early in 1945. He was on convalescent leave from an Army hospital and on his way home.

Three white soldiers were in the front seats, and one of them got up and offered his seat to the wounded veteran. But the driver overheard the remark and told the black GI to move to the back of the bus. The white soldier said that there were no empty seats there, and the driver replied: "Niggers can't sit up front in Florida!"

Still standing, the white soldier said to his two companions: "Does he sit here or doesn't he?" They called out: "He sits!" Then the white GI told the bus driver: "Either he sits down here and you drive or we'll throw your ass off the bus and I'll drive!"

The driver drove away without another word.[20]

A GI Changes His Mind

STAFF SERGEANT JOE MORTON was standing along the rail of a gray-painted transport ship as it sailed into New York harbor. He was pushing thirty-nine year of age—positively elderly for a combat soldier—and returning home from Europe to be discharged from the Army after having been overseas for two years.

Morton had been made eligible for being separated from the service as a result of a War Department edict that stated GIs thirty-eight years of age or older could get out of the Army. Now, on approaching New York City, Morton was elated over his forthcoming role as a civilian.

In the mists of early morning on the transport ship, Morton caught sight of the Statue of Liberty. For some reason he could not even explain to himself, he suddenly regretted the decision he had made. On reaching nearby Fort Dix, New Jersey, for discharge, the sergeant withdrew his application. A few days later he was back on another vessel, sailing out of New York harbor to rejoin his buddies in his old outfit in Europe.[21]

Part Six

The Lights Go On Again

A Blaze of Glory

NEW YEAR'S DAY 1945 marked the beginning of America's fourth year in a global war that had resulted in the deaths and maiming of tens of thousands of her sons. In Washington, President Roosevelt continued to be confronted by countless problems, but he and wife Eleanor, like a few million parents across the land, had their own personal worries. They had four sons in the service, all of them in combat assignments.

Franklin D. Roosevelt Jr. was executive officer (second in command) of the destroyer *Mayant* during the invasion of North Africa in November 1942. Later he commanded the destroyer *Ulvert H. Moore*, which sank a Japanese submarine off the Philippines.

James, the oldest son, was a Marine Corps officer with Carlson's Raiders, a commando-type unit that specialized in raiding Japanese positions on small Pacific islands.

The youngest son, John, was an ensign on the aircraft carrier *Hornet*, which spent fifty-two days under Japanese attack in the Pacific—and never received as much as a dent from a machine-gun bullet or shrapnel.

Elliott, the second oldest offspring, was commander of an Army Air Corps photo reconnaissance outfit that saw action in North Africa, Iceland, and the Normandy invasion.

In late 1944, Colonel Elliott Roosevelt was up for promotion to brigadier general, which would make him one of the few Air Corps officers to achieve that rank without being a trained pilot. Congress was considering the elevation, which seemed to be a certainty, when a convoluting series of events threatened to sidetrack his promotion.

It all began on January 4, 1945, when an eighteen-year-old sailor, Seaman 1st Class Leon LeRoy, arrived in New York harbor aboard a Navy tanker on which he was a gunner. When ashore he learned for the first time of the death of his father, who had been the police chief of Antioch, California, a month earlier. The sailor applied for and was granted an emergency leave to visit his mother.

Soon young LeRoy was aboard a cargo plane of the Army Transport Command (ATC), at Newark, New Jersey. When the aircraft landed at Dayton, Ohio, a large wooden crate was put aboard. It contained, the passengers learned, a bull mastiff, weighing about a hundred and thirty pounds. The crate took up the space of three seats.

Anyone boarding an ATC plane had to have papers authorizing his or her presence. The dog was no exception. The animal's papers had been handed to the flight engineer and included a top-priority A-travel designation. There were also instructions to the crew for the care, exercise, and feeding of the dog. The crate was marked for delivery to Faye Emerson, a Hollywood movie actress—who happened to be the wife of Colonel Elliott Roosevelt.

When Leon LeRoy's plane took off from Dayton for Memphis, Tennessee, there were two other passengers aboard: Sergeant David Aks, back after thirty months of duty in the Pacific, and a Navy Seabee. Aks was bound for Riverdale, California, on emergency leave, to visit his ill wife. All three servicemen were traveling on C priority, two notches below the A priority of Colonel Roosevelt's dog, Blaze, who would soon become the world's most publicized canine.

After the plane landed at Memphis, a monumental hullabaloo began. An ATC officer there examined Blaze's priority, a designation customarily reserved for the highest military officers and others of exalted eminence. The three combat veterans were "bumped" off the plane because three hundred pounds of a B-priority freight was to be taken aboard. Blaze outranked the cargo, and the cargo outranked the servicemen.

Stranded in Memphis, Leon LeRoy was determined to get home. So he began hitchhiking and slowly reached Dallas. He was angry that the hours of his leave were rapidly being consumed. Somewhere along the route, he lost his leave papers, and in Dallas, the military police took him into custody and held him for two days as a deserter.

LeRoy was released and put on another ATC plane that headed for California. After catching a ride to Antioch, word of his being bumped for a dog reached newsmen in the region. The reporters descended upon him en masse at his mother's home, and he told them his story.

Almost at once the press services went into action. Here was a news editor's dream: a dog, a teenage combat veteran, a sexy Hollywood movie star, and the son of America's First Couple. The whole affair smacked of arrogance and preferential treatment for those in high places.

Reporters all over the nation kept the telephone wires hot. LeRoy's mother told journalists she was fearful that the Navy might come down hard on her son because of the media stories.

In Granite City, Illinois, Mrs. Ola Nix added more fuel to the fire. She said that her husband, Navy Carpenter's Mate 2nd Class Maurice Nix, had been home on emergency leave because several members of his family were ill. On returning to his duty station, he could not get on an ATC plane in Dallas because a huge mastiff had had a much higher priority. Nix had to borrow a hundred dollars from the Dallas Red Cross to buy a ticket to San Francisco on a commercial plane.

Meanwhile, reporters were banging the doors of the high and mighty in Washington. Secretary of War Henry Stimson, as confused as most Americans, said only that there had been a mistake somewhere down the line. Whose mistake? He didn't know. General Harold L. George, commander of the ATC, finally admitted that somebody had committed an error of judgment. Who had done so? He didn't know.

At the White House, Stephen T. Early, press secretary to President Roosevelt and a talented spin doctor, explained that there had been a regrettable series of mistakes. Who had committed them? He didn't know.

One reporter demanded to know from Early the name of the ATC officer responsible for issuing a top-priority designation to Blaze. Early did not have an answer.

Cornered in Washington, Eleanor Roosevelt, who usually was quite talkative on any topic, said only that any ATC officer would be stupid to bump a serviceman off a plane to accommodate a dog. Who was that "stupid officer"? She was not privy to that information.

A battalion of reporters tried to locate Faye Emerson in Hollywood. Where was she? None of her associates knew—or so they claimed. Enterprising newsmen discovered that she was on a train bound for Chicago, and they pounced on her when it stopped in Albuquerque, New Mexico. Colonel Roosevelt's wife claimed ignorance, saying only that she did not believe Blaze had a high priority. The first she knew about the dog's transcontinental safari was when Blaze was delivered to her at her Hollywood home—by an Army major.

In London, reporters finally caught up with Colonel Roosevelt. For some curious reason he had been hard to locate in recent days. He explained that Blaze had been left at the White House in Washington several weeks earlier with a request that the canine be sent to Faye Emerson in Los Angeles if space was available on an empty plane that happened to be going that way.

Meanwhile, the deluge of stories about the Adventures of Blaze triggered enormous tumult and shouting across the land. Genuine war news had almost been crowded off the front pages of newspapers and took second place in radio newscasts.

Amidst the uproar, frustrated Americans found something special to kick around. In Dallas, a center of the hubbub, the Bonehead Club failed in an effort to coerce a local airline into sending to President Roosevelt a large St. Bernard dog wearing an opera hat.

The Bonehead Club passed a resolution to fly three hundred and twenty-four dogs in the Dallas pound around the country, bumping humans from the planes. Another resolution changed Groundhog Day to Ground Dog Day. On this occasion, February 2, all dogs would be grounded so people could get a chance to fly without fear of being bumped.

Now, in a masterpiece of poor timing, the War Department recommended seventy-seven colonels for promotion to the rank of brigadier general.

President Roosevelt, despite the nationwide uproar, had sent the list on to the Senate for approval even though one of the names was that of his son Elliott.

Casual observers felt that the Senate would deny Elliott Roosevelt a star, or at least postpone his promotion. But that was not to be. In their wisdom, the lawmakers concluded that there were more important things to be focused upon in the war effort than a dog. So the promotion to brigadier generals of all seventy-seven colonels was approved.

The Adventures of Blaze brought about one change in the way the Air Transport Command did business. Orders were issued not to transport dogs, cats, mice, penguins, goldfish, gorillas, snakes, or any other species of animal in airplanes.[1]

A "Byrne-out" Hits the Nation

EARLY IN 1945, James Byrnes, head of the War Mobilization Board, triggered an uproar across home-front America when he decreed that business firms would have to conform to a midnight curfew. The purpose was to conserve electricity and coal for a war that might continue for years.

Nightclub and tavern owners and others catering to the after-dark crowds had been cashing in for many months and didn't want the greenbacks bonanza to end.

Because of its huge size and reputation as the City that Never Sleeps, New York was hit hardest by what was labeled the "Byrne-out." When some bistros ignored the deadline, the Army and Navy sent in military police and shore patrols to haul servicemen out of the joints and close down the offending establishments.

The majority of citizens and officials across the land soon agreed that the Byrne-out had become a monumental snafu, in the vernacular of the era. However, everyone was stuck with it.[2]

"It Was His Duty"

IN SEATTLE ON THE MORNING OF JANUARY 31, 1945, Mr. and Mrs. A. A. Prince were tuned to a radio bulletin. It was a sketchy report about a bold raid on a Japanese prisoner-of-war camp in the Philippines in which a large number of GIs had been rescued. They conjectured that their son, Captain Robert W. Prince, might have been involved.

An hour later Mrs. Prince answered the phone, and a man who identified himself as a newspaper reporter said, "I guess you've heard about your son, Captain Prince." Her heart leaped into her throat. Had he been killed?

Then the journalist told her about one of history's most audacious rescue missions. A hundred elite Rangers led by Captain Prince and a small team of Alamo Scouts had infiltrated twenty-five miles through enemy territory to the Cabanatuan POW camp. Inside, were some five hundred sick, emaciated, and weak survivors of the Bataan disaster three years earlier. The Japanese were preparing to murder every POW if General Douglas MacArthur's army drew near.

After the Rangers stormed the compound at night and killed more than two hundred Japanese guards with the loss of only one man, the POWs were brought back to American positions, most of them being carried in oxen-pulled carts provided by Filipino guerrillas.

Listening to the telephone caller, Mrs. Prince broke out in tears of pride—and relief.

News about the "impossible mission" was broadcast across the land and plastered on the front pages of two thousand daily newspapers. For hours, the Prince telephone rang incessantly when reporters called. "Well, Bob's role doesn't surprise me," his father replied. "It was his duty, and he did it."

In Oakland, California, Mrs. Miriam L. Picotte, who had been notified by the War Department only two days earlier that her brother had been killed in the Philippines, wept again—this time tears of joy. Her husband, Captain Caryl Picotte, had been rescued from Cabanatuan.

In Chicago, white-haired Mrs. Mary Zelis hurried to the Church of the Immaculate Conception, where she had prayed every day for her son, Louis, during his thirty-two months of captivity. Kneeling at the altar, she gave thanks for Louis's delivery from death.

In Dallas, the mother of Ranger Sergeant Theodore Richardson, who had shot the lock off the main gate at Cabanatuan to permit his comrades to charge into the enclosure, stared in disbelief at a photo of her son in a local newspaper. The picture was actually one of Captain Prince, who had mistakenly been identified as the sergeant. Mrs. Richardson had not seen her son in nearly three years. She called out in astonishment: "Good Lord, what have they done to Theodore!"

In Oklahoma City, Mrs. Grace Hubbard, wife of Major Ralph W. Hubbard, heard a radio newscast. She ran all the way to a neighborhood school, barged into the first-grade class with tears streaming down her cheeks, and cried out to her son, Joe: "Your daddy's been rescued! He's safe!"[3]

A Battered Warrior Limps Home

EARLY IN 1945, thousands of awed civilians watched as the aircraft carrier *Franklin*, battered and twisted, limped into New York harbor and on to a berth in the Brooklyn Navy Yard. Because of wartime secrecy few in the public knew the story at the time.

While engaged in offensive operations against the Japanese, the *Franklin* had been hit by kamikaze (suicide) planes. Bomb and gasoline blasts wracked the huge carrier for hours, leaving her a smoking ruin. It had been one of the greatest single disasters in U.S. Navy history. Seven hundred and twenty-four men had been killed, hundreds of other wounded.

Despite this holocaust at sea, the *Franklin*'s crew brought her back home— a harrowing trek of twelve thousand miles—under her own power.[4]

Visit by a Navy Chaplain

AT HER HOME IN WASHINGTON, D.C., on February 26, 1945, Mrs. Charles Anderson responded to the ringing of her doorbell. Opening the door, she saw the grim face of a Navy chaplain. Quickly she asked: "Is it my husband or my son?"

"Your son, Marine Sergeant Charles Anderson, has been killed in action," the chaplain replied softly.

After a few moments of silence, the mother said: "A force stronger than ours has taken charge."

That afternoon she climbed into her automobile and drove into a suburb where she was a volunteer at Bethesda Naval Hospital taking care of wounded men.[5]

"Will I Be Able to See?"

LIKE THOUSANDS OF AMERICAN WIVES whose husbands were fighting overseas, twenty-five-year-old Kitty Boswell was living with her mother and father in Birmingham, Alabama. Her husband, Captain Charles Boswell, was in Germany as a company commander with the 84th "Railsplitters" Infantry Division.

Kitty constantly reminded herself that her husband would survive the rigors and dangers of the battlefield. He had been a star halfback on the University of Alabama football team and had once scored a winning touchdown in the Rose Bowl after sustaining a broken leg in that game. Charley had also been an outstanding baseball player for Alabama, and his postwar goal was to break into the outfield of the New York Yankees.

In early January 1945, Kitty glanced out of the window of her home. Her heart beat furiously. A Western Union boy was parking his bicycle in front. Like most Americans, she knew that the War Department advised the next of kin of death, wounding, or disappearance of a loved one by Western Union.

With trembling hands, Kitty took the telegram from the boy and opened it: "The War Department regrets to inform you that . . . " It was a terrific jolt, even though it said that Charley had been seriously wounded instead of killed.

A gentle young lady, Kitty also had steel in her fiber. So she took upon herself the thorny task of breaking the distressing news to her husband's parents and other family members.

As was customary, the telegram had provided no details. So Kitty would not learn until much later the agonizing pain and mental anguish Captain Boswell had endured after the Sherman tank in which he was riding was struck by a German shell and exploded.

Boswell had blacked out. Medics carried him from the battlefield, and his first conscious reaction was hearing a voice say, "Good morning." It was an 84th Division chaplain.

"Where am I?"

"You're in an Army hospital."

Boswell could feel gauze bandages covering the upper part of his body, which was racked with pain. In an alarmed voice, he whispered, "I can't see! Chaplain, why can't I see?"

When the doctors paid a visit, he again asked, "Why can't I see? What's wrong with my eyes?"

One physician replied, "You got an overdose of burns, steel splinters, and dirt. We've taken a lot of foreign matter out of your eyes, but we don't have it all yet."

"Will I be able to see?" Charley asked in a whisper.

"We're doing our best," a doctor stated.

Later Captain Boswell was taken aboard a large C-54 cargo plane that had been remodeled to carry wounded men on litters and flown to the United States. A few days after landing, he was driven to Valley Forge General Hospital, near Philadelphia. The Army had converted the medical facility to specialize in treating eye patients.

After a series of tests, an eye specialist came to his room. "Captain Boswell," he said. "Everything possible has been done to restore your sight. I'm sorry, but you'll never see again."

That night, Charley, a courageous man on the football field and in battle, plunged into deep depression, convinced that he would always be a little more than a vegetable. He was gripped by the fear of spending the rest of his life in a veterans' home.

A few days after Boswell reached Valley Forge, he asked for a telephone and called Kitty. Nothing in the letters he had written her (with the help of Red Cross women) after his wounding gave any indication that he was blind. And he had no intention of breaking the news to her over the telephone. Somehow, Kitty knew. But she gave no indication of that fact.

A few hours later Kitty climbed on a Greyhound bus that took her to Valley Forge. Arrangements had been made for someone to meet her at the main entrance and escort her to the captain's room. There was a mix-up. No one met Kitty. Instead, she meandered around the miles of corridors for a half hour, trying to find her husband. At one point, she walked through a section of the large hospital where blind soldiers were being treated. Many of the patients she saw had been in surgery and their faces were concealed by yards of gauze.

Kitty felt faint. Was Charley one of these men? She was almost in a state of shock when she finally found his room—by opening one door after another and calling out his name.

It was a joyous reunion. The couple talked far into the night. Charley's eyes were never mentioned. He couldn't think of a gentle way to tell her the news, so he rambled on about other things. In the early morning hours, Kitty left for her lodging place in a nearby town.

On the following night, Kitty walked across the room to where Charley was sitting in a large chair, sat on his lap, put her arm around his neck, and said softly: "Why don't you tell me about it? It won't make any difference."

Both of them cried for many minutes. Never in the future would Kitty or Charley talk of his sightless situation. There was no need to do so.

When it became known that Charley would be at Valley Forge for at least six months, Kitty rented a house in the country nearby. Then her parents drove up from Birmingham to deliver little daughter Kay to the couple.

On arrival at the house, the child scrambled excitedly from the car, eager to greet her father. She ran toward him, then halted abruptly a few yards away and hurried back to her grandparents. Somehow, Kay had sensed that her father was "different."

In the weeks ahead, Charley tried every trick he could think of to win over his daughter. Only gradually would she "accept" her father. All the while, he tried to conceal from Kitty the heartbreak he was suffering from the child's rejection of him.

In the days and nights ahead, Charley became steadily more despondent. He spent hours lying idle on his hospital bed. How does a blind man get by? He would have to make a living to support Kitty and little Kay. But the only sightless civilians he had ever seen were guitar players standing on street corners and holding out little tin cups. Was that to be his destiny?

Valley Forge General had done all it could for Boswell, and he was transferred to Old Farms Convalescent Hospital near West Hartford, Connecticut. Boswell's morale plunged; he thought he was being sent to some kind of old folks' home. But it proved to be dedicated to taking blind Army men through programs to make them as self-sufficient as possible.

Old Farms had about two hundred sightless Army men on hand for rehabilitation and skill-sharpening courses. Advanced courses in Braille, mental
arithmetic, and various crafts were taught—along with music. Charley told
Kitty: "You don't know what cacophony really means until you hear fifteen or
twenty boys trying to struggle through a John Philip Sousa march with instruments they had never played before!"

In the all for one, one for all, spirit of America in those war years, many
of the industrial plants nearby took on blind soldiers from Old Farms as temporary workers in order to accelerate their training and to build their confidence.
A surprise result was that the sightless men were more productive than anyone
had expected. Unlike sighted employees, they had fewer opportunities to be dis-
tracted. Moreover, the blind soldiers took great pride in doing their jobs well.

Young men at Old Farms, sadly, were regarded as curiosities by some of
the town folks. While two of the soldiers were in West Hartford with a sighted
counselor one day, they overheard two women talking nearby. One said to her
companion: "The Army must be hard up for soldiers, taking in blind men."

Weeks later Captain Boswell was discharged from the Army and returned
to Birmingham to establish a home for Kitty and Kay. He tried to mask his worries. A modest government pension was all he had to meet family needs. Moreover, he was grieving the loss of vision far more deeply than most people,
including Kitty and the couple's parents, thought. For a powerfully built man
who had known success on football and baseball fields, it was infuriating for
him to be groping around the house, bumping into objects, unable to find
items he wanted.

Charley made a great pretense of being self-sufficient, determined to make
things easier for Kitty and Kay by seeming to show that being blind was no
great problem. Actually, blindness was an agonizing difficulty—and always
would be.

Through perseverance and pluck—and Kitty's loving help—the former
sports star and war hero eventually became a successful businessman—and a
role model for countless sightless people.[6]

"Franklin Died Like a Soldier"

SPRING WAS BREAKING OUT over Washington. The mood of the city was
upbeat. Allied armies were closing in on Berlin. Soon the war in Europe was
bound to end. It was April 12, 1945.

Vice President Harry Truman was in the Capitol, presiding over a session
of the Senate. Bored by listening to a long speech, the peppery Truman began
writing a letter to his mother and sister in Independence, Missouri:

Dear Mama and Mary:

I am writing this letter from the desk of the President of the Senate while a windy Senator [Alexander Wiley] is making a speech on a subject with which he is in no way familiar.

Turn on your radio tomorrow night at 9:30 your time to hear [me] make a Jefferson Day address to the nation. I think it'll be on all the networks. It will be followed by President Roosevelt, whom I'll introduce.

Eventually, the curtain fell on Wiley's speech and Truman adjourned the Senate at 4:45 P.M. He then strolled to the office of an old crony, Speaker of the House Sam Rayburn, who handed the vice president a glass of bourbon and water. The Speaker suddenly remembered that Stephen Early, Roosevelt's press secretary, had telephoned and wanted Truman to call the White House immediately.

Early told the vice president, "Please come right over." Truman presumed that Roosevelt had returned unexpectedly from his Georgia retreat, a six-room clapboard cottage called the Little White House in Warm Springs.

Truman arrived at 1600 Pennsylvania Avenue at 5:25 P.M. and was escorted to Eleanor Roosevelt's study on the second floor. A few moments later the First Lady, dignified and composed, came into the room and put an arm around Truman's shoulder. "Harry," she said solemnly, "the president is dead."

There were several moments of silence, then the First Lady said quietly, "Franklin died like a soldier."

One minute after the announcement was made to White House reporters, the blockbuster news was flashed to the home front on radio. Unlike newspapers, the networks refused to accept advertising for three days.

In the White House, hasty preparations for swearing in the new president were rapidly completed. Soon after 7:00 P.M. Truman, with his wife Bess and daughter Margaret at his side, faced Chief Justice of the Supreme Court Harlan Fiske Stone. Truman picked up a Bible that had been put on a table, and the chief justice began reciting the oath of office. But Truman had failed to raise his right hand, and the jurist calmly reminded him to do so.

At 7:08 P.M. Harry Truman became the thirty-third president of the United States.

Reared on a farm near Independence, the sixty-year-old Missourian had been unable to afford college, and he was denied admission to West Point because of poor eyesight. So he became the only president in the twentieth century who was not a college graduate, which, his admirers held, was the reason he was always able to tackle knotty problems with a commonsense approach.

After the swearing-in ceremony, Secretary of War Henry Stimson remained, saying he had an urgent matter to discuss. "Mr. President," the World War I Army colonel who saw heavy combat said, "I want you to know about an immense project that is underway—a project looking to the development of a new explosive of unbelievable destructive power." Stimson said he could discuss the matter no longer.

When President Truman left a few minutes later for his apartment at 4701 Connecticut Avenue, he was puzzled. What did Stimson mean by this remark? Only later would Truman be told of the atomic bomb project.

Truman was now saddled with the woes of the free world. On the way to the White House the next morning, he gave Tony Vaccaro of the Associated Press a ride. The reporter thought: How many such powerful men in history would ever have given a journalist a ride to work?

Vaccaro thought the president seemed deeply occupied, perhaps awed by his new role. "Few men have equaled the one into whose shoes I'm stepping," the president declared. "I've silently prayed to God that I can measure up to the task."

Later that day Truman went to the Capitol to arrange to speak to a joint session of Congress. Page boys and reporters lined up to shake Truman's hand. "Fellows, if you ever pray, pray for me," he said in his Midwestern twang. "I feel like the moon and the stars and the planets have fallen on me."

In the meantime, Eleanor Roosevelt had flown to Georgia and was aboard a funeral train winding its way to Washington with her husband's body. Much of the day and into the night she lay in her berth, looking out at the throngs of people that had gathered at stations and in the towns to pay their final tribute to the president.

At ten o'clock on the morning of April 14, the train pulled into Union Station. Harry Truman, his wife Bess, and other top government officials got onto the train to pay their respects to Eleanor Roosevelt.

Later thousands crowded onto both sides of Constitution Avenue as a caisson drawn by six white horses carried the flag-draped coffin to the White House. Many wept openly. Others watched, grim and stoic, as though in a daze. President Truman noticed an elderly black woman, apron held to her eyes, sitting on the curb and crying as though she had just lost a son.

No president's death since Abraham Lincoln had made such a dramatic impact on the American people. Grief-stricken, they simply could not comprehend that the man who had been their president since 1933, who had taken the nation from a series of disasters to the brink of victory in Europe, was actually dead.[7]

Mama Truman Visits the White House

A MONTH AFTER HARRY TRUMAN was sworn in as president, he sent the *Sacred Cow*, his personal airplane, to bring his ninety-two-year-old mother from Grandview, Missouri, to Washington for Mother's Day on Sunday, May 13,

1945. It was her first visit to Washington and her first plane ride. "Mama got a great kick out of the trip," the president told aides.

Like her son, the mother was a rebel of sorts. The president told her that she could sleep in the bed once occupied by Abraham Lincoln. She balked. Threatened to sleep on the floor. So the son said she would put her in the large ornate Rose Room. Too fancy. She slept in a small adjoining room.[8]

GIs' Best Friend Dies in Battle

FEW, IF ANY, AMERICANS had heard of Ie Shima, an obscure flyspeck in the Pacific only three hundred and forty miles from Tokyo. But in the spring of 1945, thousands of American soldiers were locked in a death struggle with Japanese troops who fought to the death. With the GIs was war correspondent Ernie Pyle.

A thousand American correspondents covered some aspects of the global war, but Pyle was the most beloved. He was a hero to countless fighting men. Millions on the home front prayed for his safety.

Ernie never made war glamorous, and he often betrayed his own emotions when he saw young Americans being butchered in battle. He wrote of the nobility of GIs putting their lives on the line while fighting for their country. After hundreds of close brushes with death, Ernie was frail, emaciated, and his hair had gone gray. Still he refused to go home.

On April 18, Pyle was driving to the front on Ie Shima when his jeep was raked with fire from a hidden Japanese machine-gun nest. He was killed by a slug in the head.

Home-front America was shocked by Pyle's death. This simply couldn't have happened; there must have been a mistake in the media reporting. But it dawned on Americans that the "GIs' best friend," as he was known, had made the supreme sacrifice.

President Harry Truman said: "Nobody knows how many individuals in our armed forces and at home Ernie helped by his writings. But all Americans understand how wisely, how warmheartedly, how honestly he served his country and his profession."[9]

Restrained Joy Breaks Out

MORE THAN A HALF-MILLION PEOPLE gathered in Times Square in New York City to celebrate. Navy blue and Army khaki mixed with civilian browns and grays, standing shoulder to shoulder as they cheered the news flashed by elec-

(Times-Picayune)

tric bulbs that beribboned around the *New York Times* Building. It was May 8, 1945—Victory in Europe Day.

"Just like New Year's Eve before the war!" the celebrants shouted to one another. Strangers kissed and hugged. Whisky bottles were passed around. Often smiling faces were wet with tears. Confetti fluttered down from the tall structures.

At about ten o'clock that night, Mayor Fiorello La Guardia broadcast an order that Times Square be cleared. "War workers need to get to their midnight shifts," he said.

People also took to the streets in hundreds of towns large and small. Celebrations in Los Angeles concluded at about 3:00 P.M. after Mayor Fletcher Bowden asked that church bells be pealed.

"This is a time for prayer that the war in the Pacific will soon be ended," Bowden said. "This is not a holiday."

In Cleveland, the streets were littered with torn papers and long streamers dangled from office windows draped over streetcar wires. In the suburb of Parma, a man painted a fireplug red, white, and blue.

In Chicago, a gray-haired man went up to a woman behind the cigar counter in the lobby of the Stevens Hotel. "Aren't you going to celebrate?" he asked. "Celebrate what?" she replied. "I have two sons fighting in the Pacific."

There were no noisy celebrations in San Francisco. Schools closed early. The Junior Chamber of Commerce sponsored an "On to Tokyo" rally in the Civic Auditorium.

Except for a truckload of boys with musical instruments touring the heart of Des Moines, there was no revelry.

In St. Louis, church leaders held services in Memorial Plaza, and retail stores closed. In Baltimore harbor, there were impromptu celebrations aboard British and Norwegian ships, but the streets were largely empty.

In Boston, workmen tearing down the old New England Mutual Building in Post Office Square tolled the bell in the tower. It was the first time the bell had rung in years.

Minneapolis sounded its central air-raid warning siren atop the Northwestern National bank. Extra policemen were on hand in case celebrations got out of hand. But there were no celebrations, so the extras were sent home.

Many Springfield, Massachusetts, stores draped their show windows with American flags to protect glass from the expected throngs of celebrators. But there were no crowds.

Across home-front America, Victory in Europe Day had been largely subdued except for brief flurries. In Connecticut, an employee of the Seth Thomas clock factory, which had been converted to war production, reflected the mood of most people across the land: "This day really doesn't mean much to me. When I stop making fuse parts for shells and start making clock parts again, then I'll celebrate."[10]

Two Old Friends Meet

TWENTY-FOUR HOURS AFTER V-E DAY, Navy Lieutenant Cecil Sanders and an old friend from his training days two years earlier met by chance in San Francisco. Both were in the United States on leave after having seen combat in the Pacific as skippers of PT boats, the speedy little craft with the large sting in their tails.

The two young officers had dinner and a few drinks and talked over old times at Northwestern University where they had trained. Later they leisurely strolled about downtown San Francisco and saw several Soviet officers on the streets.

Sanders's friend said, "Sooner or later, we're going to have to deal with the Soviet Union." Seventeen years later, he did—as President John F. Kennedy during the Cuban missile crisis.[11]

Poll: Hang Hirohito

AN EDITORIAL HEADLINE in the *Los Angeles Times* summed up the situation: TWO DOWN [HITLER AND MUSSOLINI], ONE TO GO [EMPEROR HIROHITO].

A public opinion poll released on June 1, 1945, disclosed that home-front America wanted the war against Japan to end as quickly as possible, but not through some sort of negotiated peace. By a nine-to-one ratio, the people were in favor of continuing the conflict until Japan surrendered unconditionally.

As for the destiny of Emperor Hirohito, whom most Japanese revered as a god, nearly 50 percent of the poll's respondents wanted him hanged as a "war criminal," although no one seemed to know precisely what a war criminal was.[12]

"Your Son Is Close to Death"

IN THE HEARTLAND OF AMERICA, Doran Dole and his wife Bina were going through their daily routine in the small town of Russell, Kansas. Like other Americans, they had offered up prayers of thanks that the war in Europe was concluded. But they were constantly gripped by fear. Their son, twenty-one-year-old Lieutenant Robert J. Dole, was a patient in Winter General Hospital in Topeka, suffering from horrendous wounds he had received on April 14, 1945, while leading a platoon of the 10th Mountain Division against heavily defended Hill 913 in Italy.

At a field hospital, doctors had found that an exploding shell had destroyed Lieutenant Dole's right shoulder, fractured vertebras in his neck and spine, and riddled his body with metal slivers. His spinal cord tilted, resulting in the medical diagnosis: "Paralysis complete in all four extremities."

Army doctors doubted that the lieutenant would live. If he did survive, they concluded, he would never walk again or be able to use his arms. A heavy cast from hips to chin was fashioned on the patient.

Now the young Kansan had to summon another kind of courage with which to engage in a lonely fight to not only survive, but to one day walk again. His weapons were prayer, pluck, and perseverance.

In the weeks ahead, Dole was a patient at the 15th Evacuation Hospital in Florence, Italy; the 70th General Hospital in Casablanca, Morocco; and finally Winter General Hospital in Topeka.

Constantly flat on his back, unable to move his arms and legs, and usually in excruciating pain, Dole could do nothing but stare at the ceiling.

Bina Dole visited her son at Winter General. Seeing him in the body cast, gaunt, and helpless, she broke into tears. Then she steeled her spirit. Never again would she weep in his presence.

"Don't worry, Mom," Bob said in a soft, hoarse voice, "I'm going to be back, as good as new."

In July, Doran Dole received an urgent telephone call from a doctor at Winter General. "You might want to come here," he was told. "Your son is close to death."

Doran and Bina rushed to Topeka and kept a lonely vigil over Bob. Doctors had to remove an infected kidney.

*Lieutenant Robert J. Dole
spent two years in Army
hospitals. Parents were told
he was near death. (Courtesy
of Elizabeth Dole)*

Bob fooled the doctors, however: he refused to die. By September, an improvement was evident. Most of the burdensome body cast was hacked off, and he gained feeling in both legs. Helped by nurses and other attendants, he was able to get up, put his feet on the floor, and take a few shaky steps down the hall.

A month later, the Doles were permitted to bring their son home for a short time, back to the house where he had spent most of his boyhood in the family's basement lodging. Out of her son's hearing, Bina once broke into sobs and told a daughter, Gloria, "I'm afraid we brought him home to die!"

There was good reason for Bina's pessimism: her son looked, in the words of a boyhood friend of his, "like death warmed over." He had left Russell to go to war a vigorous, strapping athlete weighing more than a hundred and ninety pounds. Now his frame was gaunt, he weighed seventy pounds less, and he had to be carried into the house on a stretcher.

Bob remained determined to one day walk again, maybe even regain the use of his shattered arm. So just after Thanksgiving, he joined a few thousand patients at the Percy Jones Medical Center in Battle Creek, Michigan, a facility specializing in amputations, orthopedics, and neurosurgery.

The lieutenant knew that he would be striving for a near miracle, but he was determined to make the effort: he worked hard and long on exercises prescribed by therapists. Then he was stricken with a blood clot, near pneumonia, with a temperature close to 106 degrees. His life was saved by an experimental dose of streptomycin, then a new wonder drug.

Despite his travails, Dole clung to his highly developed sense of humor. He began referring to himself as "the soldier who disobeyed orders and wouldn't die when he was supposed to."

Bob astonished doctors by eventually regaining the use of both legs and what he called "my good arm." His right arm remained useless, and he was advised there was nothing more Army surgeons could do for him. So he sought a civilian surgeon, Dr. Hampar Kelikian, who specialized in bone and joint surgery, in Chicago.

Dr. Kelikian had served in the U.S. Army Medical Corps. Perhaps he felt a kinship to Dole because the doctor's brother had been killed during the war while fighting in Italy, near to the location where Dole had met his own disaster.

After studying Dole's voluminous medical charts, Kelikian agreed to perform surgery on the lieutenant, perhaps even regaining for him partial use of his right arm. Dole had no money, however, but Kelikian, a refugee from Armenia, agreed to charge no fee. Much later, the surgeon recalled: "To me, young Dole symbolized America. He had the faith to endure."

Although Kelikian had waived his fee, the Chicago hospital needed an advance for the use of its facilities. Word got around Russell that the Dole family had almost no money, so the folks at Dawson Drug Store, where Bob had worked as a teenage "soda jerk," put out an empty cigar box. A label "Bob Dole Fund" was glued to it. Eventually, quarters, dimes, and nickels added up to the needed $1,800, a sizable sum at the time, and a grateful Bob Dole left for Chicago.

Dr. Kelikian performed seven surgical procedures on Dole's right arm and hand. Amazingly, the operations, along with the Kansan's vigorous exercising, recovered 50-percent use of the arm.

After spending thirty-nine agonizing months in military hospitals, Bob Dole, who had been promoted to captain, was discharged from the Army and returned to Russell, a driven man, grimly determined to make up for lost time. That obsession would never leave him. Just the daily ordeal of buttoning a shirt reminded him that "I have to keep pushing because I'm not quite a whole person."

Dole planned to gain a law degree at Washburn College in Kansas and then enter politics. A lifelong friend said to him: "Bob, I wouldn't be surprised if one day you become the Republican nominee for president of the United States."

Both men had a good laugh over that far-fetched possibility.[13]

A Rain of Explosive Balloons

MAY 5, 1945, WAS A BEAUTIFUL SPRING DAY in Oregon as the Reverend Archie Mitchell and his wife Elyse were preparing to leave on a fishing trip in the mountains just north of the California border. Only two weeks earlier they had arrived in the small town of Bly as representatives of the Christian and Missionary Church.

The Reverend Mitchell was thirty-three years of age and Elyse, who was five months pregnant with the couple's first child, was twenty-six. Going on the outing with them were a girl and four boys from the church.

Only a day earlier, Elyse had decided not to go on the jaunt, because she decided she was too weak to keep up with the boys. But Saturday dawned with such beauty that she changed her mind and climbed into the couple's 1939 automobile with the group. They brought along fishing gear and picnic lunches.

After driving up into the mountains, the party found the narrow road blocked. A Forest Service road grader had slid into a ditch, was bogged down in thick mud, and several workers were trying to pull it out with a pickup truck. The Mitchell couple learned from one of the men that the nearby stream was far too muddy for fishing. Moreover, the road ahead was impassable.

All the passengers got out of the automobile, and the Reverend Mitchell backed it off the road to find a parking space.

Elyse and the youngsters meandered into the nearby woods. After Mitchell had gotten out of the car, he heard his wife call to him to come and look at the strange objects they had discovered.

After he had taken two steps, an explosion rocked the area. Along with three Forest Service men, Mitchell dashed into the forest and was greeted by a horrible scene. The five children, chopped up and bloody, were dead. Elyse was barely alive, and her clothes were on fire. Mitchell badly burned his hands trying to snuff out the flames. She died moments later.

Hanging from tree branches above the five mutilated bodies were bits and pieces of paper and twine. Markings on the debris seemed to indicate the material was of Japanese make. Scattered around the victims were chunks of shrapnel, an unexploded incendiary bomb, and an array of metal rings.

Elyse Mitchell and the five children had a unique but tragic distinction: they were the only casualties from enemy bombing on home-front America. Because of wartime secrecy, citizens would not learn until months later that the northwest United States was under attack by ingenious bomb-laden balloons.

Beginning in the fall of 1944, at the same time President Roosevelt was being elected for the fourth time, forest fires began raging. Tens of thousands of acres in Oregon, Washington, and northern California were destroyed.

Many people living in the region felt that careless smokers were causing the infernos. Skeptics countered that if that viewpoint were true, much of the population of the Pacific Northwest apparently was engaged in pitching lighted cigarettes into thick, dry forests.

In Washington, only President Roosevelt and a few top military and government officials knew the true reason for the conflagrations. Under the code name Fugo (windship weapons), the Japanese had been launching balloon-borne bombs into the high-altitude jet streams. The devices took sixty-eight hours to cross nine thousand miles of the Pacific.

Commanded by Major General Sueki Kusaba, Fugo would eventually launch nine thousand balloons, carrying thirty thousand bombs. Tokyo warlords were convinced that the barrage would have a demoralizing effect and create widespread panic on home-front America.

Constructed with laminated tissue paper, each balloon had some six hundred separate pieces. The armament mechanism was quite complicated. Each balloon had three explosives. The first bomb was to kill people; the second, an incendiary bomb; and the third was to self-destruct the entire apparatus. The balloons were guided by unique Seiko timing devices and Toshiba electrical systems.

Filled with hydrogen, the balloons were thirty-two-feet in diameter and seventy feet tall. Navigation was not precise. One bomb was found in a Detroit suburb, another fell on a street in a town in Idaho.

One of the airborne bombs came close to inflicting a major calamity on the United States. A balloon loaded with explosives got tangled in power lines just outside a supersecret plant near Hanford, Washington, where fuel was being refined for a revolutionary device known as an atomic bomb. A short circuit in the power for the nuclear reactor cooling pumps ensued, but backup equipment restored power rapidly. Had the cooling system been off much longer, a reactor might have collapsed and exploded, killing many workers and destroying much of the building.

Japan had no spies in the Northwest to report on the results of the balloon-borne assault, and the American media cooperated with Washington by not mentioning a word of the blazes. To do so would have informed Tokyo that Operation Fugo was a success and caused more balloon bombs to be launched.[14]

Paratroopers in Operation Firefly

WHILE THE FIRES WERE BURNING BRIGHTLY—often out of control—in the Pacific Northwest, a unit designated by the Army as the 555th Parachute Infantry Battalion (Colored) was training at Camp Mackall, North Carolina, and looking forward to taking an early crack at the Germans or Japanese. Known as the Triple Nickels, the outfit was a pioneer, America's first black paratroop unit.

Although men of the Triple Nickels were willing to put their lives on the line for America, they were reminded daily that they belonged to a Jim Crow army. However, to a man, they were deeply imbued with black pride and a grim determination to be the best parachute unit in the Army.

Lieutenant Bradley Biggs, who had grown up in a Newark, New Jersey, black ghetto and had played professional football with the New York Brown Bombers, recalled when the Triple Nickels were training at Fort Benning, Georgia:

It wasn't easy. A proud black lieutenant, sergeant, or private with polished boots and parachute wings, still had to sit in the back of the bus, use the "colored" toilets and drinking fountains in the railroad stations and theaters, and go out of our way to avoid confrontations with red-necked white police in the towns. Black captains and lieutenants found post officers' clubs closed to them. But we endured to prove ourselves as paratroopers.

In early 1945, the 555th Parachute Infantry Battalion received secret orders to report to Pendleton Air Base in Oregon for a "highly classified mission." They would play a major role in Operation Firefly, battling raging forest blazes.

After arriving at Pendleton, the battalion took a three-week crash course in forest-fire fighting by parachute, including demolitions training, tree-climbing techniques, survival in heavily timbered and mountainous locales, and the touchy business of dismantling live Japanese explosives.

In the weeks ahead, teams of paratroopers jumped into tiny clearings, often studded by boulders, where they could become trapped in the center of a conflagration. Although their dangerous mission was highly important, the Triple Nickels were deeply disappointed that their lot in the war was fighting, not the Germans or Japanese, but roaring infernos.[15]

A Purple Heart Parade

It may well have been the most distinctive and emotion-racked parade in American history. Some 500,000 people lined Fifth Avenue in New York City to watch a succession of two hundred jeeps roll past. In each vehicle sat three or four soldiers, sailors, or marines. Many had bandages wound around their heads. Some had no arms. Others were missing a leg or two. It was June 15, 1945.

This event was known as the Purple Heart Parade and had been organized by the City of New York to honor men wounded in the war. On each jeep one or more signs told the throngs in what locale the GIs had been wounded:

BATAAN, MIDWAY, SICILY, ITALY, UTAH BEACH, OKINAWA, IWO JIMA, CORAL SEA

Few other activities during the global conflict brought to the home front the horrible price the flower of America's youth was paying. Those watching were choked up and far too emotional to even cheer. Or does one "cheer" a mutilated young man? On occasion there would be sudden bursts of polite applause. Mostly the crowd stood and watched in silence.

It was eerie. For thirty minutes the procession crawled past. About the only sound was the grinding gears of the jeeps.[16]

Plane Crashes into Skyscraper

ON JULY 28, 1945, Army Air Corps Lieutenant Colonel William F. Smith Jr. was approaching the jungle of skyscrapers in Manhattan at the controls of his twin-engine B-25 bomber named *Old Feather Merchant.* He was on a training mission. A graduate of West Point in 1942, Smith had completed two years of combat in Europe and had been awarded two Distinguished Flying Crosses and four Air Medals before being routinely rotated back to the United States.

Towering among the concrete giants was perhaps the world's best-known structure, an architectural masterpiece called the Empire State Building. Built in 1931, the edifice has one hundred and two stories and is more than a quarter-mile high.

Now, on this summer day, Colonel Smith's B-25 winged in closer to the high-rise jungle. Moments later, a horrendous crash echoed throughout Manhattan. The aircraft had struck the Empire State Building between the seventy-eighth and seventy-ninth floors. An operator opened the door of her elevator just as the engines of the bomber exploded. The force blew her into a burning hall, her clothing aflame. A quick-witted woman slapped out the fire and pulled the operator into the elevator.

The woman shut the door, then turned the handle to start the elevator downward. A loud crack: the heat had snapped a cable. The elevator plunged seventy-five stories and smashed into the basement. Hours later, rescue workers used heavy tools to get inside the elevator, and they carried the two women out of the wreckage. Each had suffered a broken leg—but both were alive. A safety brake had slowed the descent of the elevator a few floors before it hit bottom.

Fourteen people, including Colonel Smith and his crew, were killed and twenty-five persons were injured seriously. Within a couple of hours, squat New York Mayor Fiorello La Guardia huffed and puffed up seventy-five floors of steps to comfort the surviving victims.

It would never be known what caused a highly experienced pilot, who had dodged German antiaircraft shells over Europe countless times, to fail to evade such a gargantuan obstacle as the Empire State Building.[17]

An Invasion of German Scientists

IN THE EARLY SUMMER OF 1945, President Harry Truman was seated in the Oval Office of the White House poring over a lengthy memorandum from John Franklin Carter Jr., who had been an unofficial intelligence advisor to Franklin Roosevelt during the war. A graduate of Yale, Carter had worked in

U.S. embassies in Rome and Constantinople, as well as in various top offices in Washington.

Carter's document stated in part:

> American armies have captured a number of top German scientists. Many of them are willing to come here and work under any terms laid down for them. However, our top [scientists] say that none of them should be brought here for fear of arousing professional jealousy. Instead, they proposed to lock up the Germans in France and say, "Work!"

At the time Washington was engulfed in preparations for an invasion of Japan, another "war" was raging behind the scenes over the topic of bringing the German scientists to the United States. Even before a decision was reached in the White House, the Pentagon began smoothing the way for offering contracts to and importing one hundred German scientists and engineers who had developed the powerful thirteen-ton missiles that had nearly destroyed London during the war.

Under a heavy veil of secrecy, Herbert Wagner, a German scientist who had designed airplanes with the Henschel Aircraft Company, was sneaked into Washington by four U.S. Navy officers in civilian clothes and registered under a phony name at a major hotel. Wagner had been "recruited" by the U.S. Navy Technical Mission, one of the several American groups that were combing the chaos in Germany in search of rocket scientists.

A report had been sent to the Pentagon explaining that Wagner's knowledge of the Hs 2T3 (a radio-controlled air-to-air missile) could be fully exploited for the war against Japan if he were brought to the United States.

For four weeks, Wagner was interrogated by Navy experts in the Washington hotel suite. Then he was taken to a secluded estate on Long Island, outside New York City, to work on a Navy top-secret missile project.

Secretly bringing German rocket scientists to work in America was endorsed by Army Chief of Staff George Marshall after he read a top-secret report from U.S. technical experts who had interviewed many of the rocket experts in Germany. "The thinking of these men is twenty-five years ahead of us," the report stated. "These [Germans] could be put to work refining a revolutionary rocket for use in the Pacific war."

Marshall dispatched two colonels to call on Assistant Secretary of State Frederick Lyon on a delicate mission. They informed Lyon that the Army planned to bring German rocket experts to the United States and, because they would technically be prisoners of war, State Department visas would not be necessary.

Moreover, Lyon was told, American intelligence in Europe had uncovered evidence that German missile blueprints and a mass of other technical materials had been passed along to the Japanese high command prior to the German collapse. So it was crucial that the German scientists and technical experts be brought to the United States to beat the Japanese in rocket development.

Most of the American scientific community was stridently opposed to the Army plan. One scientist expressed the fear that the "Nazi" group would "organize underground cells in the United States" and spread propaganda to "foment an uprising against the government in Washington."

On July 6, 1945, before an official decision had been reached, the Joint Chiefs of Staff approved Operation Overcast, a plan to import "no more than three hundred and fifty" Germans (including one hundred missile experts) to the United States. Fearful of a massive public outcry against "bringing Nazis into the country," Overcast was wrapped tightly in a veil of secrecy.

The plan stipulated that the Germans would not be treated as prisoners but rather as free men who would voluntarily come to the United States to pursue rocket research. They would be paid six dollars per day, and receive free medical care, food, and housing.

For their part, most of the rocket men were eager to come to the United States for six months. Their future in chaotic Germany was bleak indeed, including the distinct possibility of being kidnapped by the Russians and hauled off to the Soviet Union.

Pointing out that the successful prosecution of the war against Japan was uppermost in his decision, Secretary of State Edward R. Stettinius Jr. gave Overcast the green light on July 19. No doubt he had the approval of President Truman.

The first twenty German scientists and technicians disembarked in Boston. They were wearing coveralls. As they strolled down the gangplank, a reporter for the *Boston Globe* asked an Army officer, "Who are those Germans?" The reply: "They're truck drivers." A day later the newspaper carried the story.

Overcast was concealed by a tight web of secrecy. It would be more than a year before the American people knew about the project.[18]

Curious Happenings in Utah

FOLKS LIVING IN the region of Wendover, Utah, a barren expanse of desert about one hundred and ten miles from Salt Lake City, were extremely curious about what was going on at a nearby air base. In recent weeks perhaps as many as fifteen hundred Air Corps officers and men had descended upon the broad, treeless flats and trained under the utmost secrecy.

Only a handful of top officers in the Pentagon knew that this group was led by twenty-nine-year-old Colonel Paul W. Tibbets Jr., who later told his wife that he felt as though he had been set down on another planet. He had been briefed on the intricacies of a scientific theory called an atomic bomb.

The airmen at Wendover were almost as puzzled as the natives in the region. Tibbets had each one take a pledge of secrecy, but they were not told what it was they were not to reveal. Flight operations were unlike anything they had ever known. In practice runs, each plane dropped only one ten-thousand-pound bomb from precisely thirty thousand feet.[19]

A Haunting Prediction

IN LATE JULY 1945, leaders in the Pentagon were shaken after receiving a prediction from General Douglas MacArthur in Manila: a million American casualties would be suffered to conquer the Japanese homeland. That figure would be as many as U.S. forces in all branches had sustained throughout the war. Twice as many Japanese soldiers and a few million civilians would perish, MacArthur concluded.

Magic (the secret interception and decoding of Japanese messages by American monitors) seemed to confirm that awesome analysis.

"Even if the war drags on and it becomes clear that it will entail much more bloodshed, the whole country will pit itself against the [American] invaders," Foreign Minister Shinegori Togo declared in one Magic intercept.

In another intercept, War Minister Korechika Anami declared that the Japanese armed forces would "fight to the death."

Fanatical Japanese generals and admirals were preparing *Ketsu-Go* (Operation Decision), the last-ditch defense of every foot of the home islands that all Japanese held sacred, having fallen as drops from the sword of an ancient god. There were some 2.5 million soldiers, all deeply imbued with the warrior's Shintoist code that held it a duty and an honor to die in battle for Emperor Hirohito.

There would be 32 million civilian militia (including women and children) ready to die. Their weapons were ice picks, muzzle-loading rifles, butcher knives, and bamboo spears. Children were taught to strap explosives around their waists, roll under American tanks, and blow themselves to smithereens. Five thousand kamikaze (suicide) pilots were ready to crash planes into the American invasion fleet.[20]

Proposed Use of Disabling Gas

GENERAL GEORGE MARSHALL was among the Pentagon brass appalled by the frightful bloodbath that was going to be inflicted on the flower of American youth to conquer Japan. Although the use of poison gas would be in violation of the Geneva Convention, of which the United States had been a signatory in the 1920s, Marshall proposed "disabling gas" to drive the Japanese soldiers from their bunkers, caves, and foxholes. Then they could be wiped out by standard infantry weapons and artillery.

Marshall argued that gas was no more inhumane than were white phosphorous shells and flamethrowers. However, the suggestion was quietly dropped.[21]

"I Was Thinking about Our Boys"

MAJOR GENERAL LESLIE GROVES, the hulking officer who had longed for a combat command and instead had been designated to direct a project to build history's first atomic bomb, was a bundle of nerves. In the Pentagon, the cavernous structure he had been in charge of constructing prior to that assignment, he telephoned the communications room every fifteen minutes. "Any word yet?" he asked. Always the reply was the same: No. It was the night of August 6, 1945.

Like a handful of other key leaders in Washington, Groves knew that a B-29 Superfortress piloted by Colonel Paul Tibbets was to drop an A-bomb on the industrial city of Hiroshima. But no one knew whether the apparatus would explode or if Tibbets had been able to reach the target.

At 11:29 P.M. Groves received a terse radio flash from Tinian, the flyspeck island in the Pacific from where the B-29 had lifted off on the monumental mission: "Successful in all respects."

Soon after dawn, Groves met with Army Chief of Staff George Marshall. Groves was jubilant. But the low-key Marshall cautioned against excessive celebrations because so many Japanese had died.

"I was not thinking about those casualties," the outspoken Groves replied. "I was thinking about all of our boys who were murdered by the Japs on the Bataan death march!"

That was the precise view held by 98 percent of those on homefront America.[22]

"Let's Take a Second Day Off!"

IN THE WHITE HOUSE, President Harry Truman was huddled with his top military advisors when word was received that Domei, the chief Japanese news agency, began its radio broadcast to the United States: "Japan will ignore the unconditional surrender demand made by the warmonger Truman. . . . " Consequently, the American president gave the green light to drop a second nuclear device, which hit Nagasaki.

On the morning of August 15, 1945 (Tokyo time), forty-four-year-old myopic Emperor Hirohito, a figure so sacred to the Japanese that they had never heard his voice, took to Radio Tokyo with a recorded message to his people: "The enemy has begun to employ a new and most cruel bomb, the power of which to do damage is incalculable. I have ordered an end to hostilities at 4:00 P.M. today."

Within minutes word of the Japanese surrender flashed across home-front America. In Washington, a huge, boisterous crowd gathered in Lafayette Park across the street from the White House. Many joined in conga lines. Car horns honked. Thousands surged across Pennsylvania Avenue and pushed up against the iron fence that surrounds the White House.

At about 7:15 P.M. Harry and Bess Truman came out of the White House and strolled to the fountain on the north lawn. The president walked along the barrier, flashing a wide grin and tossing out V-for-victory signs in the manner of Winston Churchill. Enormous cheers echoed for blocks.

Truman went back into the White House and telephoned his mother in her home in Grandview, Missouri, not far from Kansas City. Then he called Eleanor Roosevelt and said that he wished it had been her husband who had announced the surrender news to the nation.

Truman proclaimed a two-day national holiday. "Tomorrow, August 16, 1945 [U.S. time] will be the official Victory Over Japan Day," he told the media. "But let's also take a second day off on Thursday, August 17. No school for the kids. No work for everybody."[23]

A Nation Goes Wild

A TUMULTUOUS CELEBRATION, the like of which the nation had never known, erupted across home-front America on V-J Day. Workers left their jobs, whistles blew, church bells pealed, crowds filled the streets, total strangers embraced. Less exuberant citizens went to churches and synagogues to pray, and to give thanks for victory and for peace.

In Times Square in New York City, more than a million people congregated in a wild orgy of drinking, kissing, screaming, shouting, and fondling.

In a Los Angeles neighborhood, a woman, otherwise a modest person, ran down the street shouting in a loud voice: "There's toilet paper at the A & P! There's toilet paper at the A & P!" After three years of rationing, this was an important discovery.

In Victory Square in Seattle, Mrs. Viola Lander sat on a bench, crying quietly. A passerby asked why she was not celebrating. "For mothers like me," she replied, "the war will never be over. My nineteen-year-old son, Ted, was killed in Okinawa in May."

Celebrators in New York City's Wall Street were among the million people who gathered after V-J Day was announced. (Author's collection)

In Chicago, Frances Evans Dyke broke out in tears of relief. "God bless President Truman," she told a reporter. Now all eleven of her sons in the Army, Navy, and Marine Corps—five of whom were training for an invasion of Japan— would be coming home.[24]

A GI Refugee Returns

NONE OF THOSE REJOICING over the end of the war was more euphoric than Radioman 1st class George Ray Tweed of the Navy. Nearly four years earlier, three days after the Pearl Harbor debacle, Tweed had been stationed on Guam when the Pacific island was captured by Japanese forces.

Hundreds of Americans were marched into captivity, but Tweed had managed to escape and took to the brush. Relying on skills learned as a boy on hunting trips in Oregon, he survived the long global conflict armed with only a machete and a pocketknife, a latter-day Robinson Crusoe.

On returning home, Tweed learned of more good news. He had amassed $6,000 in back pay, a small fortune in that era.[25]

"Experts" Visualize Crime Wave

AFTER REPRESENTATIVES OF EMPEROR HIROHITO signed a formal surrender document aboard the battleship *Missouri* in Tokyo Bay on September 2, 1945, millions of American servicemen and hundreds of women in uniform overseas began going home to be discharged and play catch-up in civilian pursuits.

Newspapers and magazines unleashed a collection of "experts" who wrote articles on the perceived pitfalls of young men scarred by the horrors of war on their return to civilian life. In *Good Housekeeping* magazine, a psychologist stated: "After two or three weeks the returning [GI] should be finished talking about his war experiences, with oppressive remembering. If he still goes over the same stories, reveals the same emotions, you had better consult a psychiatrist."

Other psychologists warned that the returning veterans were "trained killers," and that they would ignite a crime wave on home-front America.

What these "experts" failed to realize was that "oppressive remembering" for most fighting men would haunt them for a lifetime, but they would function as productive members of society, many in leadership roles. The prognosticators were unaware that all the "trained killers" yearned for was a huge and ongoing dose of peace and quiet.[26]

Notes and Sources

Part One—Shock Waves Hit America

1. **"On the Ground, by God!"**
   John Toland, *But Not in Shame* (New York: Random House, 1961), p. 39.
   Milwaukee Journal, December 9, 1941.
   New Orleans Times Picayune, December 9, 1941.
   San Francisco Examiner, December 8, 1941.
   Lee Kennett, *For the Duration* (New York: Scribner's, 1985), pp. 14, 69.
   "Hearings Before the Joint Committee on the Investigation of the Pearl Harbor Attack, Congress of the United States," Part 19, pp. 3504–3506. National Archives, Washington, D.C.

2. **Dispute in the President's Office**
   Thomas T. Connally, *My Name Is Tom Connally* (New York: Crowell, 1954), p. 249.
   Jack Goodman, ed., *While You Were Gone* (New York: Simon & Schuster, 1946), p. 500.
   New York Herald Tribune, December 12, 1941.

3. **Calls for Retreat to Rockies**
   Chicago Tribune, December 10, 1941.

4. **Submarines Off West Coast**
   Author's archives.

5. **Roosevelt Rallies the Nation**
   Washington Post, December 9, 1941.
   St. Louis Post-Dispatch, December 9, 1941.

6. **Eavesdropper in the German Embassy**
   Documents on German Foreign Policy series, 1940–1945.
   National Archives, Washington, D.C.

7. **A Television Pioneer**
   Author's archives.

8. **Instant Psychologists**
   Sioux City Journal, December 9, 1941.
   New York PM, December 9, 1941.
   Tulsa Daily World, December 8, 1941.
   Journal of Broadcasting, Fall, 1961.
   New York Times, December 19, 1941.

9. **Strange Doings across the Land**
   Rolla Daily News, December 14, 1941.
   Patrick S. Washburn, *A Question of Sedition* (New York: Dutton, 1986), p. 39.
   Richard Polenberg, *War and Society* (New York: Harper, 1972), p. 45.

Los Angeles Times, December 15, 1941.
New York Sun, December 10, 1941.

10. **A Stop-and-Go Railroad Trip**
Author's archives.

11. **"San Francisco Is Being Bombed!"**
New York Times, December 9, 1941.
Los Angeles Times, December 16, 1941.

12. **Watching for Enemy Paratroopers**
Atlanta Constitution, February 1, 1942.
Author's archives.

13. **A Covert Raid into Mexico**
San Francisco Examiner, December 11, 1941.
Henry L. Stimson Diaries, New Haven, Conn.: Yale University Library.
Franklin D. Roosevelt Library, Hyde Park, New York.

14. **Fear for Roosevelt's Life**
Author's archives.

15. **FBI Joins in Sinking Submarine**
FBI files in possession of author.

16. **Rounding Up Subversive Suspects**
FBI files, June 23, 1941, Washington, D.C.

17. **A Feud over Wiretapping**
Don Whitehead, *The FBI Story* (New York: Random House, 1956), p. 187.
Author's archives.

18. **Mission: Halt Ambassador's Hara-Kiri**
Fred Israel, *The War Diary of Breckenridge Long* (Lincoln: University of Nebraska Press, 1966), pp. 232, 237.
Author's archives.

19. **A Field Marshal Is Shocked**
Viscount Alanbrooke, *Diaries* (London: Collins, 1957–1958), pp. 292-293.

20. **Nazi U-Boat in New York Harbor**
Jean Noll, *The Admiral's Wolfpack* (Garden City, NY: Doubleday, 1974), p. 138.
Ladislas Farago, *The Tenth Fleet* (New York: Obolensky, 1962), p. 46.

21. **A Journalist Prowls the *Normandie***
Time, February 23, 1942.
New York PM, February 26, 1942.

22. **The Salesman's Luck Runs Out**
Ladislas Farago, *The Game of the Foxes* (New York: McKay, 1971), pp. 502–503.

Part Two—America under Siege

1. **Joe Louis Contributes Huge Purse**
New York Herald Tribune, January 22, 1942.
Author's archives.

2. **A Grieving Father Joins Navy**
Los Angeles Times, January 8, 1942.

3. **Self-Appointed Do-Gooders**
Allan M. Brandt, *No Magic Bullet* (New York: Oxford University Press, 1985), pp. 138–140.
Portland Press Herald, April 6, 9, 10, 1943.
Author's archives.

4. **A Hollywood Victory Committee**
Jean Garceau, *Gable* (New York: Grosset & Dunlap, 1961), pp. 3, 38.
Los Angeles Times, December 12, 1941.

5. **Actress Dies for Her Country**
Indianapolis News, January 16, 1942.
Washington Post, January 16, 1942.
New York Times, January 18, 1942.

6. **Dismantling a Nazi Spy Network**
Transcript of testimony taken by court reporters, February 1942.
Harper's, June 1942, pp. 10–11.
New York Times, February 14, 18, 25, 1942.
Author's archives.

7. **A Debacle in Manhattan**
Time, February 23, 1942.
John Maxtone-Graham, *The Only Way to Cross* (New York: Collier, 1972), p. 378.
New York Herald Tribune, February 21, 1942.
Author's archives.

8. **The Battle of Los Angeles**
Los Angeles Times, February 26, 1942.
San Francisco Examiner, February 27, 1942.
Author's archives.

9. **"We Poison Rats and Japs"**
Chicago Tribune, February 14, 1942.
Author interview with former FBI Assistant Director W. Raymond Wannall.
Los Angeles Times, February 15, 1942.
San Francisco Examiner, February 14, 1942.
Author's archives.

10. **Goal: Coalition of Africa and Japan**
Detroit News, March 1, 1942.
Author's archives.

11. **Mysterious Malady on Ships**
Transcript of Joseph Curran testimony before the House Committee on the Merchant Marine and Fisheries, March 25, 1942.

12. **The FBI and the OSS Feud**
Author's archives.
Author interview with former FBI Assistant Director W. Raymond Wannall.

13. **Hijinks on a Hospital Roof**
Author interview with Robert Parrish.
Author's archives.

14. **Suspicions Run Rampant**
Author's archives.
Miami Herald, February 26, 1942.

15. **"German Officers" Stalk Harbor**
    Time, February 9, 1942.

16. **Commercial Radio's First War**
    Author's archives.

17. **U-Boats "Ruining" Tourist Season**
    Miami Herald, March 23, 1942.
    Author's archives.

18. **Helping a German POW Escape**
    Don Whitehead, *The FBI Story*, p. 240.

19. **Strange Scenario in San Francisco**
    Author's archives.

20. **Silencing a Priest Rabble-Rouser**
    Kenneth P. O'Brien and Lynn H. Parsons, eds., *The Home-Front War: World War II and American Society* (Westport, CT: Greenwood, 1995), p. 19.

21. **Nazi Agents in Key Industry Posts**
    Michael Sayers and Albert E. Kahn, *Sabotage!* (New York: Harper, 1942), pp. 47–48.
    Author's archives.

22. **Blasts Rock Defense Facilities**
    New York Times, March 5, 8, 24, 1942.
    Houston Post, March 7, 1942.
    Los Angeles Times, March 8, 1942.
    Buffalo Courier Express, March 17, 1942.
    Greenville (S.C.) *News*, March 24, 1942.
    San Francisco Examiner, March 16, 1942.
    Sheboygan (Wisc.) *Press*, March 28, 1942.
    New Haven (Conn.) *Register*, March 26, 1942.

23. **Eastern America Set Ablaze**
    Author's archives.

24. **The Mysterious Shangri-la**
    New York Times, April 21, 1942.
    Author's archives.
    Washington Post, April 23, 1942.

25. **Comic Strip Puzzles Tokyo Warlords**
    Author's archives.

26. **Disaster Impacts Two U.S. Towns**
    Author's archives.

27. **"A Date with Destiny"**
    The Register, publication of Women in the Military Service for America Memorial Foundation, Fall 1995.
    Des Moines Register, July 12, 1942.
    This Fabulous Century, vol. 5 (New York: Time-Life Books, 1969), p. 176.

28. **A Tumultuous Homecoming**
    Author interview with Mrs. John D. (Alice) Bulkeley.
    New York Times, May 14, 1942.
    New York Mirror, May 18, 1942.

New York Journal-American, July 11, 1942.
New York Sun, July 6, 1942.

29. **Lord Haw-Haw and His Spies**
Author interviews with wartime members of the 509th Parachute Infantry Battalion: Colonel Carlos C. Alden (Ret.), Colonel Jack Darden (Ret.), and Kenneth Shaker.

Part Three—A Sleeping Giant Awakens

1. **Invasion Target: California**
William F. Halsey, *Admiral Halsey's Story* (New York: McGraw-Hill, 1947), p. 107.
Author's archives.
Thomas B. Buell, *Master of Seapower* (Boston: Little, Brown, 1979), p. 236.

2. **Washington: Chaotic Capital**
Washington Post, May 12, 23, June 3, 14, 1942.
New York Times, April 12, 28, June 14, 23, 1942.
Author's archives.

3. **A Young Reporter Is Awed**
David Brinkley, *A Memoir* (New York: Knopf, 1994), p. 62.
Author's archives.

4. **"Doll Woman" an Enemy Agent**
FBI files, 1942, in author's possession.
Author interview with former FBI Assistant Director W. Raymond Wannall.

5. **Panic Erupts at Concert**
St. Louis Post-Dispatch, May 24, 1942.

6. **Standard Oil Aids the Nazis**
Author's archives.

7. **A Guidebook for Nazi Spies**
Author's archives.

8. **They Came to Blow Up America**
FBI transcript of testimony at spies' trial in possession of author.
George J. Dasch, *Eight Spies Against America* (New York: McBride, 1949), pp. 96, 112.
Don Whitehead, *The FBI Story*, p. 203.
FBI memorandum, June 19, 1942, in possession of author.
Washington Post, August 8, 1942.

9. **Artillery Confrontation in Oregon**
Bert Webber, *Retaliation: Japanese Attacks on the Pacific Coast in World War II* (Corvallis: Oregon State University Press, 1975), pp. 47–48.

10. **German-American Bund Demolished**
Time, July 14, 1942.
John Roy Carlson, *The Plotters* (Chicago: Regnery, 1943), p. 252.
New York Times, August 2, 1942.

11. **First Lady Rattles Some Cages**
Chicago Tribune, July 17, 1942.
San Diego Union, July 19, 1942.

12. **"I'm Proud of You, Mom!"**
    Los Angeles Times, July 19, 1942.

13. **Horse Racing Flourishes**
    Author's archives.

14. **Psychological Saboteurs at Work**
    Author's archives.
    Don Whitehead, *The FBI Story,* p. 233.
    FBI files, 1939–1942. National Archives, Washington, D.C.

15. **Hollywood Superstars Sign Up to Fight**
    Los Angeles Times, August 13, 1942.
    Author's archives.

16. **War Hero Meets Joe Kennedy**
    Author interview with Vice Admiral John D. Bulkeley (Ret.), 1994.
    Author interview with Alice (Mrs. John D.) Bulkeley, 1997.

17. **Wants to Spotlight U.S. Spies**
    Author's archives.

18. **Government Censors Movies**
    New Republic, May 1943.
    Kenneth P. O'Brien and Lynn H. Parsons, eds., *The Home-Front War: World War II and American Society,* p. 26.
    Poynter to Mellett, November 12, 1942. OWI files. National Records Center, Suitland, Maryland.
    Author's archives.

19. **Navajo Code-Talkers**
    Collier's, January 1944.
    Alison R. Bernstein, *American Indians in World War II* (Norman: University of Oklahoma Press, 1991), p. 42.
    American Indian History Project, University of Utah, p. 11.
    Peter Iverson, *The Navajo Nation* (Westport, CT: Greenwood, 1981), p. 9.
    S. McClain, *Navajo Weapon* (Boulder: University of Colorado Press, 1994), pp. 45–46.

20. **Popular Orchestra Disbanded**
    Boston Globe, September 2, 1942.

21. **Gone with the Wind in Chicago**
    Des Moines Register, September 12, 1942.
    Chicago Tribune, September 6, 1942.

22. **Nasty Bartenders and Redneck Cops**
    Sally V. Keil, *Those Wonderful Women in Their Flying Machines* (New York: Rawson, Wade, 1979), pp. 237–238.
    Washington Post, September 11, 1942.
    New York Times, September 11, 1942.

23. **Plane Bombs Pacific Northwest**
    Author's archives.

Part Four—A Nation in Total War

1. **Covert Project on Constitution Avenue**
   Author's archives.

2. **Patton Calls on the President**
   Author's archives.

3. **Weapons Mysteriously Vanish**
   Author interview with General Mark W. Clark (Ret.), 1983.

4. **A Huge Bounty on Hitler's Head**
   Washington Post, February 5, 1943.

5. **A Tempest in a Teapot**
   Des Moines Register, February 5, 1953.

6. **Press Conference for "Women Only"**
   Author's archives.

7. **Secret Plan to Draft Females**
   Author's archives.

8. **Women in Combat Experiment**
   Author's archives.

9. **Jailbreak for a Boyfriend**
   Miami Herald, February 6, 1943.

10. **Megabucks for Jack Benny's Violin**
    New York Sun, January 28, 1943.

11. **"Mom, Keep Your Chin Up!"**
    American, January, March 1944.
    Naval History, Winter 1992.
    Chicago Herald-American, January 16, 1943.
    This Week, March 5, 1944.
    Washington Post, February 5, 1943.
    Des Moines Register, January 17, 22, 26, 1943.

12. **Firm Gets Big Payoff**
    Arch Whitehouse, *Espionage and Counterespionage* (Garden City, NY: Doubleday, 1964), pp. 150, 152.

13. **A Glamorous Nazi Agent**
    Detroit News, March 11, 1944.
    Author's archives.

14. **Marine Commander's Dilemma**
    U.S. Marine Corps pamphlet, *Marine Corps Women Reserves in World War II*, 1968. Headquarters, USMC, Washington, D.C.

15. **A Patriotic Heroine's Long Ordeal**
    New York World Telegram, December 11, 1945.
    New York Sun, December 12, 1945.
    Columbia (Mo.) *Tribune*, March 6, 1943.
    Hollywood movie, *With a Song in My Heart*, starring Susan Hayward as Jane Froman, 1951.

16. **A Platinum Smuggler's Demise**
    Don Whitehead, *The FBI Story*, pp. 225–226.
    Los Angeles Times, January 12, 1944.

17. **"Get Going! Time Is Short!"**
    War Manpower Board, "Selective Placement for the Handicapped," 1943. National
         Archives, Washington, D.C.
    Author's archives.

18. **Women Flock to War Plants**
    Author's archives.

19. **Recruiting the Blind and the Deaf**
    Author's archives.

20. **Offer to a Striptease Artist**
    Author interview with Colonel Barney Oldfield (Ret.).

21. **The FBI Arrests "Good Old Ernie"**
    New York Sun, November 6, 1943.
    Author's archives.
    FBI press release, June 27, 1943.

22. **America's Least-Known Boomtown**
    Author's archives.

23. **"Hello, America! Berlin Calling!"**
    Washington Post, July 27, 1943.
    Horst J. P. Bergmeier and Rainer E. Lotz, *Hitler's Airwaves* (London: Yale University
         Press, 1997), pp. 23, 26.
    British Broadcasting Corporation (BBC) Monitoring Service Digest, February 1940,
         January 1942, June 1944.
    Time, April 6, 1942.
    William L. Shirer, *Berlin Diary* (New York: Knopf, 1941), p. 104.

24. **A Picture Stuns the Nation**
    Life, September 20, 1943.
    Author's archives.

25. **A Tragedy in St. Louis**
    St. Louis Globe-Democrat, August 3, 1943.
    St. Louis Post-Dispatch, August 2, 1943.

26. **"Legal Kidnapping" by Soviet Thugs**
    San Francisco Examiner, September 10, 1943.
    Author's archives.

27. **Spy Nabbed a Second Time**
    Author's archives.

28. **Scoundrels in the War Effort**
    Don Whitehead, *The FBI Story*, pp. 238, 338.
    Author's archives.
    New York Times, June 28, 1943.

29. **"Bomb Japan Out of Existence"**
    Author interview with Colonel Sam Grashio (Ret.), who had spent two years as a POW
         in the Philippines.
    Washington Post, January 30, 1944.
    Chicago Tribune, January 29, 1944.

30. **War Hero Bounced from Air Corps**
    Author's archives.

31. **An Overseer of GI Morals**
    Washington Post, January 6, 1944.
    Author's archives.

32. **Top-Secret Projects Opened to Women**
    Jeanne Holm, *Women in the Military* (Novato, CA: Presidio, 1982), p. 60.
    Author interview with Major General John K. Singlaub (Ret.).

33. **Roosevelt: Chloroform Drew Pearson**
    Ted Morgan, *FDR* (New York: Dutton, 1985), p. 561.
    Charles R. Codman, *Drive* (Boston, Little, Brown, 1957), p. 154.
    Dwight Eisenhower letter to George Patton, December 17, 1943. Eisenhower Library, Abilene, Kansas.

34. **An Ace German Operative**
    Author's archives.
    Don Whitehead, *The FBI Story*, pp. 197–198.

Part Five—On the Road to Victory

1. **Hoodwinking Hitler from New York**
    Dwight Eisenhower letter to General Brehon Somervell, May 12, 1944. Eisenhower Library, Abilene, Kansas.
    Frederick Morgan, *Overture to Overlord* (London: Hodder and Stoughton, 1950), p. 127.
    Author's archives.

2. **A Spy in Allied Headquarters?**
    Author's archives.

3. **Two Broadcast Rivals Called Up**
    Kenneth Bilby, *The General* (New York: Harper & Row, 1986), p. 146.
    William S. Paley, *As It Happened* (New York: Doubleday, 1979), p. 200.

4. **Tributes to a Fallen Female Pilot**
    Sally V. Keil, *Those Wonderful Women in Their Flying Machines* (New York: Rawson, Wade, 1979), pp. 234–235.
    Author's archives.

5. **Cheers for a Lady**
    Sally V. Keil, *Those Wonderful Women in Their Flying Machines*, p. 258.
    Author's archives.

6. **D Day Anxieties and Prayers**
    Washington Post, June 7, 1944.
    Philadelphia Inquirer, June 7, 1944.
    Atlanta Constitution, June 7, 1944.
    Ohio State Journal, June 7, 1944.
    New York Herald Tribune, June 8, 1944.
    Author interview with John H. "Beaver" Thompson (1994).

7. **A Virginia Town Is Jolted**
    Author interview with Donald McKee, former National Commander of the 29th Infantry Division Association.

8. **Calamity at Port Chicago**
   San Francisco Examiner, July 19, 1944.
   Studs Terkel, *The Good War* (New York: Harper, 1958), p. 397.
   New York Times, July 20, 1944.

9. **Secret Project in a Movie Studio**
   Lou Cannon, *President Reagan* (New York: Simon and Schuster, 1991), p. 485.
   Author's archives.

10. **WASPs Test New B-29**
    Author's archives.

11. **The Fable of Fala**
    Author's archives.

12. **Roosevelt's Foe Keeps a Secret**
    Richard N. Smith, *Thomas E. Dewey and His Times* (New York: Simon & Schuster, 1982), p. 426.
    "Statement for Record of Participation by Brigadier General Carter W. Clarke in the Transmittal of Letters from General George C. Marshall to Governor Thomas E. Dewey, in September 1944," p. 3, Record Group 547. National Archives, Washington, D.C.

13. **A Father-and-Daughter Spy Team**
    FBI interrogation transcripts of interviews with Simon Emil Koedel and Marie Hedwig Koedel.
    New York Times, October 24, 26, 30, 1944, January 2, 1945.
    Author's archives.

14. **Stumbling into a World Series**
    St. Louis Post-Dispatch, September 2, 1944.
    Author's archives.

15. **A Riot Erupts in New York City**
    New York Times, October 15, 1944.
    Newsweek, November 27, 1943.
    Stars and Stripes, June 18, 1945.

16. **Dark Intruders Sneak Ashore**
    New York Times, January 2, 1945.
    David Kahn, *Hitler's Spies* (New York: Macmillan, 1975), p. 13.
    New York Herald Tribune, January 2, 1945.
    Don Whitehead, *The FBI Story*, p. 206.
    FBI transcript of interrogation of Erich Gimpel, January 2, 1945.

17. **Robot Bombs Threaten East Coast**
    New York Herald Tribune, January 9, 1945.
    Washington Post, January 9, 1945.

18. **The Führer Staggers America**
    Don Whitehead, *The FBI Story*, p. 241.
    George S. Patton, Jr., *War As I Knew It* (Boston: Houghton Mifflin, 1947), p. 247.
    Henry L. Stimson papers, December 28, 1944. Yale University Library, New Haven, Connecticut.
    Author's archives.

19. **Back Home for Christmas**
    Author's archives.

20. **Episode on a Florida Bus**
    Walter White, *A Rising Sun* (Garden City, NY: Doubleday, 1945), p. 123.

21. **A GI Changes His Mind**
    Yank magazine, February 1945.

Part Six—The Lights Go On Again

1. **A Blaze of Glory**
   Washington Post, February 3, 1945.
   New York Times, February 7, 1945.
   Author's archives.

2. **A "Byrne-out" Hits the Nation**
   Author's archives.

3. **"It Was His Duty"**
   Author interview with Robert W. Prince.
   Denver Post, February 2, 1945.

4. **A Battered Warrior Limps Home**
   Author's archives.

5. **Visit by a Navy Chaplain**
   John Delaney, *America Triumphs* (New York: Walker, 1994), p. 50.

6. **"Will I Be Able to See?"**
   Author correspondence with Charles A. Boswell Jr. and with Kitty (Mrs. Charles A. Sr.)
       Boswell.

7. **"Franklin Died Like a Soldier"**
   John Toland, *The Last 100 Days* (New York: Random House, 1968), p. 417.
   Washington Post, April 13, 15, 17, 1945.
   New York Times, April 14, 15, 1945.

8. **Mama Truman Visits the White House**
   Washington Post, May 13, 15, 1945.

9. **GIs' Best Friend Dies in Battle**
   New York Times, April 20, 1945.
   St. Louis Post-Dispatch, April 21, 1945.
   Stars and Stripes, April 20, 1945.

10. **Restrained Joy Breaks Out**
    New York Times, May 9, 1945.
    Time, May 12, 1945.

11. **Two Old Friends Meet**
    Author interview with Cecil Sanders, 1991.

12. **Poll: Hang Hirohito**
    Author's archives.

13. **"Your Son Is Close to Death"**
    Author correspondence with Robert J. Dole.
    Author's archives.

14. **A Rain of Explosive Balloons**
    Author's archives.

15. **Paratroopers in Operation Firefly**
    Author interview with Lieutenant Colonel Bradley Biggs (Ret.).

16. **A Purple Heart Parade**
    New York Times, June 16, 1945.

17. **Plane Crashes into Skyscraper**
    New York Times, June 16, 1945.

18. **An Invasion of German Scientists**
    Lucius D. Clay, *Decision in Germany* (New York: Random House, 1950), pp. 212–213.
    "History of Army Air Force's Participation in Project Paperclip [formerly Overcast],"
        August 6, 1945, Maxwell Air Force Base, Alabama.
    Frederick Ordway III and Mitchell Sharpe, *The Rocket Team* (New York: Crowell,
        1979), p. 283.
    Author interview with Dr. Walter Wiesman, a member of the German rocket team.

19. **Curious Happenings in Utah**
    Author's archives.

20. **A Haunting Prediction**
    Leslie M. Groves, *Now It Can Be Told* (New York: Da Capo, 1962), p. 324.
    Stanley Weintraub, *Long Day's Journey into War* (New York: Dutton, 1990), p. 387.
    Author's archives.

21. **Proposed Use of Disabling Gas**
    Author's archives.

22. **"I Was Thinking about Our Boys"**
    Leslie M. Groves, *Now It Can Be Told*, pp. 339–340.

23. **"Let's Take a Second Day Off!"**
    Washington Post, August 15, 1945.
    Time, August 18, 1945.
    Author's archives.

24. **A Nation Goes Wild**
    San Francisco Chronicle, August 15, 1945.
    Chicago Tribune, August 15, 1945.
    Los Angeles Times, August 15, 1945.

25. **A GI Refugee Returns**
    Author's archives.

26. **"Experts" Visualize Crime Wave**
    Author's archives.

Index